RUSSIA

UKRAINE

MOLDOVA

TURKEY

CYPRUS

LIBYA EGYPT

CHAD SUDAN

CAR

NGO-BRAZ UGAN
CONGO

GOLA ZAMBIA MALAWI

IBIA BOT ZIMB MOZ

SWAZI
SOUTH LESOTHO
AFRICA

GEORGIA
ARM AZER
TURKEY
SYRIA LEB
ISR JOR IRAQ IRAN
KUWAIT
BAH
QATAR
SAUDI UAE OMAN
ARABIA
ERITREA YEMEN
DJIB
ETHIOPIA SOMALIA

KENYA

TANZANIA

MADAGASCAR MAURITIUS

RUSSIA

KAZAKHSTAN

MONGOLIA

UZBEK
TURKMEN KIRGIZ
TAJIK
AFGH CHINA

N. KOREA
S. KOREA JAPAN

PAKISTAN NEPAL BHU

INDIA B'DESH HONG
KONG TAIWAN
MYANMAR LAOS MACAO
THAILAND VIETNAM
SRI CAMBODIA PHILIPPINES
LANKA
BRUNEI
MALAYSIA
SING
INDONESIA PAPUA
NEW GUINEA

FIJI

AUSTRALIA

NEW ZEALAND

1⁰⁰
5/23

POCKET WORLD IN FIGURES
2007 EDITION

Guide to Analysing Companies
Guide to Business Modelling
Guide to Business Planning
Guide to Economic Indicators
Guide to the European Union
Guide to Financial Markets
Guide to Investment Strategy
Guide to Management Ideas
Numbers Guide
Style Guide

Dictionary of Business
Dictionary of Economics
International Dictionary of Finance

Brands and Branding
Business Consulting
Business Ethics
Business Miscellany
Business Strategy
China's Stockmarket
Dealing with Financial Risk
Economics
Future of Technology
Globalisation
Headhunters and How to Use Them
Successful Mergers
The City
Wall Street

Essential Director
Essential Economics
Essential Investment
Essential Negotiation

Pocket
World in
Figures

2007 Edition

THE ECONOMIST IN ASSOCIATION WITH
PROFILE BOOKS LTD

Published by Profile Books Ltd,
3A Exmouth House, Pine Street, London EC1R OJH

This edition published by Profile Books in association with
The Economist, 2006

Material researched and compiled by
Andrea Burgess, Ulrika Davies, Mark Doyle, Andrew Gilbert,
Conrad Heine, Carol Howard, Stella Jones, David McKelvey,
Keith Potter, Simon Wright

Typeset in Officina by MacGuru Ltd
info@macguru.org.uk

Printed in Italy by
Graphicom

A CIP catalogue record for this book is available
from the British Library

ISBN-10: 1 86197 825 1
ISBN-13: 978 1 86197 825 7

Contents

10 **Notes**
11 **Abbreviations**

13 **Part I   World Rankings**

14 **Countries:** *natural facts*
Countries: the largest   Mountains: the highest
Rivers: the longest   Deserts: the largest   Lakes: the largest
Islands: the largest

16 **Population:** *size and growth*
Largest 2004   Largest 1950 and 2050
Fastest growing populations   Slowest growing populations
Population change 2004–2050

18 **Population:** *matters of breeding*
Highest and lowest fertility rates
Highest and lowest teenage births
Highest and lowest crude birth rates   Most male populations
Most female populations

20 **Population:** *age*
Highest median age   Lowest median age
Highest populations aged 60 and over
Highest populations aged 0–14

21 **Population:** *migrants*
International migrants: 2005, 1990, 1970

22 **Refugees and asylum**
Largest refugee nationalities
Countries with largest refugee populations
Asylum applications by origin
Industrialised countries with most asylum applications

23 **City living**
Biggest cities   Fastest growing cities   Slowest growing cities
Highest urban population   Lowest urban population
Highest % of population in a single city   Highest quality of life
Lowest quality of life

26 **The world economy**
Biggest economies   Biggest economies by purchasing power
Regional GDP   Regional purchasing power   Regional population
Regional international trade

28 **Living standards**
Highest GDP per head   Lowest GDP per head
Highest purchasing power   Lowest purchasing power

30 **The quality of life**
Highest human development index
Lowest human development index   Economic freedom index
Gender-related development index

CONTENTS

32 Economic growth
Highest economic growth   Lowest economic growth
Highest services growth   Lowest services growth

34 Trading places
Biggest exporters   Most trade dependent
Least trade dependent   Biggest visible traders
Biggest invisible traders

36 Balance of payments: *current account*
Largest surpluses   Largest deficits
Largest surpluses as % of GDP   Largest deficits as % of GDP
Workers' remittances   Official reserves

39 Exchange rates
Big Mac index

40 Inflation
Highest inflation   Lowest inflation

42 Debt
Highest foreign debt   Highest foreign debt burden
Highest debt service ratios

44 Aid
Largest donors   Largest recipients

46 Industry and services
Largest industrial output
Highest and lowest growth in industrial output
Largest manufacturing output   Largest services output

48 Agriculture
Most economically dependent on agriculture
Least economically dependent on agriculture
Highest growth   Lowest growth
Biggest producers: cereals, meat, fruit, vegetables

50 Commodities
Leading producers and consumers of: wheat, rice, sugar,
coarse grains, tea, coffee, cocoa, copper, lead, zinc, tin, nickel,
aluminium, precious metals, rubber, raw wool, cotton, major oil
seeds, oil, natural gas, coal, oil reserves

56 Energy
Largest producers   Largest consumers   Energy efficiency
Highest and lowest net importers
Largest consumption per head   Sources of electricity

58 Workers of the world
Highest % of population in labour force
Most male workforce   Most female workforce
Lowest % of population in labour force
Highest rate of unemployment

60 The business world
Global competitiveness   The business environment

62 **Business creativity and research**
Innovation index
Information and communications technology index   E-readiness
R&D expenditure   Patents granted and in force

64 **Business costs and FDI**
Office rents   Employment costs   Foreign direct investment

65 **Business burdens and corruption**
Days to register a new company   Corruption perceptions index
Business software piracy

66 **Businesses and banks**
Largest businesses   Largest banks

68 **Stockmarkets**
Largest market capitalisation
Highest growth in market capitalisation
Highest growth in value traded
Highest growth in number of listed companies

70 **Transport: *roads and cars***
Longest road networks   Densest road networks
Most crowded road networks   Most used road networks
Highest car ownership   Lowest car ownership
Most injured and killed in road accidents

74 **Transport: *planes and trains***
Most air travel   Busiest airports   Longest railway networks
Most rail passengers   Most rail freight

76 **Transport: *shipping***
Largest merchant fleets   Biggest crude oil capacity
Biggest fish catching capacity

77 **Tourism**
Most tourist arrivals   Biggest tourist spenders
Largest tourist receipts

78 **Education**
Highest primary enrolment   Lowest primary enrolment
Highest tertiary enrolment   Least literate
Highest education spending   Lowest education spending

80 **Life expectancy**
Highest life expectancy   Highest male life expectancy
Highest female life expectancy   Lowest life expectancy
Lowest male life expectancy   Lowest female life expectancy

82 **Death rates and infant mortality**
Highest death rates   Highest infant mortality
Lowest death rates   Lowest infant mortality

84 **Death and disease**
Diabetes   Heart disease   Maternal mortality rate   Tuberculosis
Measles immunisation   DPT immunisation
HIV/AIDS prevalence and deaths

86 Health
Highest health spending   Lowest health spending
Highest population per doctor   Lowest population per doctor
Most hospital beds   Highest male obesity
Highest female obesity

88 Marriage and divorce
Highest marriage rates   Lowest marriage rates
Highest divorce rates   Lowest divorce rates

90 Households and prices
Biggest number of households   Biggest households
Highest cost of living   Smallest number of households
Smallest households   Lowest cost of living

92 Consumer goods ownership
TV   Telephone   CD player   Computer   Mobile telephone

94 Books and newspapers
Cultural goods, exports and imports   Daily newspapers

95 Music and the internet
Music sales   Digital music market   Internet hosts

96 Nobel prize winners
Peace   Economics   Literature   Physiology or medicine
Physics   Chemistry

97 Olympic medal winners
Summer games, 1896–2004   Winter games, 1924–2006

98 Drinking and smoking
Beer drinkers   Wine drinkers   Alcoholic drinks
Smokers

99 Crime and punishment
Police   Crime   Prisoners

100 Stars ...
Space missions   Space vehicle launches

101 ... and Wars
Defence spending   Armed forces   UN peacekeeping missions

103 Environment
Environmental performance index   Environmental health scores
Lowest access to improved drinking water source
Highest and lowest air quality scores
Highest concentration of ozone   Biggest forests
Forests' largest share of land   Biggest loss of forested land
Biggest gain in forested land

107   **Part II   Country Profiles**

108   Algeria
110   Argentina
112   Australia
114   Austria
116   Bangladesh
118   Belgium
120   Brazil
122   Bulgaria
124   Cameroon
126   Canada
128   Chile
130   China
132   Colombia
134   Côte d'Ivoire
136   Czech Republic
138   Denmark
140   Egypt
142   Estonia
144   Finland
146   France
148   Germany
150   Greece
152   Hong Kong
154   Hungary
156   India
158   Indonesia
160   Iran
162   Ireland
164   Israel
166   Italy
168   Japan
170   Kenya
172   Latvia
174   Lithuania
176   Malaysia

178   Mexico
180   Morocco
182   Netherlands
184   New Zealand
186   Nigeria
188   Norway
190   Pakistan
192   Peru
194   Philippines
196   Poland
198   Portugal
200   Romania
202   Russia
204   Saudi Arabia
206   Singapore
208   Slovakia
210   Slovenia
212   South Africa
214   South Korea
216   Spain
218   Sweden
220   Switzerland
222   Taiwan
224   Thailand
226   Turkey
228   Ukraine
230   United Arab Emirates
232   United Kingdom
234   United States
236   Venezuela
238   Vietnam
240   Zimbabwe
242   Euro area
244   World

246   Glossary
248   List of countries
253   Sources

Notes

This 2007 edition of *The Economist Pocket World in Figures*
includes new rankings on such things as as islands, migrants,
remittances, official reserves, Big Mac index, oil reserves, e-
readiness, heart disease, trade in cultural goods, digital music
and several environmental measures. The world rankings
consider 183 countries; all those with a population of at least
1m or a GDP of at least $1bn; they are listed on pages 248–52.
The country profiles cover 67 major countries. Also included
are profiles of the euro area and the world. The extent and
quality of the statistics available varies from country to
country. Every care has been taken to specify the broad
definitions on which the data are based and to indicate cases
where data quality or technical difficulties are such that
interpretation of the figures is likely to be seriously affected.
Nevertheless, figures from individual countries may differ
from standard international statistical definitions. The term
"country" can also refer to territories or economic entities.

Some country definitions
Macedonia is officially known as the Former Yugoslav Republic
of Macedonia. Serbia includes Montenegro. Data for Cyprus
normally refer to Greek Cyprus only. Data for China do not
include Hong Kong or Macau. For countries such as Morocco
they exclude disputed areas. Congo-Kinshasa refers to the
Democratic Republic of Congo, formerly known as Zaire.
Congo-Brazzaville refers to the other Congo. Data for the EU
refer to the 15 members as at January 1 2004: Austria,
Belgium, Denmark, Finland, France, Germany, Greece,
Ireland, Italy, Luxembourg, Netherlands, Portugal, Spain,
Sweden and the United Kingdom, except where 2004 data is
now available for the 25 members ie, including Cyprus, Czech
Republic, Estonia, Hungary, Latvia, Lithuania, Malta, Poland,
Slovakia and Slovenia. The euro area includes all of the 15
except Denmark, Sweden and the United Kingdom.

Statistical basis
The all-important factor in a book of this kind is to be able to
make reliable comparisons between countries. Although this
is never quite possible for the reasons stated above, the best
route, which this book takes, is to compare data for the same
year or period and to use actual, not estimated, figures
wherever possible. Where a country's data is excessively out of
date, it is excluded, which is the reason there is no country
profile of Iraq in this edition. The research for this edition of

The Economist Pocket World in Figures was carried out in 2006 using the latest available sources that present data on an internationally comparable basis. Data, therefore, unless otherwise indicated, refer to the year ending December 31 2004.

In the country profiles, life expectancy, crude birth, death and fertility rates are based on 2005–10 averages; human development indices and energy data are for 2003; marriage and divorce data refer to the latest year for which figures are available. Employment, health and education data are for the latest year between 2000 and 2004.

Other definitions

Data shown in country profiles may not always be consistent with those shown in the world rankings because the definitions or years covered can differ. Data may also differ between two different rankings.

Most countries' national accounts are now compiled on a GDP basis so, for simplicity, the term GDP has been used interchangeably with GNP or GNI.

Statistics for principal exports and principal imports are normally based on customs statistics. These are generally compiled on different definitions to the visible exports and imports figures shown in the balance of payments section.

Definitions of the statistics shown are given on the relevant page or in the glossary on page 246. Figures may not add exactly to totals, or percentages to 100, because of rounding or, in the case of GDP, statistical adjustment. Sums of money have generally been converted to US dollars at the official exchange rate ruling at the time to which the figures refer.

Energy consumption data are not always reliable, particularly for the major oil producing countries; consumption per head data may therefore be higher than in reality. Energy exports can exceed production and imports can exceed consumption if transit operations distort trade data or oil is imported for refining and re-exported.

Abbreviations

bn	billion (one thousand million)	GNP	Gross national product
CIS	Commonwealth of Independent States	GRT	Gross tonnage
		ha	Hectare
EU	European Union	m	million
kg	kilogram	PPP	Purchasing power parity
km	kilometre	trn	trillion (one thousand billion)
GDP	Gross domestic product	...	not available
GNI	Gross national income		

World rankings

Countries: natural facts

Countries: *the largest*[a]

'000 sq km

1	Russia	17,075		31	Tanzania	945
2	Canada	9,971		32	Nigeria	924
3	China	9,561		33	Venezuela	912
4	United States	9,373		34	Namibia	824
5	Brazil	8,512		35	Pakistan	804
6	Australia	7,682		36	Mozambique	799
7	India	3,287		37	Turkey	779
8	Argentina	2,767		38	Chile	757
9	Kazakhstan	2,717		39	Zambia	753
10	Sudan	2,506		40	Myanmar	677
11	Algeria	2,382		41	Afghanistan	652
12	Congo	2,345		42	Somalia	638
13	Saudi Arabia	2,200		43	Central African Rep	622
14	Greenland	2,176		44	Ukraine	604
15	Mexico	1,973		45	Madagascar	587
16	Indonesia	1,904		46	Kenya	583
17	Libya	1,760		47	Botswana	581
18	Iran	1,648		48	France	544
19	Mongolia	1,565		49	Yemen	528
20	Peru	1,285		50	Thailand	513
21	Chad	1,284		51	Spain	505
22	Niger	1,267		52	Turkmenistan	488
23	Angola	1,247		53	Cameroon	475
24	Mali	1,240		54	Papua New Guinea	463
25	South Africa	1,226		55	Sweden	450
26	Colombia	1,142		56	Morocco	447
27	Ethiopia	1,134			Uzbekistan	447
28	Bolivia	1,099		58	Iraq	438
29	Mauritania	1,031		59	Paraguay	407
30	Egypt	1,000		60	Zimbabwe	391

Mountains: *the highest*[b]

	Name	Location	Height (m)
1	Everest	Nepal-China	8,848
2	K2 (Godwin Austen)	Pakistan	8,611
3	Kangchenjunga	Nepal-Sikkim	8,586
4	Lhotse	Nepal-China	8,516
5	Makalu	Nepal-China	8,463
6	Cho Oyu	Nepal-China	8,201
7	Dhaulagiri	Nepal	8,167
8	Manaslu	Nepal	8,163
9	Nanga Parbat	Pakistan	8,125
10	Annapurna I	Nepal	8,091
11	Gasherbrum I	Pakistan-China	8,068
12	Broad Peak	Pakistan-China	8,047
13	Xixabangma (Gosainthan)	China	8,046
14	Gasherbrum II	Pakistan-China	8,035

a Includes freshwater.
b Includes separate peaks which are part of the same massif.

Rivers: *the longest*

Name	Location	Length (km)
1 Nile	Africa	6,695
2 Amazon	South America	6,516
3 Yangtze	Asia	6,380
4 Mississippi-Missouri system	North America	6,019
5 Ob'-Irtysh	Asia	5,570
6 Yenisey-Angara	Asia	5,550
7 Hwang He (Yellow)	Asia	5,464
8 Congo	Africa	4,667
9 Parana	South America	4,500
10 Mekong	Asia	4,425

Deserts: *the largest*

Name	Location	Area ('000 sq km)
1 Sahara	Northern Africa	8,600
2 Arabia	SW Asia	2,300
3 Gobi	Mongolia/China	1,166
4 Patagonian	Argentina	673
5 Great Victoria	W and S Australia	647
6 Great Basin	SW United States	492
7 Chihuahuan	N Mexico	450
8 Great Sandy	W Australia	400

Lakes: *the largest*

Name	Location	Area ('000 sq km)
1 Caspian Sea	Central Asia	371
2 Superior	Canada/US	82
3 Victoria	E Africa	69
4 Huron	Canada/US	60
5 Michigan	US	58
6 Aral Sea	Central Asia	34
7 Tanganyika	E Africa	33
8 Great Bear	Canada	31

Islands: *the largest*

Name	Location	Area ('000 sq km)
1 Greenland	North Atlantic Ocean	2,176
2 New Guinea	South-west Pacific Ocean	809
3 Borneo	Western Pacific Ocean	746
4 Madagascar	Indian Ocean	587
5 Baffin	North Atlantic Ocean	507
6 Sumatra	North-east Indian Ocean	474
7 Honshu	Sea of Japan-Pacific Ocean	227
8 Great Britain	Off coast of north-west Europe	218

Notes: Notes: Estimates of the lengths of rivers vary widely depending on eg, the path to take through a delta. The definition of a desert is normally a mean annual precipitation value equal to 250ml or less. Australia (7.69 sq km) is defined as a continent rather than an island.

Population: size and growth

Largest populations
Millions, 2004

1	China	1,313.3		34	Kenya	32.4
2	India	1,081.2		35	Algeria	32.3
3	United States	297.0		36	Canada	31.7
4	Indonesia	222.6		37	Morocco	31.1
5	Brazil	180.7		38	Peru	27.6
6	Pakistan	157.3		39	Uganda	26.7
7	Bangladesh	149.7		40	Uzbekistan	26.5
8	Russia	142.4		41	Venezuela	26.2
9	Japan	127.8		42	Iraq	25.9
10	Nigeria	127.1		43	Nepal	25.7
11	Mexico	104.9		44	Afghanistan	24.9
12	Germany	82.5			Malaysia	24.9
	Vietnam	82.5			Saudi Arabia	24.9
14	Philippines	81.4		47	North Korea	22.8
15	Egypt	73.4		48	Taiwan	22.7
16	Ethiopia	72.4		49	Romania	22.3
17	Turkey	72.3		50	Ghana	21.4
18	Iran	69.8		51	Yemen	20.7
19	Thailand	63.5		52	Australia	19.9
20	France	60.4		53	Mozambique	19.2
21	United Kingdom	59.4			Sri Lanka	19.2
22	Italy	57.3		55	Syria	18.2
23	Congo-Kinshasa	54.4		56	Madagascar	17.9
24	Myanmar	50.1		57	Côte d'Ivoire	16.9
25	Ukraine	48.2		58	Cameroon	16.3
26	South Korea	48.0		59	Netherlands	16.2
27	South Africa	45.2		60	Chile	16.0
28	Colombia	44.9		61	Kazakhstan	15.4
29	Spain	41.1		62	Cambodia	14.5
30	Argentina	38.9		63	Angola	14.1
31	Poland	38.6		64	Burkina Faso	13.4
32	Tanzania	37.7			Mali	13.4
33	Sudan	34.3		66	Ecuador	13.2

Largest populations

1950		Millions		2050		Millions
1	China	555.0		1	India	1,592.7
2	India	358.0		2	China	1,392.3
3	United States	158.0		3	United States	395.0
4	Russia	103.0		4	Pakistan	304.7
5	Japan	84.0		5	Indonesia	284.6
6	Indonesia	80.0		6	Nigeria	258.1
7	Germany	68.0		7	Brazil	253.1
8	Brazil	54.0		8	Bangladesh	242.9
9	United Kingdom	50.0		9	Congo-Kinshasa	177.3
10	Italy	47.0		10	Ethiopia	170.2
11	Bangladesh	42.0		11	Mexico	139.0
	France	42.0		12	Philippines	127.1
13	Pakistan	37.0		13	Uganda	127.0
	Ukraine	37.0		14	Egypt	125.9

Fastest growing populations
Total growth, 2004–50, %

1	Uganda	375.7		16	West Bank and Gaza	173.0
2	Niger	304.8		17	Togo	170.0
3	Afghanistan	290.8		18	Guinea	167.4
4	Burundi	263.4		19	Sierra Leone	165.4
5	Congo-Brazzaville	260.5		20	Eritrea	160.5
6	Chad	253.9		21	Kenya	156.5
7	Guinea-Bissau	253.3		22	Mauritania	150.0
8	Congo-Kinshasa	225.7		23	Iraq	145.9
9	Benin	220.3		24	Madagascar	143.0
10	Mali	213.4		25	Malawi	139.8
11	Angola	208.5		26	Ethiopia	135.1
12	Liberia	205.7		27	Senegal	124.3
13	United Arab Emirates	193.5		28	Equatorial Guinea	117.0
14	Burkina Faso	191.8		29	Rwanda	114.1
15	Yemen	187.4		30	Qatar	110.0

Slowest growing populations
Total growth, 2004–50, %

1	Ukraine	-45.2		16	Croatia	-15.9
2	Georgia	-41.2		17	Estonia	-15.4
3	Bulgaria	-34.6		18	Hungary	-15.3
4	Belarus	-29.3		19	Kazakhstan	-14.9
5	Virgin Islands	-26.6		20	Slovakia	-14.8
6	Latvia	-26.1		21	Andorra	-14.3
7	Romania	-24.7		22	Cuba	-14.2
8	Bosnia	-23.8		23	Japan	-12.2
9	Lithuania	-23.5		24	Martinique	-11.4
10	Moldova	-23.3		25	Italy	-11.2
11	Russia	-21.5		26	Lesotho	-11.1
12	Slovenia	-20.0		27	Serbia	-10.5
13	Armenia	-19.4		28	Netherlands Antilles	-10.3
14	Poland	-17.4		29	Macedonia	-9.5
15	Czech Republic	-16.7		30	Swaziland	-9.1

Population change
2004–50, millions

Largest increase

1	India	511.5
2	Pakistan	147.4
3	Nigeria	131.0
4	Congo-Kinshasa	122.9
5	Uganda	100.3
6	United States	98.0
7	Ethiopia	97.8
8	Bangladesh	93.2
9	China	79.0
10	Afghanistan	72.4
	Brazil	72.4
12	Indonesia	62.0
13	Egypt	52.5
14	Kenya	50.7

Largest fall

1	Russia	-30.6
2	Ukraine	-21.8
3	Japan	-15.6
4	Poland	-6.7
5	Italy	-6.4
6	Romania	-5.5
7	Germany	-3.7
8	South Korea	-3.4
9	Belarus	-2.9
10	Bulgaria	-2.7
11	Kazakhstan	-2.3
12	Georgia	-2.1
13	Czech Republic	-1.7
14	Cuba	-1.6

Population: matters of breeding

Fertility rates, 2000–05

Highest av. no. of children per woman			*Lowest av. no. of children per woman*		
1	Niger	7.91	1	Macau	0.84
2	Afghanistan	7.48	2	Hong Kong	0.94
3	Guinea-Bissau	7.10	3	Ukraine	1.12
	Uganda	7.10	4	Czech Republic	1.17
5	Mali	6.92	5	Slovakia	1.20
6	Burundi	6.80	6	Slovenia	1.22
	Liberia	6.80	7	Moldova	1.23
8	Angola	6.75		South Korea	1.23
9	Congo	6.70	9	Belarus	1.24
10	Burkina Faso	6.67		Bulgaria	1.24
11	Chad	6.65	11	Greece	1.25
12	Sierra Leone	6.50	12	Latvia	1.26
13	Somalia	6.43		Poland	1.26
14	Congo-Brazzaville	6.29		Romania	1.26
15	Yemen	6.20	15	Spain	1.27
16	Malawi	6.10	16	Italy	1.28
17	Guinea	5.92		Lithuania	1.28
18	Equatorial Guinea	5.89	18	Hungary	1.30
19	Benin	5.87	19	Bosnia	1.32
	Ethiopia	5.87		Germany	1.32

Births to women under 20, 2000–05

Highest, %			*Lowest, %*		
1	Bangladesh	25	1	China	1
	Congo	25		Japan	1
	Liberia	25		Netherlands	1
	Nicaragua	25		South Korea	1
	Niger	25		Switzerland	1
6	Guinea	24	6	Algeria	2
7	Equatorial Guinea	23		Belgium	2
	Mali	23		Denmark	2
	Uganda	23		Hong Kong	2
10	Brazil	21		Italy	2
	Chad	21		Libya	2
	Côte d'Ivoire	21		Luxembourg	2
	Nepal	21		Norway	2
	Sierra Leone	21		Singapore	2
	Zimbabwe	21		Slovenia	2
16	Central African Rep	20		Sweden	2
	Costa Rica	20		Tunisia	2
	Dominican Republic	20	18	Cyprus	3
	Gabon	20		Finland	3
	Guinea-Bissau	20		Greece	3
	Jamaica	20		Israel	3
	Nigeria	20		Macau	3
	Venezuela	20		Qatar	3
				Spain	3

Crude birth rates
Average no. of live births per 1,000 population, 2000–05

Highest			Lowest		
1	Niger	55.2	1	Latvia	7.8
2	Angola	52.3	2	Bulgaria	7.9
3	Somalia	52.1	3	Slovenia	8.3
4	Uganda	50.7	4	Ukraine	8.4
5	Congo	50.2	5	Hong Kong	8.5
6	Liberia	50.0	6	Austria	8.6
7	Guinea-Bissau	49.9		Russia	8.6
	Mali	49.9	8	Estonia	8.7
9	Sierra Leone	49.6		Germany	8.7
10	Chad	48.4		Switzerland	8.7
11	Burkina Faso	47.8	11	Belarus	8.8
12	Afghanistan	47.4		Czech Republic	8.8
13	Yemen	45.0		Hungary	8.8
14	Malawi	44.6		Italy	8.8
15	Burundi	44.2		Lithuania	8.8
	Congo-Brazzaville	44.2	16	Greece	9.1
17	Rwanda	44.0	17	Japan	9.2
18	Equatorial Guinea	43.1	18	Spain	9.3
19	Guinea	42.9	19	Poland	9.6
20	Ethiopia	42.5	20	Armenia	9.7
21	Zambia	42.2		Bosnia	9.7
22	Mauritania	41.8		Macau	9.7
23	Madagascar	41.6	23	Singapore	10.2
24	Benin	41.5		Slovakia	10.2

Most male populations
Number of males per 100 females

1	United Arab Emirates	214
2	Qatar	206
3	Kuwait	150
4	Bahrain	132
5	Oman	128
6	Saudi Arabia	117
7	Greenland	113
8	Jordan	108
9	Afghanistan	107
	Andorra	107
	Brunei	107
	Faroe Islands	107
	Libya	107
14	China	106
	Pakistan	106
	Papua New Guinea	106
17	French Polynesia	105
	Guinea	105
	India	105
	New Caledonia	105
	Niger	105
	Taiwan	105

Most female populations
Number of males per 100 females

1	Latvia	84
2	Estonia	85
	Ukraine	85
4	Armenia	87
	Lesotho	87
	Lithuania	87
	Russia	87
8	Belarus	88
9	Hong Kong	89
	Netherlands Antilles	89
11	Aruba	90
	Georgia	90
	Martinique	90
14	Hungary	91
	Virgin Islands	91
16	Kazakhstan	92
	Moldova	92
	Puerto Rico	92
19	Croatia	93
	Guadeloupe	93
	Macau	93
	Swaziland	93

Population: age

Highest median age[a]
Years, 2005

1	Japan	42.9
2	Italy	42.3
3	Germany	42.1
4	Finland	40.9
5	Switzerland	40.8
6	Austria	40.6
	Belgium	40.6
	Bulgaria	40.6
	Croatia	40.6
10	Slovenia	40.2
11	Sweden	40.1
12	Channel Islands	39.7
	Greece	39.7
14	Denmark	39.5
	Latvia	39.5
16	Portugal	39.5
17	France	39.3
	Netherlands	39.3
19	Czech Republic	39.0
	Ukraine	39.0
	United Kingdom	39.0
22	Estonia	38.9
	Hong Kong	38.9
24	Hungary	38.8
25	Canada	38.6
	Spain	38.6

Lowest median age[a]
Years, 2005

1	Uganda	14.8
2	Niger	15.5
3	Mali	15.8
4	Burkina Faso	16.2
	Guinea-Bissau	16.2
6	Chad	16.3
	Congo-Kinshasa	16.3
	Congo-Brazzaville	16.3
	Liberia	16.3
	Malawi	16.3
11	Yemen	16.5
12	Angola	16.6
13	Afghanistan	16.7
	Zambia	16.7
15	Burundi	17.0
16	West Bank and Gaza	17.1
17	Eritrea	17.4
18	Ethiopia	17.5
	Nigeria	17.5
	Rwanda	17.5
21	Benin	17.6
	Equatorial Guinea	17.6
23	Mozambique	17.7
24	Madagascar	17.8
25	Kenya	17.9
	Somalia	17.9
	Togo	17.9

Highest population aged 60 and over
%, 2005

1	Japan	26.3
2	Italy	25.6
3	Germany	25.1
4	Sweden	23.4
5	Greece	23.0
6	Austria	22.7
7	Latvia	22.5
8	Belgium	22.4
	Bulgaria	22.4
10	Portugal	22.3
11	Croatia	22.1
12	Switzerland	21.8
13	Estonia	21.6
14	Spain	21.4
15	Finland	21.3
16	United Kingdom	21.2
17	Denmark	21.1
	France	21.1

Highest population aged 0–14
%, 2005

1	Uganda	50.5
2	Niger	49.0
3	Mali	48.2
4	Guinea-Bissau	47.5
5	Chad	47.3
	Congo-Kinshasa	47.3
	Malawi	47.3
8	Burkina Faso	47.2
9	Congo-Brazzaville	47.1
	Liberia	47.1
11	Afghanistan	46.5
	Angola	46.5
13	Yemen	46.4
14	Zambia	45.8
15	West Bank and Gaza	45.5
16	Burundi	45.0
17	Eritrea	44.8
18	Ethiopia	44.5

a Age at which there are an equal number of people above and below.

Population: migrants

International migrants[a]

m, 2005

1	United States	38.4	8	India	5.7
2	Russia	12.1	9	United Kingdom	5.4
3	Germany	10.1	10	Spain	4.8
4	Ukraine	6.8	11	Australia	4.1
5	France	6.5	12	Pakistan	3.3
6	Saudi Arabia	6.4	13	United Arab Emirates	3.2
7	Canada	6.1	14	Hong Kong	3.0

% of world's total, 2005

1	United States	20.2	8	India	3.0
2	Russia	6.4	9	United Kingdom	2.8
3	Germany	5.3	10	Spain	2.5
4	Ukraine	3.6	11	Australia	2.2
5	France	3.4	12	Pakistan	1.7
6	Saudi Arabia	3.3		United Arab Emirates	1.7
7	Canada	3.2	14	Hong Kong	1.6

m, 1990

1	United States	23.3	8	Saudi Arabia	4.7
2	Russia	11.5	9	Canada	4.3
3	India	7.4	10	Australia	4.0
4	Ukraine	7.1	11	Iran	3.8
5	Pakistan	6.6		United Kingdom	3.8
6	France	5.9	13	Kazakhstan	3.6
7	Germany	5.9	14	Hong Kong	2.2

% of world's total, 1990

1	United States	15.0	8	Saudi Arabia	3.1
2	Russia	7.4	9	Canada	2.8
3	India	4.8	10	Australia	2.6
4	Ukraine	4.6	11	Iran	2.5
5	Pakistan	4.2	12	United Kingdom	2.4
6	France	3.8	13	Kazakhstan	2.3
	Germany	3.8	14	Hong Kong	1.4

m, 1970

1	United States	9.7	6	Russia[b]	3.1
2	India	9.1	7	United Kingdom	2.9
3	France	5.2	8	Germany	2.6
4	Pakistan	5.1	9	Australia	2.5
5	Canada	3.3	10	Argentina	2.3

% of world's total, 1970

1	United States	11.9	5	Canada	4.0
2	India	11.2	6	Russia[b]	3.8
3	France	6.4	7	United Kingdom	3.6
4	Pakistan	6.3	8	Germany	3.2

a Residing in a country other than where they were born.
b Soviet Union.

Refugees and asylum seekers[a]

Largest refugee nationalities
'000, 2004

1	Afghanistan	2,084.9	11	Serbia	237.0
2	Sudan	730.6	12	Bosnia	229.3
3	Burundi	485.8	13	Angola	228.8
4	Congo-Kinshasa	462.2	14	Croatia	215.5
5	Somalia	389.3	15	Turkey	174.6
6	West Bank and Gaza	350.6	16	Myanmar	161.0
7	Vietnam	349.8	17	China	134.7
8	Liberia	335.5	18	Eritrea	131.1
9	Iraq	311.8	19	Iran	115.1
10	Azerbaijan	250.6	20	Sri Lanka	114.1

Countries with largest refugee populations
'000, 2004

1	Iran	1,046.0	11	Saudi Arabia	240.6
2	Pakistan	960.6	12	Kenya	239.8
3	Germany	876.6	13	Armenia	235.2
4	Tanzania	602.1	14	Congo-Kinshasa	199.3
5	United States	420.9	15	Zambia	173.9
6	China	299.4	16	Algeria	169.0
7	United Kingdom	289.1	17	India	162.7
8	Serbia	276.7	18	Sudan	141.6
9	Chad	259.9	19	Canada	141.4
10	Uganda	250.5	20	France	139.9

Origin of asylum applications to indust. countries
'000, 2004

1	Russia	30.6		Somalia	9.2
2	Serbia	22.4	12	Afghanistan	8.9
3	China	20.1		Georgia	8.9
4	Turkey	15.9	14	Algeria	8.7
5	India	12.0	15	Haiti	8.3
6	Nigeria	11.8	16	Colombia	7.6
7	Pakistan	11.0	17	Bangladesh	6.4
8	Iran	10.5	18	Moldova	5.6
9	Iraq	9.9		Sri Lanka	5.6
10	Congo-Kinshasa	9.2	20	Bosnia	5.4

Asylum applications in industrialised countries
'000, 2004

1	France	58.6	10	Slovakia	11.4
2	United States	52.4	11	Cyprus	9.9
3	United Kingdom	40.6	12	Netherlands	9.8
4	Germany	35.6	13	Italy	9.7
5	Canada	25.8	14	Poland	8.1
6	Austria	24.6	15	Norway	8.0
7	Sweden	23.2	16	Czech Republic	5.5
8	Belgium	15.4		Spain	5.5
9	Switzerland	14.3	18	Ireland	4.8

a As reported by UNHCR.

City living

Biggest cities[a]
Population m, 2005

1	Tokyo, Japan	35.3	16	Cairo, Egypt	11.1
2	Mexico City, Mexico	19.0	17	Lagos, Nigeria	11.1
3	New York, USA	18.5	18	Beijing, China	10.8
4	Mumbai, India	18.3	19	Manila, Philippines	10.7
	Sao Paulo, Brazil	18.3		Moscow, Russia	10.7
6	Delhi, India	15.3	21	Paris, France	9.9
7	Kolkata, India	14.3	22	Istanbul, Turkey	9.8
8	Buenos Aires, Argentina	13.3	23	Seoul, South Korea	9.6
9	Jakarta, Indonesia	13.2	24	Tianjin, China	9.3
10	Shanghai, China	12.7	25	Chicago, USA	8.7
11	Dhaka, Bangladesh	12.6	26	Lima, Peru	8.2
12	Los Angeles, USA	12.1	27	Bogota, Colombia	7.6
13	Karachi, Pakistan	11.8		London, UK	7.6
14	Rio de Janeiro, Brazil	11.5	29	Tehran, Iran	7.4
15	Osaka, Japan	11.3	30	Hong Kong, Hong Kong	7.2

Fastest growing cities[b]
Average annual growth, 2005–10, %

1	Niamey, Niger	5.71	15	Santa Cruz, Bolivia	4.03
2	Kabul, Afghanistan	5.39	16	Nairobi, Kenya	4.00
3	Ghaziabad, India	5.28	17	Kampala, Uganda	3.91
4	Surat, India	5.08	18	Nashik, India	3.88
5	Sana'a, Yemen	4.87	19	Conakry, Guinea	3.76
6	Lagos, Nigeria	4.63		Dhaka, Bangladesh	3.76
7	Dar es Salaam, Tanzania	4.56		Maputo, Mozambique	3.76
	Lubumbashi, Congo-Kinshasa	4.56	22	Patna, India	3.69
9	Bamako, Mali	4.52	23	Antananarivo, Madag.	3.61
10	Faridabad, India	4.46	24	Rajkot, India	3.59
11	Kinshasa, Congo	4.32	25	Jaipur, India	3.57
12	Chittagong, Bangladesh	4.29	26	Freetown, Sierra Leone	3.55
13	Toluca, Mexico	4.12	27	Ouagadougou, Burkina Faso	3.53
14	Luanda, Angola	4.11	28	Delhi, India	3.46

Slowest growing cities[b]
Average annual growth, 2005–10, %

1	Dongguan, China	-2.75		Saratov, Russia	-0.85
2	Datong, China	-0.92		Ufa, Russia	-0.85
3	Riga, Latvia	-0.87		Voronezh, Russia	-0.85
	Tbilisi, Georgia	-0.87	15	Dnepropetrovsk, Ukraine	-0.64
5	Chelyabinsk, Russia	-0.85		Donetsk, Ukraine	-0.64
	Ekaterninburg, Russia	-0.85		Kharvov, Ukraine	-0.64
	Nizhni Novgorod, Russia	-0.85		Odessa, Ukraine	-0.64
	Novosibirsk, Russia	-0.85		Zaporozhye, Ukraine	-0.64
	Omsk, Russia	-0.85	20	Taipei, Taiwan	-0.61
	Perm, Russia	-0.85	21	Yerevan, Armenia	-0.56
	Samara, Russia	-0.85	22	Seoul, South Korea	-0.48

a Urban agglomerations. Data may change from year-to-year based on reassessments of agglomeration boundaries.
b Urban agglomerations of more than 750,000.

Population living in urban areas

Highest, %, 2005 | | *Lowest, %, 2005*

	Highest				Lowest	
1	Bermuda	100.0		1	Bhutan	9.1
	Cayman Islands	100.0		2	Burundi	10.6
	Hong Kong	100.0		3	Uganda	12.4
	Singapore	100.0		4	Papua New Guinea	13.2
5	Guadeloupe	99.8		5	Nepal	15.8
6	Macau	98.9		6	Ethiopia	16.2
7	Puerto Rico	97.5		7	Malawi	17.2
8	Belgium	97.3		8	Lesotho	18.2
9	Kuwait	96.4		9	Burkina Faso	18.6
10	Martinique	96.2		10	Cambodia	19.7
11	Virgin Islands	94.1		11	Eritrea	20.8
12	Guam	94.0		12	Sri Lanka	21.0
13	Iceland	93.0		13	Laos	21.6
	Uruguay	93.0		14	Rwanda	21.8
15	Australia	92.7		15	Niger	23.3
16	Luxembourg	92.4		16	Swaziland	23.9
17	Qatar	92.3		17	Tajikistan	24.2
	Réunion	92.3		18	Afghanistan	24.3
19	Malta	92.1		19	Bangladesh	25.0
20	Israel	91.7		20	Chad	25.8
21	Andorra	91.3		21	Gambia, The	26.1
22	Argentina	90.6		22	Yemen	26.3
23	Bahrain	90.2		23	Vietnam	26.7
24	Bahamas	90.0		24	Madagascar	27.0
25	United Kingdom	89.2		25	India	28.7
26	Germany	88.5		26	Channel Islands	30.5
	Saudi Arabia	88.5		27	Myanmar	30.6
28	Venezuela	88.1		28	Thailand	32.5
29	Lebanon	88.0		29	Congo-Kinshasa	32.7
30	Chile	87.7		30	Namibia	33.5

Highest proportion of a country's population residing in a single city[a]

%, 2005

1	Hong Kong, Hong Kong	100.0		15	Brazzaville, Congo-Braz.	29.4
	Singapore, Singapore	100.0			Panama City, Panama	29.4
3	San Juan, Puerto Rico	60.2		17	Auckland, New Zealand	29.3
4	Beirut, Lebanon	49.9		18	Lima, Peru	29.2
5	Kuwait City, Kuwait	45.9		19	Asunción, Paraguay	28.4
6	Tel Aviv, Israel	45.3		20	Tokyo, Japan	27.6
7	Montevideo, Uruguay	39.1		21	Athens, Greece	27.5
8	Tripoli, Libya	36.3		22	Vienna, Austria	27.0
9	Yerevan, Armenia	35.0		23	San José, Costa Rica	26.5
10	Santiago, Chile	34.7		24	Dublin, Ireland	25.6
11	Buenos Aires, Argentina	34.0		25	Port au Prince, Haiti	24.5
12	Dubai, UAE	33.0		26	Amman, Jordan	22.5
13	Riga, Latvia	31.7		27	Baghdad, Iraq	22.3
14	Ulan Bator, Mongolia	31.6		28	San Salvador, El Salv.	21.9

a Urban agglomerations over 750,000.

Highest quality of life[a]
New York=100, Nov. 2005

1	Zurich, Switzerland	108.0	21	Perth, Australia	104.5
2	Geneva, Switzerland	108.1	22	Montreal, Canada	104.3
3	Vancouver, Canada	107.7	23	Nurnberg, Germany	104.1
4	Vienna, Austria	107.5	24	Dublin, Ireland	103.8
5	Auckland, New Zealand	107.3	25	Calgary, Canada	103.6
6	Dusseldorf, Germany	107.2	26	Hamburg, Germany	103.4
7	Frankfurt, Germany	107.0	27	Honolulu, USA	104.3
8	Munich, Germany	106.8	28	San Francisco, USA	103.2
9	Bern, Switzerland	106.5	29	Adelaide, Australia	103.1
	Sydney, Australia	106.5		Helsinki, Finland	103.1
11	Copenhagen, Denmark	106.2	31	Brisbane, Australia	102.8
12	Wellington, New Zealand	105.8		Oslo, Norway	102.8
13	Amsterdam, Netherlands	105.7	33	Paris, France	102.7
14	Brussels, Belgium	105.6	34	Singapore, Singapore	102.5
15	Toronto, Canada	105.4	35	Tokyo, Japan	102.3
16	Berlin, Germany	105.1	36	Boston, USA	101.9
17	Melbourne, Australia	105.0	37	Lyon, France	101.6
18	Luxembourg, Lux.	104.8		Yokohama, Japan	101.6
	Ottawa, Canada	104.8	39	London, UK	101.2
20	Stockholm, Sweden	104.7	40	Kobe, Japan	101.0

Lowest quality of life[a]
New York=100, Nov. 2005

1	Baghdad, Iraq	14.5	20	Bamako, Mali	43.9
2	Brazzaville, Congo-Braz.	30.3	21	Addis Ababa, Ethiopia	44.2
3	Bangui, Cen. Afr. Rep	30.6	22	Lome, Togo	44.3
4	Khartoum, Sudan	31.7	23	Baku, Azerbaijan	44.8
5	Pointe Noire, Congo-Brazzaville	33.9	24	Abidjan, Côte d'Ivoire	46.0
6	Ndjamena, Chad	37.2	25	Kazan, Russia	47.0
7	Sana'a, Yemen	38.2	26	Dar es Salaam, Tanzania	47.4
	Port Harcourt, Nigeria	38.2	27	Novosibirsk, Russia	48.2
	Nouakchott, Mauritania	38.2	28	Havana, Cuba	48.7
10	Ouagadougou, Burkina Faso	40.5		Maputo, Mozambique	48.7
11	Kinshasa, Congo-Kinshasa	40.7	30	Douala, Cameroon	48.9
12	Port au Prince, Haiti	41.1	31	Yangon, Myanmar	49.3
	Niamey, Niger	41.1	32	Minsk, Belarus	49.5
	Antananarivo, Madagascar	41.1	33	Almaty, Kazakhstan	49.8
15	Conakry, Guinea	41.2	34	Yaoundé, Cameroon	51.1
16	Dhaka, Bangladesh	41.5	35	San Pedro Sula, Honduras	51.3
17	Lagos, Nigeria	41.8	36	Tirana, Albania	51.7
18	Tashkent, Uzbekistan	43.0	37	Algiers, Algeria	52.6
19	Luanda, Angola	43.4	38	Tripoli, Libya	53.5
			39	Tehran, Iran	54.1
			40	Cotonou, Benin	54.2

a Index based on 39 factors ranging from recreation to political stability.

The world economy

Biggest economies

GDP, $bn

1	United States	11,711.8		26	Poland	242.3
2	Japan	4,622.8		27	Denmark	241.4
3	Germany	2,740.6		28	South Africa	212.8
4	United Kingdom	2,124.4		29	Greece	205.2
5	France[a]	2,046.6		30	Finland	185.9
6	China	1,931.7		31	Ireland	181.6
7	Italy	1,677.8		32	Portugal	167.7
8	Spain	1,039.9		33	Iran	163.4
9	Canada	978.0		34	Hong Kong	163.0
10	India	691.2		35	Thailand	161.7
11	South Korea	679.7		36	Argentina	153.0
12	Mexico	676.5		37	Malaysia	118.3
13	Australia	637.3		38	Israel	116.9
14	Brazil	604.0		39	Venezuela	110.1
15	Russia	581.4		40	Czech Republic	107.0
16	Netherlands	579.0		41	Singapore	106.8
17	Switzerland	357.5		42	United Arab Emirates	104.2
18	Belgium	352.3		43	Hungary	100.7
19	Sweden	346.4		44	New Zealand	98.9
20	Taiwan	305.3		45	Colombia	97.7
21	Turkey	302.8		46	Pakistan	96.1
22	Austria	292.3		47	Chile	94.1
23	Indonesia	257.6		48	Algeria	84.6
24	Saudi Arabia	250.6			Philippines	84.6
25	Norway	250.1		50	Egypt	78.8

Biggest economies by purchasing power

GDP PPP, $bn

1	United States	11,651.1		21	Argentina	510.3
2	China	7,642.3		22	South Africa	509.3
3	Japan	3,737.3		23	Iran	504.2
4	India	3,389.7		24	Poland	495.4
5	Germany	2,335.5		25	Philippines	376.6
6	United Kingdom	1,845.2		26	Pakistan	338.4
7	France	1,769.2		27	Saudi Arabia	331.1
8	Italy	1,622.4		28	Colombia	325.9
9	Brazil	1,507.1		29	Belgium	324.1
10	Russia	1,424.4		30	Egypt	305.9
11	Spain	1,069.3		31	Ukraine	303.4
12	Mexico	1,017.5		32	Sweden	265.6
13	Canada	999.6		33	Austria	263.8
14	South Korea	985.6		34	Bangladesh	260.4
15	Indonesia	785.2		35	Malaysia	255.8
16	Taiwan	615.2		36	Greece	245.5
17	Australia	610.0		37	Switzerland	244.1
18	Turkey	556.1		38	Vietnam	225.5
19	Netherlands	517.6		39	Algeria	213.7
20	Thailand	515.3		40	Hong Kong	212.1

Note: For list of all countries with their GDP see pages 248–252.

a Includes overseas departments.

Regional GDP

$bn, 2004		*% annual growth 1999-2004*	
World	41,250	World	4.0
Advanced economies	32,430	Advanced economies	2.4
G7	25,970	G7	2.2
Euro area	9,600	Euro area	1.9
Asia[a]	3,470	Asia[a]	7.5
Latin America	2,020	Latin America	2.4
Eastern Europe[b]	1,810	Eastern Europe[b]	5.9
Middle East	840	Middle East	5.0
Africa	690	Africa	4.2

Regional purchasing power

GDP, % of total		*$ per head*	
World	100.0	World	8,920
Advanced economies	54.6	Advanced economies	31,580
G7	43.0	G7	33,430
Euro area	15.3	Euro area	27,960
Asia[a]	24.6	Asia[a]	4,560
Latin America	7.5	Latin America	7,980
Eastern Europe[b]	7.2	Eastern Europe[b]	8,630
Middle East	2.8	Middle East	6,340
Africa	3.3	Africa	2,390

Regional population

% of total (6.4bn)		*No. of countries[c]*	
Advanced economies	15.4	Advanced economies	29
G7	11.4	G7	7
Euro area	4.9	Euro area	12
Asia[a]	52.1	Asia[a]	23
Latin America	8.5	Latin America	33
Eastern Europe[b]	7.4	Eastern Europe[b]	28
Middle East	4.0	Middle East	14
Africa	12.5	Africa	48

Regional international trade

Exports of goods and services, % of tot.		*Current account balances, $bn*	
Advanced economies	71.6	Advanced economies	-283.9
G7	42.3	G7	-438.8
Euro area	31.3	Euro area	75.2
Asia[a]	11.1	Asia[a]	94.7
Latin America	4.2	Latin America	17.7
Eastern Europe[b]	7.0	Eastern Europe[b]	3.2
Middle East	3.9	Middle East	103.4
Africa	2.2	Africa	0.9

a Excludes Hong Kong, Japan, Singapore, South Korea and Taiwan.
b Includes Russia and other CIS, Turkey and Malta.
c IMF definition.

Living standards

Highest GDP per head
$

1	Luxembourg	69,420	36	Brunei[ab]	18,690
2	Bermuda[a]	69,230	37	Greece	18,660
3	Channel Islands[ab]	61,900	38	French Polynesia[ab]	18,470
4	Norway	54,360	39	Israel	17,710
5	Switzerland	49,660	40	Puerto Rico	17,410
6	Ireland	45,410	41	Portugal	16,610
7	Denmark	44,710	42	Bahamas	16,590
8	Iceland	41,910	43	Slovenia	16,090
9	United States	39,430	44	Martinique[ab]	15,490
10	Sweden	38,920	45	Netherlands Antilles[a]	15,470
11	Japan	36,170	46	Macau	15,200
12	Austria	36,090	47	Guam[a]	15,150
13	United Kingdom	35,760	48	Bahrain	14,900
14	Finland	35,750	49	South Korea	14,160
15	Netherlands	35,740	50	New Caledonia[ab]	13,550
16	Belgium	34,210	51	Taiwan	13,450
17	France	33,890	52	Malta	13,430
18	United Arab Emirates	33,610	53	Czech Republic	10,490
19	Germany	33,220	54	Barbados	10,320
20	Qatar	33,000	55	Hungary	10,270
21	Cayman Islands[a]	32,350	56	Saudi Arabia	10,060
22	Australia	32,030	57	Trinidad & Tobago	9,650
23	Canada	30,850	58	Estonia	8,650
24	Italy	29,280	59	Oman	8,370
25	Aruba	26,410	60	Guadeloupe[ab]	7,930
26	Andorra[a]	26,290	61	Croatia	7,800
27	New Zealand	25,370	62	Slovakia	7,610
28	Spain	25,300	63	Lithuania	6,550
29	Singapore	24,840	64	Mexico	6,450
30	Hong Kong	22,960	65	Equatorial Guinea	6,380
31	Virgin Islands[ac]	22,940	66	Poland	6,280
32	Kuwait	21,430	67	Réunion[a]	6,270
33	Faroe Islands[ad]	21,280	68	Latvia	5,900
34	Greenland[ad]	19,640	69	Chile	5,880
35	Cyprus	19,080		Lebanon	5,880

Lowest GDP per head
$

1	Burundi	90	11	Afghanistan	230
2	Ethiopia	110	12	Madagascar	240
3	Congo-Kinshasa	120	13	Niger	250
4	Liberia	140	14	Nepal	260
5	Malawi	150		Uganda	260
6	Myanmar[a]	160	16	Gambia, The	280
7	Guinea-Bissau	190	17	Bhutan	290
8	Sierra Leone	210		Tanzania	290
9	Eritrea	220	19	Mozambique	320
	Rwanda	220	20	Tajikistan	330

a Estimate.   b 2003   c 2002   d 2001

Highest purchasing power
GDP per head in PPP (USA = 100)

1	Luxembourg	176.3		36	Macau[a]	55.4
2	Bermuda[a]	174.5		37	Aruba	54.9
3	Channel Islands[ab]	156.0		38	Faroe Islands[ac]	53.6
4	United States	100.0		39	Slovenia	52.8
5	Ireland	97.9		40	Bahrain	52.3
6	Norway	96.9		41	South Korea	51.7
7	Iceland	83.3		42	Greenland[ac]	49.5
	Switzerland	83.3		43	Portugal	49.5
9	Cayman Islands[a]	81.5		44	Czech Republic	48.9
10	Austria	81.3			Kuwait	48.9
11	Denmark	80.4		46	Equatorial Guinea[c]	48.7
12	Netherlands	80.1		47	Malta	47.6
13	Canada	78.8		48	Brunei[ab]	47.1
14	Belgium	78.4		49	French Polynesia[ab]	46.5
15	Hong Kong	77.7		50	Bahamas	44.2
	United Kingdom	77.7		51	Bahamas[d]	43.0
17	Australia	76.4		52	Hungary	42.4
18	Finland	75.5		53	Barbados	40.9
19	Sweden	74.5		54	Martinique[ab]	39.0
20	France	73.8			Netherlands Antilles[a]	39.0
21	Japan	73.7		56	Oman	38.5
22	Germany	71.3		57	Guam[a]	38.2
23	Italy	71.0		58	Slovakia	36.9
24	Singapore	70.8		59	Estonia	36.7
25	Taiwan	68.3		60	Saudi Arabia	34.8
26	Andorra[a]	66.3		61	New Caledonia[ab]	34.2
27	Qatar[a]	65.8		62	Argentina	33.5
28	Spain	63.1		63	Lithuania	33.0
29	Puerto Rico[c]	62.8		64	Poland	32.7
30	Israel	61.5		65	Croatia	30.7
31	United Arab Emirates	60.6			Trinidad & Tobago	30.7
32	New Zealand	59.0		67	Mauritius	30.3
33	Virgin Islands[ad]	57.8		68	Latvia	29.4
34	Cyprus	57.5		69	South Africa	28.2
35	Greece	56.0		70	Chile	27.4

Lowest purchasing power
GDP per head in PPP (USA = 100)

1	Somalia[a]	1.2		11	Madagascar	2.2
2	Sierra Leone	1.4			Yemen	2.2
3	Malawi	1.6		13	Liberia[a]	2.3
4	Burundi	1.7		14	West Bank and Gaza[ab]	2.4
	Tanzania	1.7			Zambia	2.4
6	Congo-Kinshasa	1.8		16	Congo-Brazzaville	2.5
	Guinea-Bissau	1.8			Eritrea	2.5
8	Ethiopia	1.9			Mali	2.5
9	Afghanistan	2.0		19	Benin	2.7
	Niger	2.0		20	Central African Rep	2.8

Note: for definition of purchasing power parity see page 247.
a Estimate.   b 2003   c 2001   d 2002

The quality of life

Human development index[a]
Highest

1	Norway	96.3		31	Czech Republic	87.4
2	Iceland	95.6		32	Malta	86.7
3	Australia	95.5		33	Brunei	86.6
4	Canada	94.9		34	Argentina	86.3
	Luxembourg	94.9		35	Hungary	86.2
	Sweden	94.9		36	Poland	85.8
7	Switzerland	94.7		37	Chile	85.4
8	Ireland	94.6		38	Estonia	85.3
9	Belgium	94.5		39	Lithuania	85.2
10	United States	94.4		40	Qatar	84.9
11	Japan	94.3			Slovakia	84.9
	Netherlands	94.3			United Arab Emirates	84.9
13	Denmark	94.1		43	Bahrain	84.6
	Finland	94.1		44	Kuwait	84.4
15	United Kingdom	93.9		45	Croatia	84.1
16	France	93.8		46	Uruguay	84.0
17	Austria	93.6		47	Costa Rica	83.8
18	Italy	93.4		48	Latvia	83.6
19	New Zealand	93.3		49	Bahamas	83.2
20	Germany	93.0		50	Cuba	81.7
21	Spain	92.8		51	Mexico	81.4
22	Hong Kong	91.6		52	Bulgaria	80.8
23	Israel	91.5		53	Panama	80.4
24	Greece	91.2		54	Trinidad & Tobago	80.1
25	Singapore	90.7		55	Libya	79.9
26	Portugal	90.4		56	Macedonia	79.7
	Slovenia	90.4		57	Malaysia	79.6
28	South Korea	90.1		58	Russia	79.5
29	Cyprus	89.1		59	Brazil	79.2
30	Barbados	87.8			Romania	79.2

Human development index[a]
Lowest

1	Niger	28.1		10	Mozambique	37.9
2	Sierra Leone	29.8		11	Congo-Kinshasa	38.5
3	Burkina Faso	31.7		12	Zambia	39.4
4	Mali	33.3		13	Malawi	40.4
5	Chad	34.1		14	Tanzania	41.8
6	Guinea-Bissau	34.8		15	Côte d'Ivoire	42.0
7	Central African Rep	35.5		16	Benin	43.1
8	Ethiopia	36.7		17	Eritrea	44.4
9	Burundi	37.8		18	Angola	44.5

a GDP or GDP per head is often taken as a measure of how developed a country is, but its usefulness is limited as it refers only to economic welfare. In 1990 the UN Development Programme published its first estimate of a Human Development Index, which combined statistics on two other indicators – adult literacy and life expectancy – with income levels to give a better, though still far from perfect, indicator of human development. In 1991 average years of schooling was combined with adult literacy to give a knowledge variable. The HDI is shown here scaled from 0 to 100; countries scoring over 80 are considered to have high human development, those scoring from 50 to 79 medium and those under 50 low.

Economic freedom index[b]

1	Hong Kong	1.28	21	Czech Republic	2.10
2	Singapore	1.56	22	Belgium	2.11
3	Ireland	1.58	23	Lithuania	2.14
4	Luxembourg	1.60	24	Malta	2.16
5	Iceland	1.74	25	Bahrain	2.23
	United Kingdom	1.74	26	Barbados	2.25
7	Estonia	1.75	27	Armenia	2.26
8	Denmark	1.78		Bahamas	2.26
9	Australia	1.84		Japan	2.26
	New Zealand	1.84	30	Botswana	2.29
	United States	1.84		Norway	2.29
12	Canada	1.85		Portugal	2.29
	Finland	1.85	33	Spain	2.33
14	Chile	1.88	34	El Salvador	2.35
15	Switzerland	1.89		Slovakia	2.35
16	Cyprus	1.90	36	Israel	2.36
	Netherlands	1.90	37	Taiwan	2.38
18	Austria	1.95	38	Slovenia	2.41
19	Germany	1.96	39	Latvia	2.43
	Sweden	1.96	40	Hungary	2.44

Gender-related development index[c]

1	Norway	96.0	21	Spain	92.2
2	Australia	95.4	22	Hong Kong	91.2
3	Iceland	95.3	23	Israel	91.1
4	Sweden	94.7	24	Greece	90.7
5	Canada	94.6	25	Slovenia	90.1
	Switzerland	94.6	26	Portugal	90.0
7	Luxembourg	94.4	27	South Korea	89.6
8	United States	94.2	28	Cyprus	88.4
9	Belgium	94.1	29	Barbados	87.6
10	Finland	94.0	30	Czech Republic	87.2
11	Ireland	93.9	31	Hungary	86.0
	Netherlands	93.9	32	Malta	85.8
13	Denmark	93.8	33	Poland	85.6
14	Japan	93.7	34	Argentina	85.4
	United Kingdom	93.7	35	Estonia	85.2
16	France	93.5	36	Lithuania	85.1
17	New Zealand	92.9	37	Slovakia	84.7
18	Italy	92.8	38	Chile	84.6
19	Austria	92.6	39	Kuwait	84.3
	Germany	92.6			

b Ranks countries on the basis of ten indicators of how government intervention can
  restrict the economic relations between individuals. The economic indicators,
  published by the Heritage Foundation, are trade policy, taxation, monetary policy,
  the banking system, foreign-investment rules, property rights, the amount of
  economic output consumed by the government, regulation policy, the size of the
  black market and the extent of wage and price controls. A country can score between
  1 and 5 in each category, 1 being the most free and 5 being the least free.
c Combines similar data to the HDI (and also published by the UNDP) to give an
  indicator of the disparities in human development between men and women in
  individual countries. The lower the index, the greater the disparity.

Economic growth

Highest economic growth, 1994–2004

Average annual % increase in real GDP

1	Equatorial Guinea	20.9		Mali	5.8
2	Bosnia	17.4	27	Latvia	5.6
3	Liberia	12.8	28	Trinidad & Tobago	5.5
4	Rwanda	10.2	29	Lithuania	5.4
5	China	9.1	30	Dominican Republic	5.3
6	Myanmar	8.2		Yemen	5.3
7	Mozambique	8.0	32	Bangladesh	5.2
8	Ireland	7.9		Belize	5.2
9	Armenia	7.6	34	Ethiopia	5.1
10	Angola	7.4		Malaysia	5.1
11	Vietnam	7.3		Singapore	5.1
12	Chad	7.0		Tanzania	5.1
13	Cambodia	6.9	38	Benin	4.9
14	Uganda	6.7		Mauritius	4.9
15	Bhutan	6.6		South Korea	4.9
	United Arab Emirates	6.6	41	Bahrain	4.8
17	Azerbaijan	6.3		Belarus	4.8
18	Laos	6.2		Luxembourg	4.8
	Sudan	6.2		Mauritania	4.8
20	India	6.1		Tunisia	4.8
21	Estonia	6.0	46	Burkina Faso	4.7
	Mongolia	6.0		Chile	4.7
23	Albania	5.9		Egypt	4.7
	Georgia	5.9	49	Malawi	4.6
25	Botswana	5.8		Senegal	4.6

Lowest economic growth, 1994–2004

Average annual % change in real GDP

1	West Bank and Gaza	-2.8		Paraguay	1.5
2	Zimbabwe	-1.9	23	Italy	1.6
3	Sierra Leone	-0.8		New Caledonia	1.6
4	Congo-Kinshasa	-0.7	25	Bulgaria	1.7
5	Turkmenistan	-0.4	26	Austria	2.1
6	Burundi	-0.1		Colombia	2.1
	Guinea-Bissau	-0.1		Côte d'Ivoire	2.1
	Haiti	0.1		Denmark	2.1
9	Papua New Guinea	0.4		Eritrea	2.1
10	Barbados	0.8		Macau	2.1
	Jamaica	0.8	32	Bahamas	2.2
	Uruguay	0.8		Belgium	2.2
13	Venezuela	1.0		Gabon	2.2
14	Argentina	1.1	35	France	2.3
	Ukraine	1.1		French Polynesia	2.3
16	Japan	1.2	37	Brazil	2.4
17	Central African Republic	1.3		Ecuador	2.4
18	Moldova	1.4		Fiji	2.4
	Switzerland	1.4		Netherlands	2.4
20	Germany	1.5		Romania	2.4
	Macedonia	1.5			

Highest economic growth, 1984–94
Average annual % increase in real GDP

1	China	10.3		Malaysia	7.0
2	Thailand	9.0	12	Bhutan	6.6
3	South Korea	8.5	13	Swaziland	6.5
4	Botswana	8.1	14	Mauritius	6.4
5	Taiwan	8.0	15	New Caledonia	6.3
6	Belize	7.9	16	Hong Kong	6.0
7	Singapore	7.7	17	Vietnam	5.9
8	Chile	7.4	18	Luxembourg	5.8
9	Macau	7.2	19	Cyprus	5.6
10	Indonesia	7.0		Papua New Guinea	5.6

Lowest economic growth, 1984–94
Average annual % increase in real GDP

1	Liberia	-20.6	12	Nicaragua	-1.8
2	Georgia	-13.9	13	Albania	-1.7
3	Tajikistan	-8.1		Cameroon	-1.7
4	Moldova	-7.9	15	Angola	-1.4
5	Rwanda	-6.2	16	Trinidad & Tobago	-1.2
6	Latvia	-4.5	17	Hungary	-1.1
7	Congo-Kinshasa	-3.7	18	Slovakia	-1.0
8	Estonia	-3.5	19	Bulgaria	-0.6
9	Romania	-2.6	20	Congo-Brazzaville	-0.5
10	Haiti	-2.0	21	Suriname	0.0
	Sierra Leone	-2.0	22	Central African Rep	0.2

Highest services growth, 1994–2004[a]
Average annual % increase in real terms

1	Bosnia	20.2	9	Uganda	7.8
2	Georgia	14.1	10	United Arab Emirates	7.7
3	Armenia	10.5	11	Iran	7.1
4	Rwanda	10.0		Mauritania	7.1
5	China	9.6	13	Ethiopia	6.9
6	Equatorial Guinea	9.4		Laos	6.9
7	India	8.4	15	Albania	6.7
8	Burkina Faso	8.2	16	Cambodia	6.6

Lowest services growth, 1994–2004[a]
Average annual % increase in real terms

1	Congo-Kinshasa	-10.2	9	Bulgaria	0.5
2	Central African Rep	-5.1	10	Papua New Guinea	0.6
3	Zimbabwe	-2.2	11	Uruguay	0.8
4	Turkmenistan	-1.5		Venezuela	0.8
5	Burundi	-0.6	13	Argentina	1.1
6	West Bank and Gaza	-0.2	14	Haiti	1.2
7	Ukraine	0.2	15	Brazil	1.3
8	Paraguay	0.4		Switzerland	1.3

a Or nearest available years.
Note: Rankings of highest industrial growth 1994-2004 can be found on page 46 and highest agricultural growth on page 49.

Trading places

Biggest exporters
% of total world exports (visible & invisible)

1	Euro area	17.03		23	India	1.14
2	United States	12.06		24	Saudi Arabia	1.07
3	Germany	9.33		25	Australia	1.00
4	United Kingdom	6.20		26	Denmark	0.98
5	Japan	5.91			Hong Kong	0.98
6	China	5.33		28	Norway	0.96
7	France	5.08		29	Thailand	0.93
8	Italy	3.85		30	Brazil	0.88
9	Netherlands	3.49		31	Luxembourg	0.85
10	Canada	3.21		32	Poland	0.77
11	Belgium	2.69			United Arab Emirates	0.77
12	South Korea	2.43		34	Turkey	0.74
13	Spain	2.35		35	Indonesia	0.72
14	Switzerland	1.99		36	Finland	0.64
15	Russia	1.69		37	Czech Republic	0.62
	Taiwan	1.69		38	Hungary	0.53
17	Mexico	1.63		39	South Africa	0.47
18	Ireland	1.53		40	Portugal	0.46
19	Sweden	1.52		41	Puerto Rico	0.43
20	Austria	1.42		42	Israel	0.42
21	Singapore	1.22		43	Greece	0.41
22	Malaysia	1.16		44	Iran	0.38

Most trade dependent
Trade as % of GDP[a]

1	Aruba	152.0
2	Iraq	151.4
3	Liberia	115.3
4	Equatorial Guinea	102.0
5	Malaysia	95.4
6	Singapore	84.9
7	Swaziland	80.4
8	Lesotho	76.5
9	United Arab Emirates	73.9
10	Suriname	68.6
11	Puerto Rico	68.5
12	Belgium	68.3
13	Belarus	65.3
14	Congo-Brazzaville	64.7
15	Czech Republic	62.9
16	Vietnam	62.7
17	Bahrain	62.5
18	Estonia	61.9
19	Faroe Islands	61.8
20	Qatar	59.0
21	Malta	58.5

Least trade dependent
Trade as % of GDP[a]

1	North Korea	4.9
2	Somalia	9.5
3	Rwanda	9.6
4	United States	9.8
5	Japan	10.2
6	Central African Rep	10.3
7	Bermuda	11.0
8	Cuba	11.7
9	Brazil	13.2
10	Euro area	14.1
11	Hong Kong	14.5
12	Australia	15.1
	Niger	15.1
14	Greece	15.4
15	Pakistan	15.7
16	Uganda	15.9
17	Tanzania	16.0
18	Peru	16.3
19	Burkina Faso	16.6
20	Cameroon	16.7
21	Colombia	16.9

Notes: The figures are drawn from balance of payment statistics and, therefore, have differing technical definitions from trade statistics taken from customs or similar sources. The invisible trade figures do not show some countries due to unavailable data. For Hong Kong and Singapore, domestic exports and retained imports only are used.

Biggest visible traders
% of world visible exports

1	Euro area	15.61	24	Singapore	1.10
2	Germany	10.11	25	India	1.09
3	United States	9.02	26	Brazil	1.07
4	China	6.60		Thailand	1.07
5	Japan	5.99	28	United Arab Emirates	1.01
6	France	4.68	29	Australia	0.97
7	Italy	3.92	30	Norway	0.92
8	United Kingdom	3.89	31	Poland	0.91
9	Canada	3.67	32	Denmark	0.83
10	Chile	3.56	33	Indonesia	0.80
11	Netherlands	3.38	34	Czech Republic	0.74
12	South Korea	2.87		Turkey	0.74
13	Belgium	2.73	36	Finland	0.68
14	Mexico	2.09	37	Hungary	0.62
15	Spain	2.05	38	Puerto Rico	0.61
16	Russia	2.04	39	South Africa	0.54
17	Taiwan	1.92	40	Iran	0.49
18	Switzerland	1.54	41	Philippines	0.43
19	Malaysia	1.41		Venezuela	0.43
20	Saudi Arabia	1.40	43	Israel	0.41
21	Sweden	1.39	44	Portugal	0.41
22	Austria	1.25	45	Argentina	0.38
23	Ireland	1.11	46	Ukraine	0.37

Biggest invisible traders
% of world invisible exports

1	Euro area	19.26	24	Australia	1.00
2	United States	18.30	25	Norway	0.98
3	United Kingdom	11.12	26	Greece	0.92
4	Germany	6.98	27	Russia	0.78
5	France	5.68	28	Turkey	0.68
6	Japan	5.36	29	Thailand	0.56
7	Netherlands	3.54	30	Portugal	0.54
8	Italy	3.48	31	Malaysia	0.53
9	Switzerland	2.92	32	Finland	0.51
10	Spain	2.90	33	Indonesia	0.48
11	Hong Kong	2.65		Mexico	0.48
12	Belgium	2.43	35	Israel	0.44
13	Ireland	2.40	36	Brazil	0.40
	Luxembourg	2.40		Poland	0.40
15	China	2.11	38	Egypt	0.38
16	Canada	1.96	39	Czech Republic	0.32
17	Austria	1.72	40	Hungary	0.29
	Sweden	1.72		South Africa	0.29
19	Singapore	1.44	42	Lebanon	0.28
20	South Korea	1.27	43	Croatia	0.26
21	Denmark	1.25		Kuwait	0.26
22	India	1.17	45	Saudi Arabia	0.25
23	Taiwan	1.04	46	New Zealand	0.24

a Average of imports plus exports of goods as % of GDP.

Balance of payments: current account

Largest surpluses
$m

1	Japan	172,060	26	Ukraine	6,804
2	Germany	103,770	27	Denmark	5,941
3	China	68,659	28	Macau	4,163
4	Switzerland	60,246	29	Iran	3,989
5	Russia	59,935	30	Egypt	3,922
6	Saudi Arabia	51,488	31	Brunei	3,879
7	Norway	34,445	32	Libya	3,705
8	Singapore	27,897	33	Argentina	3,353
9	South Korea	27,613	34	Indonesia	3,108
10	Sweden	27,485	35	Luxembourg	2,709
11	Netherlands	23,172	36	Philippines	2,080
12	Canada	22,000	37	Israel	1,474
13	Kuwait	18,884	38	Dominican Republic	1,399
14	Taiwan	18,658	39	Chile	1,390
15	Hong Kong	16,357	40	Uzbekistan	989
16	Malaysia	14,770	41	Trinidad & Tobago[a]	985
17	Belgium	14,011	42	Morocco	922
18	Venezuela	13,830	43	Austria	765
19	Nigeria	12,264	44	Angola	686
20	Brazil	11,738	45	Gabon[a]	575
21	Algeria	11,120	46	Namibia	573
22	United Arab Emirates	10,096	47	Kazakhstan	533
23	Qatar	7,552	48	Botswana	483
24	Finland	7,529	49	Oman	443
25	Thailand	7,080	50	Bahrain	415

Largest deficits
$m

1	United States	-668,070	21	Bulgaria	-2,053
2	Spain	-49,225	22	Serbia[a]	-2,005
3	United Kingdom	-41,880	23	Bosnia	-1,918
4	Australia	-39,658	24	Latvia	-1,673
5	Turkey	-15,543	25	Croatia	-1,641
6	Italy	-15,137	26	Lithuania	-1,590
7	Greece	-13,148	27	Slovakia	-1,447
8	India	-12,948	28	Estonia	-1,432
9	Portugal	-12,682	29	Ireland	-1,423
10	Iraq	-12,218	30	Guatemala	-1,188
11	Poland	-10,357	31	Panama	-1,104
12	Hungary	-8,812	32	Iceland	-1,055
13	Mexico	-7,409	33	Belarus	-1,043
14	South Africa	-6,892	34	Colombia	-952
15	New Zealand	-6,199	35	Cuba	-915
16	Czech Republic	-5,595	36	Cyprus	-915
17	Romania	-5,589	37	Sudan	-871
18	France	-4,830	38	Costa Rica	-832
19	Lebanon	-4,797	39	Pakistan	-808
20	Azerbaijan	-2,589	40	Nicaragua	-772

a 2000   b 2002

Largest surpluses as % of GDP

%

1	Macau	61.5	26	Botswana	5.4
2	Brunei	56.7	27	Egypt	5.0
3	Qatar	37.0	28	Swaziland	4.8
4	Kuwait	33.9	29	Thailand	4.4
5	Singapore	26.1	30	South Korea	4.1
6	Saudi Arabia	20.5	31	Belgium	4.0
7	Nigeria	17.0		Finland	4.0
8	Switzerland	16.9		Netherlands	4.0
9	Norway	13.8	34	Eritrea	3.9
10	Algeria	13.1	35	Bahrain	3.8
11	Libya	12.7		Germany	3.8
12	Venezuela	12.6	37	Japan	3.7
13	Malaysia	12.5	38	China	3.6
14	Ukraine	10.5	39	Angola	3.5
15	Russia	10.3	40	Bolivia	3.3
16	Hong Kong	10.0	41	Denmark	2.5
	Namibia	10.0		Philippines	2.5
18	United Arab Emirates	9.7	43	Iran	2.4
19	Luxembourg	8.5	44	Argentina	2.2
20	Uzbekistan	8.3		Canada	2.2
21	Gabon[a]	8.0	46	Côte d'Ivoire	2.0
22	Sweden	7.9	47	Brazil	1.9
	Trinidad & Tobago[a]	7.9	48	Morocco	1.8
24	Dominican Republic	7.5		Oman	1.8
25	Taiwan	6.1	50	Yemen	1.7

Largest deficits as % of GDP

%

1	Iraq	-96.9	21	Bulgaria	-8.5
2	Mauritania	-36.2	22	Serbia[a]	-8.4
3	Azerbaijan	-30.4	23	Zimbabwe	-8.3
4	Bosnia	-22.5	24	Bhutan	-8.2
5	Lebanon	-22.0		Georgia	-8.2
6	Equatorial Guinea[a]	-21.9	26	Benin	-8.1
7	Nicaragua	-17.0	27	Panama	-8.0
8	Belize	-16.7	28	Togo[a]	-7.9
9	Estonia	-12.7	29	Macedonia	-7.7
10	Suriname	-12.4	30	Portugal	-7.6
11	Latvia	-12.3		Romania	-7.6
12	Barbados	-12.0	32	Lithuania	-7.1
13	Gambia, The	-11.3		Madagascar[a]	-7.1
14	Malawi[b]	-10.7	34	Sierra Leone	-6.9
15	Malta	-10.3	35	Chad	-6.8
16	Mozambique	-10.0	36	Greece	-6.4
17	Ethiopia	-9.4	37	New Zealand	-6.3
18	Hungary	-8.8	38	Australia	-6.2
	Niger[a]	-8.8	39	Burkina Faso[c]	-6.0
20	Iceland	-8.6	40	Cyprus	-5.9

a 2003   b 2002   c 2001

Workers' remittances

$m

1	India[a]	21,595	24	Sudan	1,401
2	Mexico	16,613	25	Bosnia	1,312
3	Philippines	8,961	26	Yemen	1,283
4	Spain	5,189	27	Honduras	1,135
5	China	4,627	28	Peru	1,123
6	Morocco	4,221	29	Russia	1,098
7	Pakistan	3,943	30	Greece	894
8	Bangladesh	3,572	31	Croatia	851
9	Egypt	3,341	32	Haiti[a]	811
10	Colombia	3,170	33	Turkey	804
11	Portugal	3,032	34	Nepal	793
12	Guatemala	2,551	35	Albania[a]	778
13	El Salvador	2,548	36	Syria	690
14	Brazil	2,459	37	Austria	641
15	Poland	2,347	38	Japan	600
16	Nigeria	2,273	39	Nicaragua	519
17	Dominican Republic	2,200	40	France	510
18	Jordan	2,059	41	Senegal[a]	448
19	Indonesia	1,700	42	Uganda	306
20	Ecuador	1,604	43	Costa Rica	302
21	Sri Lanka	1,564	44	Italy	283
22	Jamaica	1,466	45	Argentina	266
23	Tunisia	1,432	46	Tajikistan	252

Official reserves[b]

$m, end-2004

1	Japan	844,666	24	Poland	36,773
2	China	622,953	25	Indonesia	36,310
3	Taiwan	242,476	26	Canada	34,478
4	South Korea	199,196	27	Saudi Arabia	29,304
5	United States	190,466	28	Czech Republic	28,451
6	India	131,631	29	Israel	27,094
7	Russia	126,258	30	Sweden	24,740
8	Hong Kong	123,569	31	Venezuela	23,408
9	Singapore	112,232	32	Netherlands	21,052
10	Germany	97,169	33	Spain	19,761
11	France	77,353	34	Argentina	19,659
12	Switzerland	74,568	35	United Arab Emirates	18,530
13	Malaysia	66,896	36	Nigeria	17,257
14	Mexico	64,202	37	Morocco	16,647
15	Italy	62,387	38	Philippines	16,234
16	Brazil	52,937	39	Romania	16,095
17	Thailand	49,847	40	Chile	15,997
18	United Kingdom	49,738	41	Hungary	15,951
19	Algeria	45,690	42	Egypt	15,338
20	Norway	44,308	43	Slovakia	14,912
21	Denmark	39,960	44	South Africa	14,884
22	Turkey	37,304	45	Belgium	13,992
23	Australia	36,924	46	Colombia	13,537

a 2003   b Foreign exchange, SDRs, IMF position and gold at market prices.

Exchange rates

The Economist's Big Mac index

		Big Mac prices in local currency	in $	Implied PPP[a] of the $	Actual $ exchange rate	Under (-)/ over (+) valuation against $, %
Countries with the most under-valued currencies, May 2006						
1	China	10.50	1.31	3.39	8.03	-58
2	Macau	11.12	1.39	3.59	7.99	-55
3	Malaysia	5.50	1.52	1.77	3.63	-51
4	Argentina	4.75	1.55	1.53	3.06	-50
	Hong Kong	12.00	1.55	3.87	7.75	-50
	Thailand	60.00	1.56	19.35	38.45	-50
7	Indonesia	14,600.00	1.57	4,709.68	9,325.00	-49
8	Philippines	85.00	1.62	27.42	52.63	-48
9	Egypt	9.50	1.65	3.06	5.77	-47
	Paraguay	9,000.00	1.63	2,903.23	5,505.00	-47
11	Ukraine	8.50	1.68	2.74	5.05	-46
12	Moldova	23.00	1.75	7.42	13.16	-44
13	Russia	48.00	1.77	15.48	27.06	-43
	Uruguay	42.28	1.77	13.64	23.93	-43
15	Dominican Rep	60.00	1.84	19.35	32.60	-41
16	Sri Lanka	190.00	1.85	61.29	102.96	-40
17	Honduras	35.95	1.90	11.60	18.90	-39
18	Bulgaria	2.99	1.94	0.96	1.54	-37
	Slovakia	57.98	1.97	18.70	29.50	-37
20	Macedonia	95.00	1.98	30.65	47.90	-36
Countries with the most over-valued or least under-valued currencies, May 2006						
1	Norway	43.00	7.05	13.87	6.10	+127
2	Iceland	459.00	6.37	148.06	72.04	+106
	Oman	2.46	6.39	0.79	0.39	+106
4	Switzerland	6.30	5.21	2.03	1.21	+68
5	Denmark	27.75	4.77	8.95	5.82	+54
6	Sweden	33.00	4.53	10.65	7.28	+46
7	Euro area[b]	2.94	3.77	1.05[c]	1.28[c]	+22
8	Jordan	2.59	3.66	0.84	0.71	+18
	United Kingdom	1.94	3.65	1.60[d]	1.88[d]	+18
10	Canada	3.52	3.14	1.14	1.12	+1
11	Chile	1,560.00	2.94	503.23	529.95	-5
12	Peru	9.50	2.91	3.06	3.26	-6
13	Morocco	24.54	2.82	7.92	8.71	-9
14	Brazil	6.40	2.78	2.06	2.30	-10
15	Aruba	4.95	2.77	1.60	1.79	-11
	New Zealand	4.45	2.75	1.44	1.62	-11
	Slovenia	520.00	2.76	167.74	188.58	-11
18	Hungary	560.00	2.71	180.65	206.34	-12
	Turkey	4.20	2.72	1.35	1.54	-12

a Purchasing-power parity: local price divided by price in United States ($3.10, average of four cities).
b Weighted average of prices in euro area.
c Dollars per euro.
d Dollars per pound.

Inflation

Consumer price inflation

Highest, 2005, %

1	Zimbabwe[a]	140.1
2	Dominican Republic[b]	51.5
3	Angola[c]	23.0
	Suriname	23.0
5	Madagascar	18.5
6	Zambia	18.3
7	Venezuela	16.0
8	Haiti	15.7
9	Malawi	15.4
10	Jamaica	15.3
11	Ghana	15.1
12	Gambia, The[b]	14.2
13	Costa Rica	13.8
14	Nigeria	13.5
	Ukraine	13.5
16	Iran	13.4
17	Mongolia	13.0
18	Mozambique[b]	12.7
	Russia	12.7
20	Burundi[b]	12.6
21	Mauritania	12.1
	Sierra Leone	12.1

Lowest, 2005, %

1	Chad[b]	-5.4
2	Libya[b]	-2.2
3	Central African Rep[b]	-2.1
4	Japan	-0.3
5	Macedonia	0.0
6	Gabon	0.1
7	Panama[b]	0.4
8	Singapore	0.5
	Sweden	0.5
10	Armenia	0.6
11	Saudi Arabia	0.7
12	Finland	0.9
	Guinea-Bissau[b]	0.9
14	Morocco	1.0
	Syria[a]	1.0
16	Hong Kong	1.1
17	Oman	1.2
	Switzerland	1.2
19	Congo-Brazzaville	1.3
	Israel	1.3
21	Norway	1.5

Inflation, 2000–05

Highest average annual consumer price inflation, %

1	Zimbabwe[d]	106.0
2	Angola	79.2
3	Congo[e]	60.9
4	Belarus	30.9
5	Myanmar[e]	28.4
6	Turkey	26.9
7	Suriname[f]	25.3
8	Dominican Republic[e]	21.9
9	Venezuela	20.6
10	Ghana	20.2
11	Haiti	20.0
12	Zambia	19.2
13	Romania	18.3
14	Nigeria	15.7
15	Russia	14.8
16	Malawi	14.7
17	Iran	14.0
18	Mozambique[e]	12.9
19	Ecuador	12.0
20	Yemen[f]	11.7
21	Costa Rica	11.2
	Sierra Leone	11.2

Lowest average annual consumer price inflation, %

1	Libya[e]	-5.8
2	Hong Kong	-1.3
3	Japan	-0.4
4	Oman	-0.1
5	Saudi Arabia	0.1
6	Bahrain[e]	0.6
	Singapore	0.6
8	Taiwan	0.7
10	Lithuania	0.8
	Panama[e]	0.8
	Switzerland	0.8
13	Guinea Bissau[e]	0.9
14	Gabon	1.0
15	China[e]	1.2
	Finland	1.2
17	Morocco	1.4
18	Senegal	1.5
	Sweden	1.5
20	Germany	1.6

a 2002   b 2004   c 2003   d 2000–02   e 2000–04   f 2000–03

Lowest inflation, 2005

Consumer price inflation, %

1	Libya[a]	-9.8		Morocco[b]	1.2
2	Guinea-Bissau[b]	-3.5		Netherlands	1.2
3	Chad[b]	-1.9	29	Panama[b]	1.4
4	Mali[b]	-1.4	30	South Africa	1.4
5	Togo[b]	-1.0	31	Benin[b]	1.5
6	Burkina Faso	-0.4		Malaysia	1.5
	Hong Kong	-0.4	33	Barbados[b]	1.6
	Israel	-0.4		Bhutan[b]	1.6
	Macedonia	-0.4	35	Germany	1.7
	Oman	-0.4		Singapore	1.7
11	Japan	0.0	37	Canada	1.8
	Senegal[b]	0.0	38	Netherlands Antilles[b]	2.0
13	Finland	0.2	39	Austria	2.1
14	Niger	0.3		Belgium	2.1
15	Saudi Arabia	0.4		Euro area	2.1
	Sweden	0.4		France	2.1
17	Gabon[c]	0.5	43	Ireland	2.2
	Norway	0.5		Italy	2.2
19	Switzerland	0.8		Luxembourg	2.2
20	Syria[a]	1.0	46	Albania	2.3
21	Chile	1.1		Australia	2.3
	Kuwait	1.1		Cyprus	2.3
23	Bahrain[a]	1.2		Jordan[b]	2.3
	China[b]	1.2		New Zealand	2.3
	Denmark	1.2		Qatar[b]	2.3
	Lithuania	1.2	52	Portugal	2.4

Lowest inflation, 2000–05

Average annual consumer price inflation, %

1	Libya[d]	-7.2		Qatar[e]	1.4
2	Hong Kong	-2.3	18	Germany	1.5
3	Oman[e]	-0.8		Malaysia	1.5
4	Japan	-0.5		Senegal[e]	1.5
5	Saudi Arabia	-0.2	21	Belize[e]	1.6
6	Syria[d]	0.0		Israel	1.6
7	Bahrain[d]	0.3		Morocco[e]	1.6
	China[e]	0.3		Niger	1.6
9	Lithuania	0.5		Sweden	1.6
	Taiwan	0.5	26	Barbados[e]	1.7
11	Singapore	0.8		Burkina Faso	1.7
12	Switzerland	0.9		Cameroon[d]	1.7
13	Panama[e]	1.0		Finland	1.7
14	Congo-Brazzaville	1.1		Jordan[e]	1.7
15	Cambodia	1.4		Thailand	1.7
	Kuwait	1.4	32	France	1.9

a 2002 b 2003 c 2000 d 1999–2002 e 1999–2003
Notes: Inflation is measured as the % change in the consumer price index. The five-year figures shown are based on the changes in the average level of the index during the relevant years

Debt

Highest foreign debt[a]

$bn, 2004

1	China	248.93	25	Croatia	31.55
2	Brazil	222.03	26	Peru	31.30
3	Russia	197.34	27	United Arab Emirates	30.65
4	Argentina	169.25	28	Egypt	30.29
5	Turkey	161.60	29	Romania	30.03
6	South Korea	144.81	30	South Africa	28.50
7	Indonesia	140.65	31	Singapore	23.64
8	Mexico	138.69	32	Lebanon	22.18
9	India	122.72	33	Slovakia	22.07
10	Poland	99.19	34	Algeria	21.99
11	Taiwan	81.89	35	Ukraine	21.65
12	Israel	75.78	36	Syria	21.52
13	Hong Kong	67.86	37	Bangladesh	20.34
14	Hungary	63.16	38	Sudan	19.33
15	Philippines	60.55	39	Tunisia	18.70
16	Malaysia	52.15	40	Vietnam	17.83
17	Thailand	51.31	41	Morocco	17.67
18	Czech Republic	45.56	42	Ecuador	16.87
19	Chile	44.06	43	Serbia	15.88
20	Colombia	37.73	44	Bulgaria	15.66
21	Nigeria	35.89	45	Slovenia	14.81
22	Pakistan	35.69	46	Iran	13.62
23	Venezuela	35.57	47	Latvia	12.66
24	Kazakhstan	32.31	48	Uruguay	12.38

Highest foreign debt

As % of exports of goods and services, average, 2002–04

1	Burundi	3,069	21	Uganda	379
2	Liberia	1,891	22	Laos	365
3	Rwanda	964	23	Uruguay	338
4	Sierra Leone	903	24	Madagascar	330
5	Guinea-Bissau	791	25	Mozambique	310
6	Congo-Kinshasa	765	26	Cameroon	296
7	Central African Rep	730	27	Nicaragua	283
8	Malawi	584	28	Bolivia	275
9	Zambia	530	29	Benin	268
10	Mauritania	526	30	Zimbabwe	264
11	Sudan	478	31	Eritrea	260
12	Lebanon	470	32	Mali	251
13	Ethiopia	460	33	Syria	250
14	Nigeria	452	34	Peru	245
15	Argentina	451	35	Latvia	243
16	Burkina Faso	432	36	Togo	242
17	Bhutan	431	37	Kyrgyzstan	240
18	Guinea	416	38	Brazil	239
19	Gambia, The	398	39	Myanmar	233
	Tanzania	398	40	Congo-Brazzaville	230

a Foreign debt is debt owed to non-residents and repayable in foreign currency; the figures shown include liabilities of government, public and private sectors. Developed countries have been excluded.

Highest foreign debt burden
Foreign debt as % of GDP, average, 2002–04

1	Liberia	674	23	Syria	102
2	Guinea-Bissau	331	24	Laos	101
3	Burundi	227	25	Guinea	100
4	Congo-Brazzaville	214	26	Belize	99
5	Congo-Kinshasa	208		Bhutan	99
6	Malawi	188	28	Mozambique	98
7	Gambia, The	186	29	Ethiopia	97
8	Sierra Leone	177	30	Rwanda	96
9	Zambia	170	31	Ghana	95
10	Mauritania	161		Honduras	95
11	Argentina	141	33	Central African Rep	91
12	Nicaragua	127		Côte d'Ivoire	91
13	Estonia	116	35	Eritrea	90
	Lebanon	116	36	Mali	83
	Sudan	116	37	Bulgaria	81
16	Kyrgyzstan	114		Cameroon	81
	Mongolia	114		Moldova	81
18	Croatia	113	40	Cambodia	80
19	Latvia	112		Gabon	80
20	Kazakhstan	107		Hungary	80
21	Togo	106	43	Jamaica	79
22	Uruguay	104		Tunisia	79

Highest debt service ratios[b]
%, average, 2002–04

1	Burundi	195	23	Algeria	22
2	Lebanon	92		Bulgaria	22
3	Belize	65		Romania	22
4	Brazil	58		Uzbekistan	22
5	Kazakhstan	52	27	Peru	21
6	Guinea-Bissau	46	28	Cameroon	20
7	Turkey	45		Ethiopia	20
8	Poland	44		Gambia, The	20
9	Ecuador	42		Guinea	20
	Uruguay	42		Slovakia	20
11	Colombia	38		Venezuela	20
12	Argentina	33	34	Angola	19
	Croatia	33		Papua New Guinea	19
14	Chile	32	36	Kyrgyzstan	18
15	Hungary	31		Lithuania	18
	Zambia	31	38	India	16
17	Indonesia	26		Jamaica	16
	Latvia	26		Morocco	16
19	Mexico	25		Panama	16
20	Bolivia	23		Paraguay	16
	Pakistan	23		Tunisia	16
	Philippines	23			

b Debt service is the sum of interest and principal repayments (amortisation) due on outstanding foreign debt. The debt service ratio is debt service expressed as a percentage of the country's exports of goods and services.

Aid

Largest bilateral and multilateral donors[a]
$m

1	United States	19,705	14	Switzerland	1,545
2	Japan	8,906	15	Belgium	1,463
3	France	8,473	16	Australia	1,460
4	United Kingdom	7,883	17	Portugal	1,031
5	Germany	7,534	18	Austria	678
6	Netherlands	4,204	19	Finland	655
7	Sweden	2,722	20	Ireland	607
8	Canada	2,599	21	Greece	465
9	Italy	2,462	22	South Korea	423
10	Spain	2,437	23	Taiwan	421
11	Norway	2,199	24	Turkey	339
12	Denmark	2,037	25	Luxembourg	236
13	Saudi Arabia	1,734	26	New Zealand	212

Largest recipients of bilateral and multilateral aid
$m

1	Iraq	4,658	35	Jordan	581
2	Afghanistan	2,190	36	French Polynesia	580
3	Vietnam	1,830	37	Nigeria	573
4	Ethiopia	1,823	38	Mali	567
5	Congo-Kinshasa	1,815	39	Niger	536
6	Tanzania	1,746	40	New Caledonia	525
7	China	1,661	41	Sri Lanka	519
8	Poland	1,525	42	Colombia	509
9	Egypt	1,458	43	Peru	487
10	Pakistan	1,421	44	Israel	479
11	Bangladesh	1,404	45	Cambodia	478
12	Ghana	1,358	46	Malawi	476
13	Russia	1,313	47	Rwanda	468
14	Madagascar	1,236	48	Philippines	463
15	Nicaragua	1,232	49	Nepal	427
16	Mozambique	1,228	50	Benin	378
17	Serbia	1,170	51	Albania	362
18	Uganda	1,159	52	Sierra Leone	360
19	Angola	1,144		Ukraine	360
20	West Bank and Gaza	1,136	54	Burundi	351
21	Zambia	1,081	55	Tunisia	328
22	Senegal	1,052	56	Chad	319
23	Romania	916	57	Georgia	315
24	Sudan	882	58	Algeria	313
25	Bolivia	767	59	Hungary	303
26	Cameroon	762	60	Malaysia	290
27	Morocco	706	61	Brazil	285
28	India	691	62	Czech Republic	280
29	Bosnia	671	63	Guinea	279
30	Honduras	642	64	Laos	270
31	Kenya	635	65	Papua New Guinea	266
32	Bulgaria	622	66	Kazakhstan	265
33	South Africa	617		Lebanon	265
34	Burkina Faso	610	68	Mongolia	262

Largest bilateral and multilateral donors[a]
% of GDP

1	Norway	0.87	14	Germany	0.28
2	Denmark	0.85	15	Canada	0.27
3	Luxembourg	0.83	16	Australia	0.25
4	Sweden	0.78	17	Spain	0.24
5	Netherlands	0.73	18	Austria	0.23
6	Saudi Arabia	0.69		Greece	0.23
7	Portugal	0.63		New Zealand	0.23
8	Belgium	0.41	21	Japan	0.19
	France	0.41	22	Iceland	0.18
	Switzerland	0.41	23	United States	0.17
11	Ireland	0.39	24	Italy	0.15
12	United Kingdom	0.36	25	Taiwan	0.13
13	Finland	0.35	26	Czech Republic	0.11

Largest recipients of bilateral and multilateral aid
$ per head

1	French Polynesia	2,416	34	Sierra Leone	67
2	New Caledonia	2,386	35	Ghana	66
3	West Bank and Gaza	337	36	Mozambique	65
4	Nicaragua	225	37	Mauritania	63
5	Iraq	189	38	Liberia	62
6	Bosnia	175	39	Equatorial Guinea	61
7	Bahrain	146	40	Eritrea	59
8	Serbia	144		Lebanon	59
9	Macedonia	121	42	Lesotho	57
10	Albania	114	43	Benin	56
11	Jordan	109		Rwanda	56
12	Barbados	108	45	Suriname	54
13	Mongolia	106	46	Guinea-Bissau	51
14	Swaziland	105		Kyrgyzstan	51
15	Zambia	104	48	Burkina Faso	50
16	Senegal	103	49	Burundi	49
17	Estonia	101		Mali	49
18	Netherlands Antilles	98		Tanzania	49
19	Honduras	92	52	Laos	48
20	Bhutan	90		Papua New Guinea	48
21	Namibia	89	54	Cameroon	47
22	Bolivia	87	55	Niger	46
23	Angola	85		Uganda	46
24	Armenia	83	57	Gambia, The	44
25	Bulgaria	80		Slovakia	44
26	Cyprus	78	59	Malawi	43
27	Fiji	76	60	Romania	42
28	Afghanistan	73	61	Poland	40
	Lithuania	73	62	Tajikistan	38
	Madagascar	73	63	Chad	37
31	Israel	72	64	Cambodia	36
32	Latvia	71	65	Guinea	35
33	Georgia	69	66	Congo-Kinshasa	34

a China also provides aid, but does not disclose amounts.

Industry and services

Largest industrial output
$bn

1	United States[a]	2,271	26	Poland	69
2	Japan[a]	1,308	27	Iran	67
3	China	893	28	South Africa	61
4	Germany	721	29	Malaysia	60
5	United Kingdom	496	30	United Arab Emirates	57
6	Italy	417	31	Ireland[a]	56
7	France	399		Turkey	56
8	Canada	285	33	Denmark	51
9	Spain	274	34	Argentina	50
10	South Korea	247		Finland	50
11	Brazil	211	36	Algeria	44
12	Russia	182	37	Greece	42
13	India	171	38	Venezuela[a]	41
14	Mexico	162	39	Nigeria	40
15	Saudi Arabia	147	40	Portugal	39
16	Netherlands	132	41	Chile	38
17	Australia[a]	124	42	Czech Republic	37
18	Indonesia	113	43	Singapore	35
19	Taiwan	90	44	Colombia	27
20	Norway	87		Egypt	27
	Sweden	87		Philippines	27
22	Austria	81	47	New Zealand	25
23	Belgium	80	48	Kuwait[a]	24
24	Switzerland[b]	76		Romania	24
25	Thailand	70			

Highest growth in industrial output
Average annual real % growth, 1994–2004[c]

1	Equatorial Guinea	36.8		Myanmar	10.5
2	Mozambique	16.5	11	Bhutan	10.3
3	Georgia	15.6	12	Uganda	10.0
4	Bosnia	15.3	13	Albania	8.4
5	Cambodia	15.3		Azerbaijan	8.4
6	Rwanda	12.0	15	Angola	8.3
7	Laos	10.7		Mongolia	8.3
	Vietnam	10.7	17	Trinidad & Tobago	8.1
9	China	10.5	18	Eritrea	7.6

Lowest growth in industrial output
Average annual real % growth, 1994–2004[c]

1	West Bank and Gaza	-8.8		Uruguay	-0.1
2	Zimbabwe	-5.0	12	Jamaica	0.1
3	Congo-Kinshasa	-3.6	13	Haiti	0.4
4	Moldova	-2.4	14	Germany	0.5
5	Tajikistan	-1.9		Japan	0.5
6	Papua New Guinea	-1.5	16	Turkmenistan	0.6
7	Burundi	-0.8	17	Colombia	0.7
8	Lebanon	-0.4	18	Iran	0.8
9	Venezuela	-0.3		Switzerland	0.8
10	Bulgaria	-0.1		United Kingdom	0.8

Largest manufacturing output
$bn

1	United States[a]	1,523	21	Belgium[a]		49
2	Japan[a]	894	22	Austria[a]		45
3	China	889	23	Sweden[b]		44
4	Germany[a]	495	24	Ireland[a]		42
5	United Kingdom	319	25	Poland		41
6	Italy	295	26	South Africa		38
7	France	255	27	Malaysia		37
8	Canada	177	28	Turkey		35
9	South Korea	174	29	Argentina		34
10	Spain	153	30	Finland[a]		32
11	Russia	138	31	Denmark[a]		29
12	Mexico	111		Singapore		29
13	India	101	33	Czech Republic		25
14	Taiwan	78		Saudi Arabia		25
15	Indonesia	73	35	Portugal[a]		22
16	Netherlands[a]	68	36	Philippines		20
17	Australia[a]	57		Romania		20
	Brazil	57	38	Norway[b]		19
19	Thailand	56	39	Greece[a]		18
20	Switzerland[b]	53		Iran		18

Largest services output
$bn

1	United States[a]	7,807	26	Norway	130
2	Japan[a]	2,920	27	Greece	127
3	Germany	1,729	28	South Africa	124
4	France	1,391	29	Finland	106
5	United Kingdom	1,371	30	Indonesia	105
6	Italy	1,045	31	Portugal	101
7	China	786	32	Saudi Arabia	93
8	Canada	672	33	Iran	77
9	Spain	630		Ireland[a]	77
10	Mexico	426	35	Argentina	76
11	Netherlands	370	36	Thailand	75
12	Australia[a]	341	37	Singapore	65
13	South Korea	335	38	New Zealand	64
14	India	326	39	Czech Republic	56
15	Russia	310	40	Colombia	51
16	Brazil	261	41	Hungary	47
17	Belgium	230		Malaysia	47
18	Sweden	210		Pakistan[a]	47
	Taiwan	210	44	Philippines	46
20	Switzerland[b]	182	45	Chile	45
21	Austria	175	46	United Arab Emirates	44
22	Turkey	163	47	Egypt	36
23	Denmark	151		Peru	36
24	Poland	136	49	Venezuela[a]	35
25	Hong Kong[a]	134	50	Romania	32

a 2003   b 2002   c Or nearest available years.

Agriculture

Most economically dependent on agriculture
% of GDP from agriculture

1	Guinea-Bissau	62.6	24	Cambodia	32.9
2	Sierra Leone[a]	58.4	25	Uganda	32.2
3	Congo-Kinshasa[b]	58.3	26	Gambia, The	32.0
4	Myanmar[a]	57.2	27	Uzbekistan	31.1
5	Central African Rep	55.6	28	Burkina Faso	30.8
6	Burundi	51.5	29	Papua New Guinea[c]	29.0
7	Ethiopia	46.9	30	Madagascar	28.8
8	Laos	46.8	31	Haiti	27.4
9	Chad[c]	45.6	32	Paraguay	27.2
10	Tanzania	44.8	33	Kenya	26.8
11	Cameroon	44.2	34	Guinea	24.9
12	Liberia[b]	42.7	35	Albania	24.7
13	Togo	41.2	36	Tajikistan	24.2
14	Rwanda	40.5	37	Armenia	23.4
15	Nepal	40.3	38	Syria	23.0
16	Niger[c]	39.9	39	Guatemala	22.5
17	Sudan	39.3	40	Pakistan	22.4
18	Malawi	39.1	41	Côte d'Ivoire	22.1
19	Ghana	37.9	42	Vietnam	21.8
20	Benin	36.9	43	Mozambique	21.6
21	Kyrgyzstan	36.6	44	Moldova	21.3
22	Mali	35.6	45	India	21.1
23	Bhutan[c]	33.2			

Least economically dependent on agriculture
% of GDP from agriculture

1	Hong Kong[c]	0.1	24	Ireland[c]	2.7
	Singapore	0.1		Slovenia[c]	2.7
3	Kuwait[c]	0.5		United Arab Emirates	2.7
4	Luxembourg	0.6	27	Jordan	2.8
5	Puerto Rico[d]	0.7	28	Czech Republic	3.1
6	Trinidad & Tobago	0.9	29	Finland	3.2
7	United Kingdom	1.0	30	Hungary[c]	3.3
8	Germany	1.1	31	Australia[c]	3.4
9	United States[c]	1.2		Poland	3.4
10	Japan[c]	1.3		South Africa	3.4
11	Belgium	1.4	34	Spain	3.5
	Switzerland[b]	1.4	35	Slovakia	3.6
13	Norway	1.6	36	Portugal	3.7
14	Taiwan	1.7		South Korea	3.7
15	Sweden	1.8	38	Chile	3.8
16	Austria	1.9	39	Saudi Arabia	4.0
	Oman	1.9	40	Latvia	4.1
18	Canada[d]	2.2		Mexico	4.1
19	Denmark	2.3	42	Estonia	4.3
20	Netherlands	2.4	43	Venezuela[c]	4.5
21	France	2.5	44	French Polynesia[a]	4.7
22	Botswana	2.6	45	Russia	5.0
	Italy	2.6	46	Barbados[c]	5.4

a 2000   b 2002   c 2003   d 2001

Highest growth
Average annual real % growth, 1994–2004ª

1	Angola	11.7	10	Dominican Republic	6.4
2	Kuwait	10.3	11	Yemen	6.1
3	Rwanda	9.7	12	Algeria	6.0
4	Malawi	9.0		Myanmar	6.0
5	United Arab Emirates	8.5	14	Benin	5.7
6	Sudan	7.9	15	Kyrgyzstan	5.6
7	Mozambique	7.0	16	Bulgaria	5.5
8	Cameroon	6.5	17	Gambia, The	4.9
	Equatorial Guinea	6.5	18	Belize	4.7

Lowest growth
Average annual real % growth, 1994–2004ª

1	West Bank and Gaza	-7.1	9	Singapore	-2.1
2	Georgia	-5.2	10	Kazakhstan	-1.7
3	Haiti	-4.1		Luxembourg	-1.7
4	Eritrea	-2.7	12	Trinidad & Tobago	-1.6
5	Chile	-2.6	13	Barbados	-1.4
	Jamaica	-2.6	14	Zimbabwe	-0.8
7	Switzerland	-2.5	15	Taiwan	-0.7
8	Japan	-2.4	16	Estonia	-0.5

Biggest producers
'000 tonnes

Cereals
1	China	413,166	6	Indonesia	65,314
2	United States	389,066	7	Brazil	63,812
3	India	232,360	8	Canada	52,684
4	Russia	76,231	9	Germany	51,097
5	France	70,534	10	Bangladesh	41,044

Meat
1	China	74,306	6	India	6,032
2	United States	38,891	7	Spain	5,531
3	Brazil	19,919	8	Mexico	5,040
4	Germany	6,798	9	Russia	4,981
5	France	6,255	10	Canada	4,592

Fruit
1	China	83,238	6	Spain	16,687
2	India	47,031	7	Mexico	14,759
3	Brazil	36,015	8	Indonesia	14,748
4	United States	30,197	9	Iran	13,143
5	Italy	17,922	10	Philippines	12,372

Vegetables
1	China	423,395	5	Italy	16,355
2	India	80,529	6	Egypt	15,900
3	United States	39,185	7	Russia	15,504
4	Turkey	25,235	8	Iran	13,495

a Or nearest available years.

Commodities

Wheat

Top 10 producers
'000 tonnes

1	EU25	136,100
2	China	91,000
3	India	72,100
4	United States	58,700
5	Russia	45,300
6	Canada	25,900
7	Australia	22,600
8	Pakistan	19,000
9	Turkey	18,000
10	Ukraine	16,500

Top 10 consumers
'000s tonnes

1	EU25	117,200
2	China	104,300
3	India	71,900
4	Russia	38,000
5	United States	31,900
6	Pakistan	20,400
7	Turkey	17,700
8	Egypt	14,900
9	Iran	13,800
10	Ukraine	12,300

Rice[a]

Top 10 producers
'000 tonnes

1	China	125,363
2	India	85,310
3	Indonesia	34,250
4	Bangladesh	25,600
5	Vietnam	22,716
6	Thailand	17,070
7	Myanmar	9,570
8	Philippines	9,445
9	Brazil	8,996
10	Japan	7,944

Top 10 consumers
'000 tonnes

1	China	135,100
2	India	82,510
3	Indonesia	35,850
4	Bangladesh	26,900
5	Vietnam	18,250
6	Philippines	10,400
7	Myanmar	10,300
8	Thailand	9,480
9	Brazil	9,001
10	Japan	8,300

Sugar[b]

Top 10 producers
'000 tonnes

1	Brazil	28,248
2	EU25	21,843
3	India	14,432
4	China	10,912
5	United States	7,647
6	Thailand	7,462
7	Mexico	5,672
8	Australia	5,530
9	Pakistan	4,481
10	Colombia	2,740

Top 10 consumers
'000 tonnes

1	India	19,858
2	EU25	17,691
3	China	11,613
4	Brazil	10,857
5	United States	8,994
6	Russia	6,700
7	Mexico	5,300
8	Pakistan	4,004
9	Indonesia	3,915
10	Egypt	2,600

Coarse grains[c]

Top 5 producers
'000 tonnes

1	United States	319,500
2	EU25	150,500
3	China	139,700
4	Brazil	37,800
5	India	32,000

Top 5 consumers
'000 tonnes

1	United States	240,200
2	EU25	142,000
3	China	135,700
4	Brazil	43,600
5	Mexico	38,900

Tea

Top 10 producers '000 tonnes		*Top 10 consumers* '000 tonnes	
1 China	835	1 India	671
2 India	820	2 China	558
3 Kenya	325	3 Russia	171
4 Sri Lanka	308	4 Turkey	165
5 Indonesia	165	5 Japan	155
Turkey	165	6 United Kingdom	129
7 Japan	100	7 Pakistan	120
8 Vietnam	95	8 United States	99
9 Argentina	63	9 Iran	84
10 Bangladesh	56	10 Egypt	72

Coffee

Top 10 producers '000 tonnes		*Top 10 consumers* '000s tonnes	
1 Brazil	2,357	1 United States	1,255
2 Vietnam	831	2 Brazil	929
3 Colombia	684	3 Germany	595
4 Indonesia	443	4 Japan	428
5 Ethiopia	300	5 Italy	335
6 India	231	6 France	305
7 Guatemala	222	7 Spain	177
8 Mexico	204	8 United Kingdom	133
9 Uganda	165	9 Poland	130
10 Honduras	155	10 Indonesia	120

Cocoa

Top 10 producers '000 tonnes		*Top 10 consumers* '000 tonnes	
1 Côte d'Ivoire	1,407	1 United States	775
2 Ghana	737	2 Germany	289
3 Indonesia	430	3 France	230
4 Nigeria	180	4 United Kingdom	220
5 Brazil	163	5 Russia	177
6 Cameroon	162	6 Japan	163
7 Ecuador	117	7 Italy	101
8 Dominican Republic	47	8 Brazil	94
9 Mexico	44	9 Spain	90
10 Papua New Guinea	39	10 Canada	72

a Milled.
b Raw.
c Includes: maize (corn), barley, sorghum, rye, oats and millet.

Copper

Top 10 producers[a]
'000 tonnes

1	Chile	5,413
2	United States	1,160
3	Peru	1,036
4	Australia	854
5	Indonesia	842
6	Russia	767
7	China	742
8	Canada	563
9	Poland	531
10	Kazakhstan	468

Top 10 consumers[b]
'000 tonnes

1	China	3,364
2	United States	2,410
3	Japan	1,279
4	Germany	1,100
5	South Korea	940
6	Italy	715
7	Taiwan	690
8	France	536
9	Russia	526
10	Mexico	475

Lead

Top 10 producers[a]
'000 tonnes

1	China	944
2	Australia	678
3	United States	445
4	Peru	306
5	Mexico	117
6	Canada	77
7	Ireland	66
8	Sweden	54
9	Poland	53
10	India	51

Top 10 consumers[b]
'000 tonnes

1	United States	1,480
2	China	1,399
3	Germany	396
4	South Korea	358
5	Japan	291
6	Italy	275
7	United Kingdom	261
8	Mexico	254
9	Spain	226
10	France	189

Zinc

Top 10 producers[a]
'000 tonnes

1	China	2,024
2	Australia	1,334
3	Peru	1,209
4	Canada	791
5	United States	739
6	Ireland	444
7	Mexico	424
8	Kazakhstan	361
9	India	341
10	Sweden	197

Top 10 consumers[c]
'000 tonnes

1	China	2,551
2	United States	1,097
3	Japan	621
4	Germany	549
5	South Korea	420
6	Belgium	404
7	Italy	389
8	India	353
9	Taiwan	342
10	Spain	253

Tin

Top 5 producers[a]
'000 tonnes

1	China	118.2
2	Indonesia	78.4
3	Peru	41.6
4	Bolivia	18.1
5	Brazil	12.5

Top 5 consumers[b]
'000 tonnes

1	China	92.9
2	United States	53.6
3	Japan	33.1
4	Germany	20.3
5	South Korea	16.2

Nickel

Top 10 producers[a]		*Top 10 consumers[b]*	
'000 tonnes		*'000 tonnes*	
1 Russia	289.2	1 Japan	194.9
2 Canada	186.7	2 China	143.9
3 Australia	185.0	3 United States	129.4
4 New Caledonia	118.2	4 South Korea	122.6
5 Indonesia	96.6	5 Germany	94.5
6 China	75.6	6 Taiwan	91.4
7 Cuba	75.5	7 Italy	69.5
8 Colombia	48.8	8 Finland	59.4
9 Brazil	47.4	9 Spain	48.3
10 South Africa	39.9	10 Belgium	43.4

Aluminium

Top 10 producers[d]		*Top 10 consumers[e]*	
'000 tonnes		*'000 tonnes*	
1 China	6,689	1 China	6,043
2 Russia	3,594	2 United States	5,800
3 Canada	2,592	3 Japan	2,319
4 United States	2,517	4 Germany	1,795
5 Australia	1,895	5 South Korea	1,118
6 Brazil	1,457	6 Russia	1,020
7 Norway	1,322	7 Italy	987
8 South Africa	864	8 India	861
9 India	861	9 Canada	761
10 United Arab Emirates	683	10 France	749

Precious metals

Gold [a]		*Silver* [a]	
Top 10 producers		*Top 10 producers*	
tonnes		*tonnes*	
1 South Africa	340.4	1 Peru	3,060
2 Australia	259.0	2 Mexico	2,531
3 United States	258.0	3 Australia	2,183
4 China	194.4	4 China	2,000
5 Russia	180.5	5 Chile	1,360
6 Peru	173.2	6 Canada	1,338
7 Indonesia	164.4	7 Poland	1,330
8 Canada	130.7	8 United States	1,246
9 Uzbekistan	86.0	9 Kazakhstan	690
10 Papua New Guinea	73.5	10 Bolivia	413

Platinum		*Palladium*	
Top 3 producers		*Top 3 producers*	
tonnes		*tonnes*	
1 South Africa	154.6	1 Russia	127.5
2 Russia	26.4	2 South Africa	78.1
3 North America	10.6	3 North America	32.2

a Mine production. b Refined consumption. c Slab consumption.
d Primary refined production. e Primary refined consumption.

Rubber (natural and synthetic)

Top 10 producers		*Top 10 consumers*	
'000 tonnes		*'000 tonnes*	
1 Thailand	3,114	1 China	4,068
2 United States	2,325	2 United States	3,050
3 Indonesia	2,051	3 Japan	1,961
4 China	1,964	4 India	968
5 Japan	1,616	5 Germany	867
6 Malaysia	1,189	6 Brazil	712
7 Russia	1,112	7 South Korea	691
8 Germany	905	8 France	650
9 India	837	9 Russia	614
10 France	776	10 Malaysia	542

Raw wool

Top 10 producers[a]		*Top 10 consumers[a]*	
'000 tonnes		*'000 tonnes*	
1 Australia	335	1 China	358
2 China	171	2 India	120
3 New Zealand	167	3 Italy	110
4 Argentina	43	4 Turkey	69
5 India	38	5 United Kingdom	31
6 United Kingdom	31	6 Japan	30
7 Uruguay	29	7 Russia	29
8 South Africa	27	8 Iran	26
Turkey	27	9 Belgium	25
10 Iran	24	10 New Zealand	23

Cotton

Top 10 producers		*Top 10 consumers*	
'000 tonnes		*'000 tonnes*	
1 China	6,320	1 China	8,330
2 United States	5,060	2 India	3,300
3 India	4,130	3 Pakistan	2,340
4 Pakistan	2,480	4 Turkey	1,550
5 Brazil	1,300	5 United States	1,460
6 Uzbekistan	1,130	6 Brazil	900
7 Turkey	900	7 Indonesia	490
8 Australia	660	8 Thailand	470
9 Greece	390	9 Mexico	450
10 Syria	330	10 Bangladesh	380

Major oil seeds[b]

Top 5 producers		*Top 5 consumers*	
'000 tonnes		*'000 tonnes*	
1 United States	94,850	1 China	76,705
2 Brazil	56,584	2 United States	60,315
3 China	53,660	3 EU25	35,879
4 Argentina	44,070	4 Brazil	34,356
5 India	25,370	5 Argentina	32,682

Oil[c]

Top 10 producers
'000 barrels per day

1	Saudi Arabia[d]	10,584
2	Russia	9,285
3	United States	7,241
4	Iran[d]	4,081
5	Mexico	3,824
6	China	3,490
7	Norway	3,188
8	Canada	3,085
9	Venezuela[d]	2,980
10	United Arab Emirates[d]	2,667

Top 10 consumers
'000 barrels per day

1	United States	20,517
2	China	6,684
3	Japan	5,288
4	Germany	2,625
5	Russia	2,574
6	India	2,555
7	South Korea	2,280
8	Canada	2,206
9	France	1,975
10	Mexico	1,896

Natural gas

Top 10 producers
Billion cubic metres

1	Russia	589.1
2	United States	542.9
3	Canada	182.8
4	United Kingdom	95.9
5	Iran[d]	85.5
6	Algeria[d]	82.0
7	Norway	78.5
8	Indonesia[d]	73.3
9	Netherlands	68.8
10	Saudi Arabia[d]	64.0

Top 10 consumers
Billion cubic metres

1	United States	646.7
2	Russia	402.1
3	United Kingdom	98.0
4	Canada	89.5
5	Iran[d]	87.1
6	Germany	85.9
7	Italy	73.3
8	Japan	72.2
9	Ukraine	70.7
10	Saudi Arabia[d]	64.0

Coal

Top 10 producers
Million tonnes oil equivalent

1	China	989.8
2	United States	567.2
3	Australia	199.4
4	India	188.8
5	South Africa	136.9
6	Russia	127.6
7	Indonesia[d]	81.4
8	Poland	69.8
9	Germany	54.7
10	Kazakhstan	44.4

Top 10 consumers
Million tonnes oil equivalent

1	China	956.9
2	United States	564.3
3	India	204.8
4	Japan	120.8
5	Russia	105.9
6	South Africa	94.5
7	Germany	85.7
8	Poland	57.7
9	Australia	54.4
10	South Korea	53.1

Oil[c]

Top 10 shares of proved reserves
% of world total

1	Saudi Arabia[d]	22.1		5	United Arab Emirates[d]	8.2
2	Iran[d]	11.1		6	Venezuela[d]	6.5
3	Iraq[d]	9.7		7	Russia	6.1
4	Kuwait[d]	8.3				

a Clean basis.   b Soybeans, sunflower seed, cottonseed, groundnuts and rapeseed.
c Includes crude oil, shale oil, oil sands and natural gas liquids.   d Opec members.

Energy

Largest producers
Million tonnnes oil equivalent, 2003

1	United States	1,631.4	16	Algeria	163.3
2	China	1,380.8	17	United Arab Emirates	159.2
3	Russia	1,106.9	18	South Africa	154.5
4	Saudi Arabia	533.7	19	France	136.0
5	India	453.1	20	Germany	134.5
6	Canada	385.3	21	Kuwait	120.7
7	Iran	265.4	22	Kazakhstan	105.5
8	Australia	253.5	23	Japan	84.6
9	Indonesia	250.0	24	Argentina	84.3
10	United Kingdom	246.1	25	Malaysia	83.8
11	Mexico	242.5	26	Poland	80.0
12	Norway	233.2	27	Libya	77.5
13	Nigeria	214.6	28	Ukraine	75.5
14	Venezuela	179.6	29	Colombia	74.4
15	Brazil	171.1	30	Iraq	68.4

Largest consumers
Million tonnnes oil equivalent, 2003

1	United States	2,280.8	16	Spain	136.1
2	China	1,409.4	17	Ukraine	132.6
3	Russia	639.7	18	Saudi Arabia	130.8
4	India	553.4	19	South Africa	118.6
5	Japan	517.1	20	Australia	112.6
6	Germany	347.1	21	Nigeria	97.8
7	France	271.3	22	Poland	93.7
8	Canada	260.6	23	Thailand	88.8
9	United Kingdom	232.0	24	Netherlands	80.8
10	South Korea	205.3	25	Turkey	79.0
11	Brazil	193.2	26	Pakistan	69.3
12	Italy	181.0	27	Argentina	59.9
13	Indonesia	161.6	28	Belgium	59.2
14	Mexico	160.0	29	Malaysia	56.7
15	Iran	136.4	30	Venezuela	54.2

Energy efficiency[a]

Most efficient
GDP per unit of energy use, 2003

1	Peru	11.3
2	Hong Kong	10.9
3	Uruguay	10.5
4	Bangladesh	10.4
5	Morocco	10.2
6	Colombia	10.1
7	Costa Rica	9.9
	Namibia	9.9
9	Ireland	9.3
10	Sri Lanka	8.8
11	Italy	8.2

Least efficient
GDP per unit of energy use, 2003

1	Uzbekistan	0.8
2	Trinidad & Tobago	1.2
3	Nigeria	1.3
	Tanzania	1.3
	Turkmenistan	1.3
6	Zambia	1.4
7	Kuwait	1.8
8	Kazakhstan	1.9
	Moldova	1.9
	Russia	1.9
	Ukraine	1.9

a PPP$, per kg of oil equivalent.

Net energy importers
% of commercial energy use, 2003

Highest			Lowest		
1	Hong Kong	100	1	Congo-Brazzaville	-1,078
2	Singapore	99	2	Norway	-899
3	Moldova	98	3	Gabon	-637
4	Israel	96	4	Angola	-457
4	Lebanon	96	5	Kuwait	-427
5	Jordan	95	6	Algeria	-395
7	Morocco	94	7	Oman	-379
8	Jamaica	88	8	Libya	-331
9	Ireland	87	9	Saudi Arabia	-308
10	Belarus	86	10	United Arab Emirates	-306
11	Italy	85	11	Yemen	-284

Largest consumption per head
Kg of oil equivalent, 2003

1	United Arab Emirates	9,707	12	Norway	5,100
2	Kuwait	9,566	13	Oman	4,975
3	Trinidad & Tobago	8,553	14	Netherlands	4,962
4	Canada	8,240	15	France	4,519
5	United States	7,843	16	Russia	4,424
6	Finland	7,204	17	New Zealand	4,333
7	Sweden	5,754	18	Czech Republic	4,324
8	Belgium	5,701	19	South Korea	4,291
9	Australia	5,668	20	Germany	4,205
10	Saudi Arabia	5,607	21	Austria	4,086
11	Singapore	5,359	22	Japan	4,053

Sources of electricity
% of total, 2003

Oil			Gas		
1	Yemen	100.0	1	Turkmenistan	100.0
2	Iraq	98.5	2	Trinidad & Tobago	99.7
3	Benin	97.4	3	United Arab Emirates	99.4
4	Jamaica	96.9	4	Algeria	96.8
5	Cuba	94.3	5	Belarus	95.5

Hydropower			Nuclear power		
1	Paraguay	100.0	1	Lithuania	82.2
2	Nepal	99.8	2	France	78.5
3	Congo-Brazzaville	99.7	3	Slovakia	57.7
	Congo-Kinshasa	99.7	4	Belgium	56.7
	Mozambique	99.7	5	Sweden	49.7

Coal		
1	Poland	95.1
2	South Africa	93.5
3	Estonia	92.2
4	China	79.4
5	Hong Kong	77.7

Workers of the world

Highest % of population in labour force

1	Cayman Islands	68.9	21	Russia	50.6
2	Bermuda	59.4	22	Slovenia	50.5
3	China	57.8	23	Czech Republic	50.3
4	Switzerland	57.5	24	United Kingdom	50.2
5	Thailand	55.7	25	Finland	50.0
6	Canada	55.4	26	Cyprus	49.9
	Denmark	54.4	27	South Korea	49.7
8	Iceland	54.0	28	Slovakia	49.4
9	Norway	52.9	29	Ecuador	49.3
10	Netherlands	52.6	30	Austria	49.0
11	Brazil	52.4		Latvia	49.0
	Portugal	52.4	32	Turkey	48.7
	Singapore	52.4	33	Germany	48.5
14	Hong Kong	52.0	34	Estonia	48.6
	Japan	52.0	35	Ghana	47.8
16	Macau	51.8	36	Belgium	47.6
17	New Zealand	51.7		Spain	47.6
18	United States	50.9	38	Ireland	47.5
19	Australia	50.8	39	Bahrain	47.4
20	Sweden	50.7	40	Brunei	47.3

Most male workforce

Highest % men in workforce

1	Pakistan	83.9
2	West Bank and Gaza	83.4
3	Algeria	83.0
4	Oman	81.6
5	Syria	80.6
6	Bahrain	78.3
7	Egypt	78.1
8	Bangladesh	77.7
9	Guatemala	77.4
10	Tunisia	74.3
11	Turkey	73.7
12	Morocco	72.9
13	Malta	69.2
	Nicaragua	69.2
15	India	68.4
16	Sri Lanka	66.5
17	Honduras	66.3
18	Costa Rica	65.4
	Mauritius	65.4
20	Malaysia	65.3
21	Mexico	64.5
22	Chile	64.4
23	Suriname	63.1
24	Panama	62.7
25	Philippines	62.2

Most female workforce

Highest % women in workforce

1	Belarus	53.3
2	Benin	53.1
3	Moldova	51.0
	Mongolia	51.0
	Tanzania	51.0
6	Malawi	50.2
7	Cayman Islands	49.7
8	Ghana	49.6
9	Armenia	49.5
	Madagascar	49.5
11	Bahamas	49.4
	Estonia	49.4
13	Guadeloupe	49.1
	Lithuania	49.1
	Russia	49.1
16	Kazakhstan	49.0
17	Ukraine	48.9
18	Barbados	48.7
	Latvia	48.7
20	Bermuda	48.5
21	Zimbabwe	48.2
22	Papua New Guinea	47.9
	Sweden	47.9
24	Azerbaijan	47.7
	Finland	47.7

Lowest % of population in labour force

1	West Bank and Gaza	21.9	21	Moldova	39.6
2	Algeria	27.6	22	Chile	39.7
3	Syria	29.3	23	El Salvador	40.1
4	Pakistan	29.6		Sri Lanka	40.1
5	Egypt	30.5	25	Croatia	40.8
6	Congo-Brazzaville	32.3	26	Honduras	40.9
7	Armenia	32.4		Macedonia	40.9
8	Suriname	34.6	28	Malaysia	41.3
9	Bangladesh	34.7	29	Zimbabwe	41.5
10	Botswana	35.0	30	Mexico	41.7
	Guatemala	35.0	31	Hungary	42.0
	Tunisia	35.0	32	Israel	42.1
13	Nicaragua	36.5	33	Italy	42.2
14	Puerto Rico	37.0	34	Costa Rica	42.3
15	Oman	37.3	35	Albania	42.4
16	Morocco	37.4	36	Argentina	42.7
17	India	39.1		Bulgaria	42.7
18	Georgia	39.3		Greece	42.7
	Mongolia	39.3	39	Luxembourg	43.0
20	Malta	39.5	40	Poland	44.1

Highest rate of unemployment

% of labour force[a]

1	Macedonia	37.2	26	Georgia	12.6
2	Namibia	33.8	27	Kyrgyzstan	12.5
3	South Africa	27.1	28	Iran	12.3
4	West Bank and Gaza	26.7		Panama	12.3
5	Guadeloupe	24.7	30	Nicaragua	12.2
6	Ethiopia	22.9	31	Bulgaria	12.0
7	Martinique	22.4	32	Morocco	11.9
8	Botswana	19.6	33	Syria	11.7
9	Poland	19.0	34	Yemen	11.5
10	Dominican Republic	18.4	35	Jamaica	11.4
11	Slovakia	18.1	36	Egypt	11.0
12	Algeria	17.7		Germany	11.0
13	Uruguay	16.9		Spain	11.0
14	Venezuela	15.8	39	Philippines	10.9
15	Argentina	15.6	40	Bahamas	10.8
16	Albania	15.2	41	Israel	10.7
	Serbia	15.2	42	Puerto Rico	10.6
18	Netherlands Antilles	15.1	43	Peru	10.5
19	Tunisia	14.3	44	Latvia	10.4
20	Burundi	14.0		Trinidad & Tobago	10.4
	Suriname	14.0	46	Turkey	10.3
22	Croatia	13.8	47	France	9.9
23	Colombia	13.6	48	Barbados	9.8
24	Jordan	13.2	49	Brazil	9.7
25	Lithuania	12.8		Estonia	9.7

a ILO definition.

The business world

Global competitiveness

	Overall	*Government*	*Infrastructure*
1	United States	Hong Kong	United States
2	Hong Kong	Singapore	Japan
3	Singapore	Denmark	Denmark
4	Iceland	Iceland	Switzerland
5	Denmark	Finland	Singapore
6	Australia	Australia	Sweden
7	Canada	Ireland	Finland
8	Switzerland	Switzerland	Norway
9	Luxembourg	Canada	Germany
10	Finland	Norway	Iceland
11	Ireland	Estonia	Canada
12	Norway	New Zealand	Austria
13	Austria	Chile	Belgium
14	Sweden	United States	Hong Kong
15	Netherlands	Austria	Israel
16	Japan	Luxembourg	Netherlands
17	Taiwan	China	Australia
18	China	Netherlands	Taiwan
19	Estonia	Malaysia	France
20	United Kingdom	Thailand	Luxembourg
21	New Zealand	Sweden	United Kingdom
22	Malaysia	Slovakia	South Korea
23	Chile	Taiwan	New Zealand
24	Israel	United Kingdom	Ireland
25	Germany	South Africa	Czech Republic
26	Belgium	Japan	Spain
27	India	Israel	Malaysia
28	Czech Republic	Germany	Hungary
29	Thailand	Czech Republic	Greece
30	France	India	Portugal
31	Spain	Colombia	Estonia
32	South Korea	Belgium	Slovenia
33	Slovakia	Jordan	China
34	Colombia	Spain	Italy
35	Hungary	Hungary	Jordan
36	Greece	Portugal	Colombia
37	Portugal	Bulgaria	Slovakia
38	South Africa	Russia	Chile
39	Slovenia	Philippines	Poland
40	Jordan	Greece	Bulgaria
41	Bulgaria	South Korea	Argentina
42	Philippines	France	Thailand
43	Turkey	Slovenia	Croatia
44	Brazil	Mexico	Russia

Notes: Rankings reflect assessments for the ability of a country to achieve sustained high rates of GDP growth per head. Column 1 is based on 259 criteria covering: the openness of an economy, the role of the government, the development of financial markets, the quality of infrastructure, technology, business management and judicial and political institutions and labour-market flexibility. Column 2 looks at the extent to which government policies are conducive to competitiveness. Column 3 is based on the extent to which a country is integrated into regional trade blocks.

The business environment

		2006–10 score	2001–2005 score	2001–2005 ranking
1	Denmark	8.82	8.69	1
2	Finland	8.70	8.55	6
3	Canada	6.86	8.63	2
4	Singapore	8.66	8.62	3
5	Ireland	8.65	8.44	10
	Netherlands	8.65	8.51	7
7	United Kingdom	8.64	8.59	4
8	United States	8.63	8.56	5
9	Switzerland	8.60	8.45	9
10	Hong Kong	8.57	8.50	8
11	Sweden	8.49	8.29	11
12	Australia	8.44	8.14	13
13	New Zealand	8.36	8.18	12
14	Germany	8.33	7.95	14
15	Belgium	8.23	7.89	15
16	Norway	8.21	7.82	17
17	Austria	8.16	7.81	18
	France	8.16	7.83	16
19	Taiwan	8.08	7.52	21
20	Estonia	7.93	7.65	19
21	Spain	7.87	7.45	22
22	Chile	7.81	7.64	20
23	Israel	7.79	6.84	30
24	Slovakia	7.54	6.77	31
25	Malaysia	7.46	7.34	23
	South Korea	7.46	7.10	25
27	Czech Republic	7.45	6.92	28
28	Japan	7.41	6.95	27
29	Portugal	7.35	6.75	32
	Slovenia	7.35	7.16	24
	United Arab Emirates	7.35	6.71	35
32	Qatar	7.30	6.90	29
33	Hungary	7.29	6.72	34
34	Latvia	7.17	6.69	36
35	Lithuania	7.16	6.60	39
36	Bahrain	7.15	6.98	26
37	Poland	7.14	6.64	38
38	Italy	7.07	6.45	41
39	Cyprus	7.01	6.73	33
40	Thailand	6.98	6.66	37
41	South Africa	6.92	6.14	45
42	Mexico	6.88	6.46	40
43	Bulgaria	6.77	5.87	49
44	Greece	6.75	6.25	44
45	Brazil	6.74	6.37	42
46	Kuwait	6.65	6.32	43

Note: Scores reflect the opportunities for, and hindrances to, the conduct of business, measured by countries' rankings in ten categories including market potential, tax and labour-market policies, infrastructure, skills and the political environment. Scores reflect average and forecast average over given date range.

Business creativity and research

Innovation index[a]

1	United States	6.66	13	Singapore	4.47
2	Finland	6.43	14	Iceland	4.45
3	Taiwan	6.19	15	Australia	4.36
4	Sweden	5.89	16	United Kingdom	4.35
5	Japan	5.74	17	Netherlands	4.33
6	Israel	5.38	18	New Zealand	4.22
7	Switzerland	5.37	19	Belgium	4.20
8	South Korea	5.29	20	France	4.05
9	Germany	4.92	21	Austria	3.97
10	Denmark	4.70	22	Ireland	3.82
11	Canada	4.69	23	Slovenia	3.60
12	Norway	4.62	24	Greece	3.54

Information and communications technology index[b]

1	Denmark	5.90	13	Luxembourg	5.19
2	Iceland	5.88	14	Norway	5.12
3	United States	5.72	15	United Kingdom	4.98
4	Sweden	5.66	16	Canada	4.89
5	Finland	5.61	17	Japan	4.75
6	Taiwan	5.51	18	Austria	4.74
7	Netherlands	5.43	19	New Zealand	4.71
8	Singapore	5.40	20	Germany	4.63
9	Australia	5.27	21	Estonia	4.56
10	Hong Kong	5.23	22	France	4.46
	South Korea	5.23	23	Israel	4.37
12	Switzerland	5.21	24	Ireland	4.33

E-readiness[c]
Score out of 10, 2006

1	Denmark	9.00		New Zealand	8.19
2	United States	8.88	16	Ireland	8.09
3	Switzerland	8.81	17	Belgium	7.99
4	Sweden	8.74	18	South Korea	7.90
5	United Kingdom	8.64	19	France	7.86
6	Netherlands	8.60	20	Bermuda	7.81
6	Finland	8.55	21	Japan	7.77
8	Australia	8.50	22	Israel	7.59
9	Canada	8.37	23	Taiwan	7.51
10	Hong Kong	8.36	24	Spain	7.34
11	Norway	8.35	25	Italy	7.14
12	Germany	8.34	26	Portugal	7.07
13	Singapore	8.24	27	Estonia	6.71
14	Austria	8.19	28	Slovenia	6.43

a The innovation index is a measure of the adoption of new technology, and the interaction between business and the scientific sector. It includes measures of the number of patents granted and higher education enrolment rates.

b The information and communications technology (ICT) index is a measure of ICT usage and includes per capita measures of telephone lines, internet usage, personal computers and mobile phone users.

c E-Readiness measures how amenable a country is to internet-based business. The factors considered include broadband and mobile-phone penetration, as well as government regulation.

Total expenditure on R&D
% of GDP, 2003

1	Israel	4.35		24	Russia	1.28
2	Sweden	4.27		25	Czech Republic	1.26
3	Finland	3.44		26	New Zealand	1.25
4	Japan	3.12		27	Ireland	1.13
5	Iceland	3.10		28	Italy	1.11
6	South Korea	2.64		29	Brazil	1.04
7	United States	2.59		30	Spain	1.02
8	Switzerland	2.57		31	Hungary	0.95
9	Denmark	2.54		32	Portugal	0.94
10	Germany	2.51		33	India	0.84
11	Taiwan	2.45		34	Estonia	0.83
12	Belgium	2.33		35	South Africa	0.74
13	France	2.26		36	Chile	0.69
14	Austria	2.17			Malaysia	0.69
15	Singapore	2.13		38	Turkey	0.66
16	Netherlands	1.88		39	Greece	0.65
	United Kingdom	1.88		40	Hong Kong	0.60
18	Canada	1.85		41	Poland	0.59
19	Luxembourg	1.71		42	Slovakia	0.58
20	Norway	1.67		43	Venezuela	0.46
21	Australia	1.59		44	Colombia	0.40
22	Slovenia	1.50			Mexico	0.40
23	China	1.31		46	Argentina	0.39

Patents

No. of patents granted to residents		*No. of patents in force*	
Total, 2002		*Per 100,000 people, 2002*	
1 Japan	110,053	1 Luxembourg	5,804
2 United States	86,551	2 Switzerland	1,152
3 Taiwan	26,964	3 Sweden	1,105
4 South Korea	24,984	4 Singapore	864
5 Germany	19,593	5 Japan	860
6 Russia	14,454	6 Belgium	851
7 France	10,737	7 Taiwan	834
8 China	5,913	8 Ireland	831
9 United Kingdom	4,452	9 Netherlands	776
10 Netherlands	2,929	10 Denmark	701
11 Italy	2,298	11 France	602
12 Sweden	1,795	12 Canada	554
13 Switzerland	1,746	13 United Kingdom	551
14 Spain	1,564	14 South Korea	516
15 Australia	1,415	15 United States	511
16 Austria	1,349	16 Australia	502
17 Canada	1,193	17 Germany	457
18 Poland	875	18 Finland	394
19 Belgium	783	19 Spain	377
20 Romania	696	20 Portugal	281

a 2001   b 2000   c 1997   d 1998   e 1996

Business costs and FDI

Office rents

Occupation cost[a], $ per square metre, August 2005

1	London (West End), UK	1,923	15	Frankfurt, Germany	684
2	Tokyo (Inner Central), Japan	1,411	16	Bristol, UK	680
3	Tokyo (Outer Central), Japan	1,328	16	Glasgow, UK	680
			18	Paris (La Defense), France	679
4	London (City), UK	1,282	19	Seoul, South Korea	665
5	Paris, France	964	20	Milan, Italy	656
6	Moscow, Russia	918	21	Aberdeen, UK	617
7	Dublin, Ireland	874	22	Munich, Germany	615
8	Edinburg, UK	816	23	Mumbai, India	607
8	Hong Kong	816	24	Geneva, Switzerland	599
10	Manchester, UK	796	25	Luxembourg City, Luxembourg	588
11	Leeds, UK	748	26	Jersey, UK	583
12	Zurich, Switzerland	731	27	New York (MT Manhattan), US	578
13	Birmingham, UK	728	28	Madrid, Spain	569
14	Dubai, UAE	704			

Employment costs

Pay, social security and other benefits, $ per hr. worked for a production worker

1	Norway	37.33	11	Australia	24.88
2	Denmark	34.51	12	France	24.70
3	Germany	32.52	13	United States	24.42
4	Finland	31.96	14	Canada	23.87
5	Netherlands	31.25	15	Ireland	23.08
6	Switzerland	30.77	16	Japan	21.67
7	Belgium	30.73	17	Italy	21.17
8	Austria	28.94	18	Spain	17.70
9	Sweden	28.78	19	New Zealand	15.44
10	United Kingdom	25.54	20	Singapore	7.92

Foreign direct investment[b]

Inflow, $m, 2004

1	United States	95,859	19	Canada	6,293
2	United Kingdom	78,399	20	Poland	6,159
3	China	60,630	21	India	5,335
4	Luxembourg	57,000	22	Romania	5,174
5	Australia	42,594	23	Austria	4,865
6	Belgium	34,366	24	Azerbaijan	4,769
7	Hong Kong	34,035	25	Finland	4,648
8	France	24,318	26	Malaysia	4,624
9	Spain	18,361	27	Switzerland	4,478
10	Brazil	18,166	28	Czech Republic	4,463
11	Italy	16,815	29	Kazakhstan	4,269
12	Mexico	16,602	30	Argentina	4,254
13	Singapore	16,060	31	Hungary	4,167
14	Russia	11,672	32	Bermuda	3,800
15	Ireland	9,120	33	Cayman Islands	3,000
16	Japan	7,816	34	Colombia	2,739
17	South Korea	7,687	35	Turkey	2,733
18	Chile	7,603	36	Bulgaria	2,488

Business burdens and corruption

Number of days taken to register a new company

Highest			Lowest		
1	Haiti	203	1	Australia	2
2	Laos	198	2	Canada	3
3	Congo	155	3	Denmark	5
4	Mozambique	153		Iceland	5
5	Brazil	152		United States	5
6	Indonesia	151	6	Singapore	6
7	Angola	146	7	Afghanistan	7
8	Venezuela	116		Puerto Rico	7
9	Azerbaijan	115	9	France	8
10	Botswana	108	10	Jamaica	9
11	West Bank and Gaza	106		Turkey	9
12	Peru	102	12	Hong Kong	11
13	Zimbabwe	96		Morocco	11
14	Namibia	95		Netherlands	11
15	Lesotho	92		Romania	11
16	Eritrea	91	16	New Zealand	12

Corruption perceptions index[c]

2005, 10 = least corrupt

Lowest			Highest		
1	Iceland	9.7	1	Bangladesh	1.7
2	Finland	9.6		Chad	1.7
	New Zealand	9.6	3	Haiti	1.8
4	Denmark	9.5		Myanmar	1.8
5	Singapore	9.4		Turkmenistan	1.8
6	Sweden	9.2	6	Equatorial Guinea	1.9
7	Switzerland	9.1		Ivory Coast	1.9
8	Norway	8.9		Nigeria	1.9
9	Australia	8.8	9	Angola	2.0
10	Austria	8.7	10	Congo	2.1
11	Netherlands	8.6		Kenya	2.1
	United Kingdom	8.6		Pakistan	2.1
13	Luxembourg	8.5		Paraguay	2.1
14	Canada	8.4		Somalia	2.1
15	Hong Kong	8.3		Sudan	2.1
				Tajikistan	2.1

Business software piracy

% of software that is pirated, 2004

1	Vietnam	92	7	Nigeria	84
2	Ukraine	91		Tunisia	84
3	China	90	9	Algeria	83
	Zimbabwe	90		Kenya	83
5	Indonesia	87		Paraguay	83
	Russia	87	12	Pakistan	82

a Total rent, taxes and operating expenses.
b Investment in companies in a foreign country.
c This index ranks countries based on how much corruption is perceived by business
   people, academics and risk analysts to exist among politicians and public officials.

Businesses and banks

Largest businesses
By sales, $bn

1	Wal-Mart Stores	United States	288.0
2	BP	United Kingdom	285.1
3	Exxon Mobil	United States	270.8
4	Royal Dutch/Shell Group	United Kingdom/Netherlands	268.7
5	General Motors	United States	193.5
6	DaimlerChrysler	United States	176.7
7	Toyota Motor	Japan	172.6
8	Ford Motor	United States	172.2
9	General Electric	United States	152.9
10	Total Fina Elf	France	152.6
11	ChevronTexaco	United States	148.0
12	ConocoPhillips	United States	121.7
13	AXA	France	121.6
14	Allianz	Germany	118.9
15	Volkswagen	Germany	110.6
16	Citigroup	United States	108.3
17	ING Group	Netherlands	105.9
18	Nippon Telegraph & Telephone	Japan	100.5
19	American Intl. Group	United States	98.0
20	IBM	United States	96.3
21	Siemens	Germany	91.5
22	Carrefour	France	90.4
23	Hitachi	Japan	84.0
24	Assicurazioni Generali	Italy	83.3
25	Matsushita Electric Industrial	Japan	81.1
26	McKesson	United States	80.5
27	Honda Motor	Japan	80.5
28	Hewlett-Packard	United States	79.9
29	Nissan Motor	Japan	79.8
30	Fortis	Netherlands	75.5
31	Sinopec	China	75.1
32	Berkshire Hathaway	United States	74.4
33	ENI	Italy	74.2
34	Home Depot	United States	73.1
35	Aviva	United Kingdom	73.0
36	HSBC Holdings	United Kingdom	72.6
37	Deutsche Telekom	Germany	72.0
38	Verizon Communications	United States	71.6
39	Samsung Electronics	South Korea	71.6
40	State Grid	China	71.3
41	Peugeot	France	70.6
42	Metro-Goldwyn-Mayer	United States	70.2
43	Nestlé	Switzerland	69.8
44	U.S. Postal Service	United States	69.0

Notes: Industrial and service corporations. Figures refer to the year ended December 31, 2004, except for Japanese companies, where figures refer to year ended March 31, 2005. They include sales of consolidated subsidiaries but exclude excise taxes, thus differing, in some instances, from figures published by the companies themselves.

Largest banks
By capital, $m

1	Citigroup	United States	74,415
2	J.P. Morgan Chase	United States	68,621
3	HSBC Holdings	United Kingdom	67,259
4	Bank of America Corp	United States	64,281
5	Crédit Agricole Groupe	France	63,422
6	Royal Bank of Scotland	United Kingdom	43,828
7	Mitsubishi Tokyo Financial Group	Japan	39,932
8	Mizuho Financial Group	Japan	38,864
9	HBOS	United Kingdom	36,587
10	BNP Paribas	France	35,685
11	Bank of China	China	34,851
12	Santander Central Hispano	Spain	33,259
13	Barclays Bank	United Kingdom	32,178
14	Rabobank Group	Netherlands	30,810
15	Sumitomo Mitsui Financial Group	Japan	30,389
16	Wells Fargo & Co.	United States	29,060
17	ING Bank	Netherlands	28,792
18	Wachovia Corporation	United States	28,583
19	UBS	Switzerland	27,440
20	ABN-Amro Bank	Netherlands	26,993
21	Deutsche Bank	Germany	25,507
22	Groupe Caisse d'Epargne	France	25,056
23	Société Générale	France	25,008
24	Crédit Mutuel	France	24,773
25	China Construction Bank	China	23,530
26	Lloyds TSB Group	United Kingdom	22,644
27	Credit Suisse Group	Switzerland	21,736
28	UFJ Holdings	Japan	21,550
29	HypoVereinsbank	Germany	21,412
30	Banca Intesa	Italy	21,199
31	MetLife	United States	20,968
32	Industrial and Commercial Bank of China	China	20,170
33	Banco Bilbao Vizcaya Argentaria	Spain	20,033
34	Fortis Bank	Belgium	19,489
35	Norinchukin Bank	Japan	18,493
36	Groupe Banques Populaires	France	18,280
37	Agricultural Bank of China	China	16,670
38	Washington Mutual	United States	16,368
39	UniCredit	Italy	16,175
40	National Australia Bank	Australia	15,044
41	Dexia	Belgium	15,014
42	Sanpaolo IMI	Italy	14,792
43	US Bancorp	United States	14,720
44	Nordea Group	Sweden	14,432
45	Commerzbank	Germany	14,279
46	Scotiabank	Canada	14,135

Notes: Capital is essentially equity and reserves.
Figures for Japanese banks refer to the year ended March 31, 2005. Figures for all other countries refer to the year ended December 31, 2004.

Stockmarkets

Largest market capitalisation
$m, end 2005

1	United States	16,997,982		27	Norway	190,952
2	Japan	4,736,513		28	Malaysia	181,236
3	United Kingdom	3,058,182		29	Denmark	178,038
4	France	1,710,029		30	Turkey	161,537
5	Canada	1,480,891		31	Greece	145,013
6	Germany	1,221,250		32	Chile	136,446
7	Hong Kong	1,006,228		33	Kuwait	130,080
8	Spain	960,024		34	Austria	126,324
9	Switzerland	938,624		35	Thailand	123,539
10	Australia	804,074		36	Israel	120,114
11	Italy	798,167		37	Ireland	114,134
12	China	780,763		38	Poland	93,873
13	Netherlands	727,515		39	Qatar	87,316
14	South Korea	718,180		40	Indonesia	81,428
15	Saudi Arabia	646,104		41	Egypt	79,672
16	South Africa	565,408		42	Portugal	66,981
17	India	553,074		43	Argentina	61,478
18	Russia	548,579		44	Luxembourg	51,254
19	Taiwan	485,617		45	Colombia	46,016
20	Brazil	474,647		46	Pakistan	45,937
21	Sweden	403,948		47	New Zealand	40,620
22	Belgium	327,065		48	Philippines	40,153
23	Mexico	239,128		49	Iran	38,724
24	United Arab Emirates	225,568		50	Czech Republic	38,345
25	Finland	209,504		51	Jordan	37,639
26	Singapore	208,300		52	Peru	35,995

Highest growth in market capitalisation, $ terms
% increase, 2000–05

1	Macedonia	9,129		21	Lithuania	415
2	United Arab Emirates	3,839		22	Kenya	398
3	Amenia[a]	2,050		23	Colombia	381
4	Romania	1,826		24	Croatia	371
5	Qatar	1,595		25	Ecuador	357
6	Georgia	1,379			Nigeria	357
7	Russia	1,309		27	Latvia	349
8	Ukraine	1,228		28	Oman	341
9	Kyrgyzstan	950		29	Austria	322
10	Saudi Arabia	862		30	South Korea	319
11	Bulgaria	724			Thailand	319
12	Kazakhstan	684			Zambia	319
13	Jordan	661		33	Trinidad & Tobago	292
14	Serbia[b]	637		34	India	274
15	Pakistan	598		35	Jamaica	264
16	Iceland	526		36	Slovakia	261
	Kuwait	526		37	Czech Republic	249
18	West Bank and Gaza	483		38	Peru	241
19	Sri Lanka	433		39	Barbados	226
20	Iran	427		40	Papua New Guinea[a]	220

Highest growth in value traded
$ terms, % increase, 2000–05

1	United Arab Emirates	121,194	23	Iceland	626
2	Serbia	13,220	24	Czech Republic	524
3	Qatar	11,639	25	Oman	481
4	Saudi Arabia	6,274	26	Jamaica	466
5	Jordan	5,623	27	Austria	389
6	Bulgaria	2,293	28	Trinidad & Tobago	364
7	Kuwait	2,133	29	Ghana	350
8	Colombia	1,503	30	Ireland	348
9	Barbados	1,433	31	Pakistan	328
10	Romania	1,340	32	Croatia	324
11	Ecuador	1,209	33	Thailand	284
12	Georgia	1,167	34	Morocco	279
13	Kazakhstan	1,110	35	Lithuania	267
14	West Bank and Gaza	1,008	36	Norway	224
15	Kenya	974	37	Chile	210
16	Papua New Guinea[b]	750	38	Belgium	199
17	Sri Lanka	690	39	Indonesia	193
18	Russia	684	40	Bahrain	188
19	Lebanon	683	41	El Salvador	181
20	Estonia	660	42	Argentina	176
21	Iran	659	43	Australia	172
22	Nigeria	637	44	South Africa	159

Highest growth in number of listed companies
% increase, 2000–05

1	Serbia	14,300.0	25	Malta	30.0
2	Macedonia	5,600.0	26	Papua New Guinea[a]	28.6
3	Uzbekistan	2,180.0	27	Malaysia	28.3
4	Kazakhstan	260.9	28	Japan	28.0
5	Spain	223.8	29	China	27.7
6	Slovenia	205.3	30	South Korea	23.9
7	Canada	162.4	31	Australia	23.5
8	Uganda[a]	150.0	32	Barbados	23.5
9	Croatia	126.6	33	Jordan	23.3
10	Armenia[a]	88.6	34	Thailand	22.8
11	Kuwait	85.7	35	Cyprus	20.0
12	Ukraine	59.0	36	Russia	18.9
13	Tanzania	50.0	37	Bangladesh	18.6
14	United Arab Emirates	46.3	38	West Bank and Gaza	16.7
15	United Kingdom	44.9	39	Indonesia	15.5
16	Hong Kong	44.5	40	Zimbabwe	14.5
17	Qatar	40.9	41	Botswana	12.5
18	Bolivia	38.5	42	Bahrain	11.9
19	Iran	38.2	43	Poland	10.2
20	Trinidad & Tobago	37.0	44	Nigeria	9.7
21	Ghana	36.4	45	New Zealand	8.5
22	Singapore	33.3	46	Ecuador[b]	6.7
	Zambia	33.3		Fiji	6.7
24	Taiwan	31.5	48	Norway	5.8

a 2001–05   b 2002–05

Transport: roads and cars

Longest road networks
Km, 2003 or latest

1	United States	6,378,154	21	Bangladesh	239,226
2	India	3,851,440	22	Germany	231,581
3	China	1,809,829	23	Vietnam	215,628
4	Brazil	1,724,929	24	Argentina	215,471
5	Canada	1,408,900	25	Philippines	200,037
6	Japan	1,177,278	26	Romania	198,817
7	France	891,290	27	Nigeria	194,394
8	Australia	811,601	28	Iran	178,152
9	Spain	666,292	29	Ukraine	169,739
10	Russia	537,289	30	Hungary	159,568
11	Italy	479,688	31	Congo-Kinshasa	157,000
12	Sweden	424,981	32	Saudi Arabia	152,044
13	Poland	423,997	33	Belgium	149,757
14	United Kingdom	387,674	34	Austria	133,718
15	Indonesia	368,360	35	Czech Republic	127,672
16	South Africa	362,099	36	Netherlands	116,500
17	Turkey	354,421	37	Greece	116,470
18	Mexico	349,038	38	Colombia	112,988
19	Kazakhstan	258,029	39	Algeria	104,000
20	Pakistan	254,410	40	Bulgaria	102,016

Densest road networks
Km of road per km^2 land area, 2003 or latest

1	Macau	20.3		Trinidad & Tobago	1.6
2	Malta	7.1		United Kingdom	1.6
3	Bahrain	5.1	24	Slovakia	1.5
4	Singapore	5.0		Sri Lanka	1.5
5	Belgium	4.9	26	Ireland	1.4
6	Barbados	3.7		Poland	1.4
7	Japan	3.1	28	Cyprus	1.3
8	Netherlands	2.8		Estonia	1.3
9	Puerto Rico	2.6		Spain	1.3
10	Luxembourg	2.0	31	India	1.2
11	Slovenia	1.9		Lithuania	1.2
12	Bangladesh	1.7	33	Latvia	1.1
	Denmark	1.7	34	Mauritius	1.0
	Hong Kong	1.7		South Korea	1.0
	Hungary	1.7	36	Bulgaria	0.9
	Jamaica	1.7		Greece	0.9
	Switzerland	1.7		Sweden	0.9
18	Austria	1.6	39	Israel	0.8
	Czech Republic	1.6		Portugal	0.8
	France	1.6		Romania	0.8
	Italy	1.6			

Most crowded road networks
Number of vehicles per km of road network, 2003 or latest

1	Hong Kong	286.7	26	Tunisia	45.5
2	Qatar	283.6	27	Guatemala	44.8
3	Germany	206.0	28	Greece	41.1
4	Singapore	181.8	29	France	40.0
5	Macau	181.2	30	Ukraine	39.1
6	Kuwait	178.7	31	Belgium	36.5
7	South Korea	150.0	32	Serbia	36.2
8	Brunei	135.6	33	Cyprus	36.1
9	Malta	112.1		United States	36.1
10	Israel	110.4	35	Spain	34.4
11	Malaysia	87.6	36	Austria	33.0
12	Bahrain	76.9	37	Poland	31.9
13	United Kingdom	75.6	38	Denmark	31.7
14	Italy	73.3	39	Czech Republic	31.3
15	Mauritius	72.1	40	New Zealand	31.0
16	Jordan	71.1	41	Cambodia	30.9
17	Portugal	65.7	42	Finland	30.0
18	Japan	63.0	43	Honduras	28.4
19	Barbados	62.6	44	Panama	27.1
20	Luxembourg	59.7	45	Chile	26.9
21	Mexico	58.9	46	Norway	26.2
22	Netherlands	57.9	47	Moldova	25.9
23	Switzerland	57.1	48	Bulgaria	25.7
24	Croatia	50.3	49	Swaziland	25.6
25	Russia	47.3	50	Slovenia	25.5

Most used road networks
'000 vehicle-km per year per km of road network, 2003 or latest

1	Hong Kong	5,888.0	16	Pakistan	921.8
2	Indonesia	5,741.9	17	Switzerland	829.1
3	Singapore	5,097.6	18	Luxembourg	781.2
4	Germany	2,759.7	19	South Korea	691.7
5	Bhutan	2,651.4	20	Greece	681.5
6	Israel	2,220.4	21	Japan	671.7
7	Puerto Rico	1,666.1	22	Denmark	647.5
8	Bahrain	1,528.0	23	United States	647.3
9	Portugal	1,322.5	24	Finland	636.6
10	United Kingdom	1,250.3	25	Croatia	633.3
11	Malta	1,245.8	26	France	615.8
12	Belgium	1,045.9	27	Cambodia	585.1
13	Tunisia	1,012.3	28	Chile	482.4
14	Kuwait	1,000.0	29	China	464.7
15	Netherlands	943.8	30	Ecuador	453.8

Highest car ownership
Number of cars per 1,000 population[a]

1	New Zealand	619	26	Czech Republic	358
2	Luxembourg	574		Denmark	358
3	Canada	564	28	Brunei	353
4	Iceland	557	29	Estonia	334
5	Italy	547	30	Greece	331
6	Germany	546	31	Bahrain	327
7	Switzerland	521	32	Kuwait	312
8	Malta	518	33	Barbados	305
9	Austria	500	34	Croatia	294
10	France	492	35	Bulgaria	292
11	Belgium	473	36	Poland	291
12	United States	468	37	Netherlands Antilles	285
13	Sweden	458	38	Latvia	282
14	Spain	455	39	Hungary	281
15	Slovenia	445	40	Slovakia	251
16	United Kingdom	439	41	Israel	241
17	Portugal	437	42	Malaysia	225
18	Finland	434	43	South Korea	215
19	Japan	432	44	Belarus	167
20	Norway	430	45	Macau	143
21	Qatar	383		Serbia	143
22	Ireland	382	47	Russia	142
23	Cyprus	379	48	Romania	138
24	Netherlands	376	49	Mexico	131
25	Lithuania	370	50	Brazil	130

Lowest car ownership
Number of cars per 1,000 population[a]

1	Ethiopia	1	20	Swaziland	40
2	Sierra Leone	2	21	Namibia	42
	West Bank and Gaza	2	22	Morocco	43
4	Bolivia	3	23	Azerbaijan	44
5	Bhutan	4		Zimbabwe	44
6	India	6	25	Albania	47
	Gambia, The	6		Ecuador	47
8	Pakistan	7	27	Georgia	50
9	Kenya	8	28	Moldova	59
10	Philippines	9	29	Tunisia	60
11	China	10	30	Jordan	65
12	Syria	12	31	Turkey	66
13	Sri Lanka	13	32	Panama	73
14	Nicaragua	16	33	Kazakhstan	75
15	Cambodia	22	34	Chile	89
16	Mongolia	24	35	Mauritius	90
17	Peru	30	36	South Africa	93
18	Botswana	36	37	Costa Rica	98
19	Kyrgyzstan	37	38	Singapore	99

a Latest available year between 1999 and 2003.

Most injured in road accidents
Number of people injured per 100,000 population[a]

1	Qatar	9,681	27	Chile	291
2	Kuwait	2,155	28	Sri Lanka	290
3	Rwanda	1,764	29	Iceland	284
4	Costa Rica	1,438	30	Israel	282
5	Saudi Arabia	1,353	31	Peru	278
6	Panama	1,262	32	New Zealand	277
7	Jordan	1,023	33	Mongolia	275
8	Barbados	763	34	Botswana	273
9	Japan	749	35	Czech Republic	266
10	United States	704	36	Malta	261
11	Serbia	638	37	Spain	249
12	Slovenia	600	38	United Arab Emirates	244
13	Austria	543	39	Bahrain	237
14	South Korea	517		Nicaragua	237
15	Canada	509	41	Hong Kong	232
16	Swaziland	501	42	Bolivia	230
17	Belgium	461	43	Lesotho	221
18	Oman	434	44	Latvia	217
	Namibia	434	45	Greece	212
20	Germany	432	46	Sweden	207
21	Italy	412	47	Malaysia	204
22	Portugal	408	48	Netherlands	200
23	Croatia	385	49	Hungary	194
24	United Kingdom	375	50	Mauritius	178
25	Switzerland	334		Norway	178
26	Cyprus	310			

Most deaths in road accidents
Number of people killed per 100,000 population[a]

1	Botswana	30		South Korea	16
2	South Africa	29		Tunisia	16
	United Arab Emirates	29	23	Croatia	15
4	Malaysia	28		Greece	15
5	Oman	25		Jordan	15
6	Russia	24		Kazakhstan	15
	Swaziland	24		Kyrgyzstan	15
8	Gabon	23		Poland	15
9	Latvia	21		Portugal	15
	Saudi Arabia	21		United States	15
11	Lithuania	20	31	Belgium	14
12	Qatar	19		Czech Republic	14
13	Belarus	18		Panama	14
	Kuwait	18	34	Algeria	13
15	Colombia	17		Egypt	13
	Lesotho	17		Hungary	13
	Mongolia	17		Mauritius	13
	Namibia	17		Morocco	13
19	Suriname	16		Puerto Rico	13
20	Jamaica	16		Spain	13

a Latest available year between 1999 and 2003.

Transport: planes and trains

Most air travel
Million passenger-km[a] per year

1	United States	1,148,383	16	Spain	50,299
2	Japan	243,982	17	Brazil	47,986
3	United Kingdom	182,401	18	Thailand	36,828
4	China	151,962	19	Belgium	31,408
5	Germany	127,382	20	South Africa	31,171
6	France	90,496	21	Saudi Arabia	29,217
7	Hong Kong	83,733	22	United Arab Emirates	29,135
8	Australia	76,159	23	Switzerland	29,087
9	South Korea	72,935	24	Mexico	28,197
10	Canada	70,937	25	New Zealand	24,323
11	Singapore	70,030	26	India	23,850
12	Russia	62,417	27	Turkey	20,051
13	Netherlands	56,056	28	Austria	19,895
14	Italy	54,035	29	Ireland	19,471
15	Malaysia	52,206	30	Indonesia	19,306

Busiest airports

Total passengers, m

1	Atlanta, Hartsfield	85.9
2	Chicago, O'Hare	76.5
3	London, Heathrow	67.9
4	Tokyo, Haneda	63.3
5	Los Angeles, Intl.	61.5
6	Dallas, Ft. Worth	59.1
7	Paris, Charles de Gaulle	53.8
8	Frankfurt, Main	52.2
9	Las Vegas, McCarran Intl.	44.3
10	Amsterdam, Schipol	44.2
11	Denver, Intl.	43.3
12	Madrid, Barajas Intl.	41.9

Total cargo, m tonnes

1	Memphis, Intl.	3.60
2	Hong Kong, Intl.	3.44
3	Anchorage, Intl.	2.61
4	Tokyo, Narita	2.29
5	Seoul, Inchon	2.15
6	Frankfurt, Main	1.96
7	Los Angeles, Intl.	1.93
8	Shanghai, Pudong Intl.	1.86
9	Singapore, Changi	1.85
10	Louisville, Standiford Fd.	1.81
11	Paris, Charles de Gaulle	1.77
12	Miami, Intl.	1.76

Average daily aircraft movements, take-offs and landings

1	Atlanta, Hartsfield	2,686
2	Chicago, O'Hare	2,664
3	Dallas, Ft. Worth	1,950
4	Los Angeles, Intl.	1,783
5	Las Vegas, McCarran Intl.	1,658
6	Houston, George Bush Intercont.	1,542
7	Denver, Intl.	1,532
8	Phoenix, Skyharbor Intl.	1,521
9	Philadelphia, Intl.	1,468
10	Minneapolis, St Paul	1,458
11	Paris, Charles de Gaulle	1,432
12	Detroit, Metro	1,430
13	Charlotte/Douglas, Intl.	1,430
14	Washington, Dulles Intl.	1,396
15	Cincinnati, Intl.	1,360
16	Frankfurt, Main	1,343
17	London, Heathrow	1,309
18	Salt Lake City	1,248
19	Newark	1,198
20	Amsterdam, Schiphol	1,152

a Air passenger–km data refer to the distance travelled by each aircraft of national origin.

Longest railway networks
'000 km

1	United States	231.2	21	Sweden	9.9
2	Russia	85.5	22	Australia	9.5
3	India	63.2		Czech Republic	9.5
4	China	61.0	24	Turkey	8.7
5	Canada	57.7	25	Hungary	8.0
6	Germany	34.7	26	Iran	6.4
7	Argentina	34.2	27	Austria	5.8
8	France	29.3	28	Finland	5.7
9	Mexico	26.5	29	Belarus	5.5
10	Brazil	22.1		Sudan	5.5
11	Ukraine	22.0	31	Egypt	5.2
12	Japan	20.1	32	Cuba	4.8
	South Africa	20.1	33	Congo-Kinshasa	4.5
14	Poland	19.6		North Korea	4.5
15	United Kingdom	16.5	35	Bulgaria	4.3
16	Italy	16.2		Philippines	4.3
17	Spain	14.4	37	Indonesia	4.2
18	Kazakhstan	13.8	38	Norway	4.1
19	Pakistan	11.5		Serbia	4.1
20	Romania	10.8		Uzbekistan	4.1

Most rail passengers
Km per person per year

1	Japan	1,897	11	Italy	797
2	Switzerland	1,672	12	Kazakhstan	783
3	Belarus	1,418	13	Hungary	731
4	France	1,219	14	United Kingdom	709
5	Russia	1,099	15	Sweden	701
6	Ukraine	1,098	16	Finland	645
7	Austria	1,021	17	Czech Republic	642
8	Netherlands	865	18	South Korea	593
9	Germany	852	19	Egypt	552
10	Belgium	826	20	Luxembourg	532

Most rail freight
Million tonnes-km per year

1	United States	2,427,268	11	France	45,121
2	China	1,828,548	12	Australia	42,300
3	Russia	1,664,300	13	Belarus	40,331
4	India	381,241	14	Japan	22,200
5	Canada	338,661	15	Italy	21,579
6	Ukraine	233,961	16	United Kingdom	20,700
7	Kazakhstan	163,420	17	Austria	19,047
8	South Africa	106,549	18	Uzbekistan	18,428
9	Germany	77,640	19	Iran	18,182
10	Poland	47,847	20	Latvia	16,877

Transport: shipping

Merchant fleets
By country of registration, gross tonnage, million

1	Panama	141.8	11	Japan	12.6
2	Liberia	59.6	12	Italy	11.6
3	Bahamas	38.4	13	Germany	11.5
4	Singapore	31.0	14	United Kingdom	11.2
5	Greece	30.7	15	United States	11.1
6	Hong Kong	29.8	16	South Korea	9.3
7	Malta	23.0	17	Russia	8.3
8	China	22.3	18	Denmark	8.1
9	Cyprus	19.0		India	8.1
10	Norway	17.5	20	Bermuda	7.3

Merchant fleets
By country of ownership, gross tonnage, million

1	Greece	95.6	11	Denmark	15.2
2	Japan	89.3	12	Singapore	14.3
3	Germany	54.4	13	Russia	13.0
4	China	41.5	14	Italy	12.3
5	United States	36.0	15	Switzerland	9.6
6	Norway	33.4	16	India	8.3
7	Hong Kong	26.4	17	Malaysia	7.5
8	United Kingdom	22.1	18	Turkey	6.9
9	South Korea	19.3	19	Belgium	6.8
10	Taiwan	16.1			

Crude oil capacity
By country of registration, gross tonnage, '000

1	Panama	24,735	11	France	2,093
2	Liberia	21,708	12	Cyprus	2,065
3	Greece	14,136	13	China	1,872
4	Singapore	12,489	14	Japan	1,704
5	Bahamas	12,100	15	Belgium	1,594
6	Hong Kong	5,312	16	United States	1,479
7	Malta	4,980	17	Malaysia	1,458
8	India	3,767	18	Kuwait	1,443
9	Norway	3,655	19	Italy	997
10	Iran	3,067	20	Taiwan	809

Fish catching capacity
By country of registration, gross tonnage, '000

1	Russia	1,822		Peru	179
2	United States	711	12	Iceland	172
3	Japan	429	13	United Kingdom	162
4	South Korea	411	14	Panama	161
	Spain	411	15	China	154
6	Norway	362	16	Philippines	141
7	Argentina	205	17	Canada	139
8	Chile	193	18	Honduras	133
9	Belize	187	19	Denmark	127
10	Netherlands	179		Ukraine	127

Tourism

Most tourist arrivals
Number of arrivals, '000

1	France	75,121	20	Russia	9,164
2	Spain	53,599	21	Saudi Arabia	8,580
3	United States	46,077	22	Macau	8,324
4	China	41,761	23	Croatia	7,912
5	Italy	37,071	24	Ireland	6,982
6	United Kingdom	27,755	25	South Africa	6,815
7	Hong Kong	21,811	26	Belgium	6,710
8	Mexico	20,618	27	Japan	6,138
9	Germany	20,137	28	Czech Republic	6,061
10	Austria	19,373	29	Tunisia	5,998
11	Canada	19,150	30	South Korea	5,818
12	Turkey	16,826	31	Morocco	5,501
13	Malaysia	15,703	32	Indonesia	5,321
14	Ukraine	15,629	33	Finland	4,875
15	Poland	14,290	34	Brazil	4,725
16	Hungary	12,212	35	Norway	3,600
17	Thailand	11,651	36	Puerto Rico	3,541
18	Portugal	11,617	37	Dominican Republic	3,450
19	Netherlands	9,646			

Biggest tourist spenders
$m

1	Germany	67,198	11	Austria	13,152
2	United States	60,592	12	Canada	12,734
3	United Kingdom	55,347	13	Hong Kong	11,707
4	Japan	28,415	14	Spain	9,683
5	France	27,191	15	Denmark	9,015
6	Italy	24,122	16	South Korea	8,949
7	China	19,862	17	Sweden	8,608
8	Russia	17,927	18	Norway	8,576
9	Netherlands	16,797	19	Switzerland	7,976
10	Belgium	14,477	20	Australia	7,205

Largest tourist receipts
$m

1	United States	74,481	11	Greece	12,872
2	Spain	45,247	12	Canada	12,843
3	France	40,842	13	Japan	11,202
4	Italy	35,656	14	Mexico	10,753
5	Germany	27,657	15	Switzerland	10,413
6	United Kingdom	27,299	16	Netherlands	10,260
7	China	25,739	17	Thailand	10,034
8	Turkey	15,888	18	Belgium	9,185
9	Austria	15,351	19	Hong Kong	9,007
10	Australia	12,952	20	Malaysia	8,198

Education

Highest primary enrolment
Number enrolled as % of relevant age group

1	Brazil	147	17	Peru	118
2	Uganda	141		Russia	118
3	Malawi	140	19	Ecuador	117
4	Gabon	132	20	Laos	116
5	Equatorial Guinea	126	21	Aruba	115
	Lesotho	126		Bolivia	115
	Suriname	126		China	115
8	Cambodia	124		Portugal	115
	Dominican Republic	124		Syria	115
10	Belize	122	26	Libya	114
	Rwanda	122	27	El Salvador	113
12	Togo	121	28	Indonesia	112
13	Madagascar	120		Israel	112
14	Argentina	119		Panama	112
	Nepal	119		Philippines	112
	Nigeria	119			

Lowest primary enrolment
Number enrolled as % of relevant age group

1	Niger	44	15	Côte d'Ivoire	78
2	Burkina Faso	46	16	Sierra Leone	79
3	Congo-Brazzaville	50	17	Congo-Kinshasa	80
4	Mali	58		Senegal	80
5	Sudan	60	19	Guinea	81
6	Eritrea	63		Oman	81
7	Central African Rep	66	21	Zambia	82
8	Saudi Arabia	67	22	Ghana	83
9	Pakistan	68		Yemen	83
10	Ethiopia	70	24	Gambia, The	85
	Guinea-Bissau	70	25	Moldova	86
12	Papua New Guinea	75	26	Mauritania	88
13	Chad	76	27	Georgia	90
14	Burundi	77	28	Turkey	91

Highest tertiary enrolment[a]
Number enrolled as % of relevant age group

1	Finland	88		Latvia	73
2	South Korea	85	11	Lithuania	72
3	Sweden	83	12	Russia	69
	United States	83	13	Slovenia	68
5	Macau	81	14	Denmark	67
	Norway	81	15	Estonia	66
7	New Zealand	77	16	United Kingdom	64
8	Greece	74	17	Iceland	63
9	Australia	73			

Notes: Latest available year 2000–04. The gross enrolment ratios shown are the actual number enrolled as a percentage of the number of children in the official primary age group. They may exceed 100 when children outside the primary age group are receiving primary education.

Least literate
% adult literacy rate, latest year 2000–04

1	Burkina Faso	12.8	17	Morocco	50.7
2	Niger	14.4	18	Haiti	51.9
3	Mauritania	15.2	19	Togo	53.0
4	Mali	19.0	20	Ghana	54.1
5	Chad	25.5	21	Egypt	55.6
6	Sierra Leone	29.6	22	Liberia	55.9
7	Benin	33.6	23	Papua New Guinea	57.3
8	Senegal	39.3	24	Burundi	58.9
9	Bangladesh	41.1	25	Sudan	59.0
10	Ethiopia	41.5	26	India	61.0
11	Mozambique	46.5	27	Rwanda	64.0
12	Côte d'Ivoire	48.1	28	Malawi	64.1
13	Central African Rep	48.6	29	Congo-Brazzaville	65.3
	Nepal	48.6	30	Angola	66.8
15	Pakistan	48.7		Nigeria	66.8
16	Yemen	49.0			

Highest education spending
% of GDP

1	Yemen	9.5	12	Namibia	7.2
2	Cuba	9.0	13	Swaziland	7.1
	Mongolia	9.0	14	Kenya	7.0
4	Lesotho	8.9	15	New Zealand	6.7
5	Denmark	8.5	16	Morocco	6.5
6	Malaysia	8.1	17	Finland	6.4
7	Sweden	7.7		Tunisia	6.4
8	Barbados	7.6	19	Belgium	6.3
	Iceland	7.6		Bolivia	6.3
	Norway	7.6		Cyprus	6.3
11	Israel	7.5			

Lowest education spending
% of GDP

1	Equatorial Guinea	0.6		Papua New Guinea	2.3
2	Ecuador	1.0	15	Bangladesh	2.4
3	Indonesia	1.2	16	Albania	2.6
4	Myanmar	1.3		Togo	2.6
5	United Arab Emirates	1.6		Uruguay	2.6
6	Cambodia	1.8	19	Lebanon	2.7
	Guinea	1.8	20	Andorra	2.8
	Pakistan	1.8		Gambia, The	2.8
9	Zambia	2.0		Laos	2.8
10	Botswana	2.2		Macau	2.8
	Georgia	2.2		Rwanda	2.8
12	Dominican Republic	2.3		Tajikistan	2.8
	Niger	2.3			

a Tertiary education includes all levels of post-secondary education including courses
  leading to awards not equivalent to a university degree, courses leading to a first
  university degree and postgraduate courses.

Life expectancy

Highest life expectancy
Years, 2005–10

#	Country	Value		#	Country	Value
1	Andorra[a]	83.5			Guadeloupe	79.2
2	Japan	82.8		27	Aruba[a]	79.1
3	Hong Kong	82.2			Luxembourg	79.1
4	Iceland	81.4			Malta	79.1
5	Switzerland	81.1			United Arab Emirates	79.1
6	Australia	81.0		31	Channel Islands	79.0
7	Sweden	80.8			Netherlands	79.0
8	Canada	80.7			United Kingdom	79.0
	Macau	80.7		34	Costa Rica	78.8
10	Israel	80.6		35	Greece	78.7
	Italy	80.6		36	Chile	78.6
12	Norway	80.2			Cuba	78.6
13	Spain	80.1		38	Ireland	78.5
14	Cayman Islands[a]	80.0		39	South Korea	78.2
	France	80.0		40	Portugal	77.9
16	New Zealand	79.8			United States	77.9
17	Austria	79.7		42	Bermuda[a]	77.8
18	Belgium	79.6			Denmark	77.8
19	Martinique	79.4		44	Kuwait	77.6
	Singapore	79.4		45	Taiwan	77.3
21	Finland	79.3		46	Slovenia	77.2
	Germany	79.3		47	Brunei	77.1
	Virgin Islands	79.3		48	Netherlands Antilles	76.9
24	Cyprus	79.2		49	Puerto Rico	76.8
	Faroe Islands[a]	79.2		50	Barbados	76.4

Highest male life expectancy
Years, 2005–10

#	Country	Value		#	Country	Value
1	Andorra[a]	80.6		9	Canada	78.2
2	Iceland	79.5			Switzerland	78.2
3	Hong Kong	79.3		11	Norway	77.8
4	Japan	79.1		12	New Zealand	77.7
5	Macau	78.6		13	Singapore	77.6
	Sweden	78.6		14	Italy	77.5
7	Australia	78.5		15	United Arab Emirates	77.4
8	Israel	78.4		16	Cayman Islands[a]	77.3

Highest female life expectancy
Years, 2005–10

#	Country	Value		#	Country	Value
1	Andorra[a]	86.6			Virgin Islands	83.2
2	Japan	86.4		11	Canada	83.1
3	Hong Kong	85.1		12	Sweden	83.0
4	Spain	83.8		13	Aruba[a]	82.7
	Switzerland	83.8			Belgium	82.7
6	Italy	83.6			Faroe Islands[a]	82.7
7	France	83.5			Macau	82.7
8	Australia	83.4		17	Cayman Islands[a]	82.6
9	Iceland	83.2			Israel	82.6

a 2005 estimate.

Lowest life expectancy
Years, 2005–10

1	Swaziland	29.9		26	Ethiopia	48.5
2	Botswana	33.9		27	Somalia	48.8
3	Lesotho	34.3		28	Burkina Faso	49.3
4	Zimbabwe	37.3			Mali	49.3
5	Zambia	39.1		30	Kenya	50.3
6	Central African Rep	39.5		31	Uganda	52.1
7	Malawi	41.1		32	Gabon	53.3
8	Equatorial Guinea	41.5		33	Congo-Brazzaville	53.5
9	Mozambique	41.8			Haiti	53.5
10	Angola	41.9		35	Guinea	54.4
	Sierra Leone	41.9		36	Mauritania	54.5
12	Liberia	42.5		37	Togo	55.8
13	South Africa	44.1		38	Benin	55.9
14	Nigeria	44.2		39	Eritrea	56.0
15	Chad	44.3		40	Madagascar	56.2
16	Rwanda	44.6		41	Laos	56.5
17	Congo-Kinshasa	44.7		42	Sudan	56.9
18	Niger	45.4		43	Papua New Guinea	57.1
19	Guinea-Bissau	45.5			Senegal	57.1
20	Burundi	45.6		45	Gambia, The	57.7
21	Namibia	45.9		46	Cambodia	58.0
22	Côte d'Ivoire	46.2		47	Ghana	58.1
23	Cameroon	46.3		48	Iraq	61.0
24	Tanzania	46.6		49	Myanmar	61.8
25	Afghanistan	47.7		50	Yemen	62.7

Lowest male life expectancy
Years, 2005–10

1	Swaziland	30.8		11	Mozambique	41.7
2	Lesotho	34.2		12	Liberia	41.9
3	Botswana	35.0		13	Rwanda	43.1
4	Zimbabwe	38.2		14	Chad	43.3
5	Central African Rep	39.0		15	Congo-Kinshasa	43.6
6	Zambia	39.6		16	Nigeria	44.1
7	Angola	40.5		17	South Africa	44.2
	Sierra Leone	40.5		18	Guinea-Bissau	44.3
9	Equatorial Guinea	41.4		19	Burundi	44.5
10	Malawi	41.6		20	Niger	45.4

Lowest female life expectancy
Years, 2005–10

1	Swaziland	29.2		10	Liberia	43.1
2	Botswana	32.7		11	Sierra Leone	43.3
3	Lesotho	34.3		12	Angola	43.4
4	Zimbabwe	36.3		13	South Africa	43.8
5	Zambia	38.6		14	Nigeria	44.3
6	Central African Rep	40.0		15	Namibia	45.1
7	Malawi	40.6		16	Chad	45.4
8	Equatorial Guinea	41.6			Niger	45.4
9	Mozambique	41.9		18	Congo-Kinshasa	45.8

Death rates and infant mortality

Highest death rates
Number of deaths per 1,000 population, 2005–10

#	Country	Rate		#	Country	Rate
1	Swaziland	31.2		49	Laos	11.3
2	Botswana	28.4			Togo	11.3
3	Lesotho	26.4		51	Madagascar	11.2
4	Zimbabwe	23.0			Serbia	11.2
5	Sierra Leone	22.5		53	Czech Republic	11.1
6	Central African Rep	21.8		54	Kazakhstan	11.0
7	Zambia	21.2		55	Portugal	10.9
8	Angola	21.1			Sudan	10.9
9	Equatorial Guinea	20.9		57	Gambia, The	10.8
10	South Africa	20.6			Moldova	10.8
11	Liberia	20.3		59	Germany	10.7
12	Malawi	19.9			North Korea	10.7
	Mozambique	19.9			Senegal	10.7
14	Chad	19.5		62	Denmark	10.6
	Niger	19.5			Italy	10.6
16	Congo-Kinshasa	19.2		64	Greece	10.5
17	Guinea-Bissau	19.0		65	Slovenia	10.4
18	Nigeria	18.4		66	Ghana	10.3
19	Afghanistan	18.0		67	Belgium	10.2
20	Burundi	17.9			United Kingdom	10.2
	Rwanda	17.9		69	Cambodia	10.1
22	Ukraine	16.9			Eritrea	10.1
23	Cameroon	16.8			Poland	10.1
24	Côte d'Ivoire	16.7			Sweden	10.1
25	Mali	16.4		73	Bosnia	9.9
	Namibia	16.4		74	Austria	9.8
27	Tanzania	16.3			Finland	9.8
28	Somalia	16.1			Slovakia	9.8
29	Russia	16.0		77	Armenia	9.6
30	Burkina Faso	15.8			France	9.6
31	Ethiopia	15.4			Papua New Guinea	9.6
32	Belarus	15.0		80	Channel Islands	9.5
33	Bulgaria	14.5		81	Myanmar	9.3
34	Kenya	13.8			Norway	9.3
35	Estonia	13.6		83	Netherlands	9.1
	Latvia	13.6			Spain	9.1
37	Uganda	13.5		85	Uruguay	9.0
38	Gabon	13.0		86	Macedonia	8.9
39	Guinea	12.9		87	Japan	8.8
40	Hungary	12.9			Switzerland	8.8
41	Mauritania	12.8		89	Faroe Islands[a]	8.7
42	Haiti	12.7		90	Trinidad & Tobago	8.5
43	Romania	12.6		91	Iraq	8.4
44	Congo-Brazzaville	12.2			Malta	8.4
	Lithuania	12.2			United States	8.4
46	Croatia	12.1		94	India	8.3
47	Georgia	11.8			Puerto Rico	8.3
48	Benin	11.6				

Note: Both death and, in particular, infant mortality rates can be underestimated in certain countries where not all deaths are officially recorded.   a 2005 estimate.

Highest infant mortality
Number of deaths per 1,000 live births, 2005–10

1	Sierra Leone	159.8	21	Central African Rep	93.2
2	Niger	145.4	22	Ethiopia	90.9
3	Afghanistan	141.9	23	Cameroon	90.7
4	Angola	141.6	24	Mozambique	90.6
5	Liberia	132.0	25	Zambia	88.4
6	Mali	125.8	26	Mauritania	88.1
7	Burkina Faso	115.6	27	Togo	87.5
8	Côte d'Ivoire	113.8	28	Cambodia	87.3
9	Somalia	113.1	29	Tajikistan	85.2
10	Congo-Kinshasa	112.5	30	Iraq	81.5
11	Rwanda	112.3	31	Laos	79.6
12	Chad	111.5	32	Senegal	77.2
13	Guinea-Bissau	111.0	33	Uganda	76.6
14	Nigeria	108.1	34	Turkmenistan	74.7
15	Tanzania	104.0	35	Azerbaijan	72.2
16	Malawi	102.6	36	Madagascar	71.2
17	Burundi	98.9	37	Pakistan	70.5
18	Benin	97.6	38	Congo-Brazzaville	68.0
19	Guinea	96.7		Gambia, The	68.0
20	Equatorial Guinea	94.5	40	Myanmar	66.4

Lowest death rates
No. deaths per 1,000 pop., 2005–10

1	United Arab Emirates	1.3
2	Kuwait	1.9
3	Brunei	2.8
	Oman	2.8
5	Qatar	2.9
6	Bahrain	3.4
	Syria	3.4
8	Saudi Arabia	3.7
	West Bank and Gaza	3.7
10	Jordan	4.0
11	Costa Rica	4.1
	Libya	4.1
13	Mexico	4.5
14	Malaysia	4.7
	Nicaragua	4.7
16	Cayman Islands[a]	4.8
	Macau	4.8
	Paraguay	4.8
	Philippines	4.8
20	Algeria	4.9
21	French Polynesia	5.0
	Guam	5.0
	New Caledonia	5.0
	Panama	5.0
	Venezuela	5.0

Lowest infant mortality
No. deaths per 1,000 live births, 2005–10

1	Singapore	3.0
2	Iceland	3.1
	Japan	3.1
4	Sweden	3.2
5	Norway	3.3
6	South Korea	3.6
7	Finland	3.7
	Hong Kong	3.7
9	Andorra[a]	4.1
	Belgium	4.1
11	France	4.3
	Germany	4.3
	Switzerland	4.3
14	Austria	4.4
	Netherlands	4.4
	Spain	4.4
17	Australia	4.6
18	Denmark	4.7
19	Canada	4.8
	Israel	4.8
21	Cuba	4.9
22	Italy	5.0
	Luxembourg	5.0
	New Zealand	5.0
	United Kingdom	5.0

a 2005 estimate.

Death and disease

Diabetes
% of population aged 20–79, 2003

1	United Arab Emirates	20.1
2	Cuba	13.2
	Puerto Rico	13.2
4	Kuwait	12.8
5	Singapore	12.3
6	Oman	11.4
7	Mauritius	10.7
8	Germany	10.2
9	Bulgaria	10.0
	Dominican Republic	10.0
11	Latvia	9.9
	Spain	9.9
13	Egypt	9.8
14	Estonia	9.7
	Hungary	9.7
	Ukraine	9.7
17	Austria	9.6
	Bosnia	9.6
	Slovenia	9.6

Heart disease
Deaths per 100,000 population, 2002

1	Ukraine	686
2	Belarus	601
3	Georgia	503
4	Russia	468
5	Estonia	466
6	Moldova	435
7	Latvia	426
8	Lithuania	423
9	Kazakhstan	336
10	Bulgaria	329
11	Hungary	297
12	Armenia	277
13	Romania	271
	Slovakia	271
15	Azerbaijan	269
16	Croatia	263
17	Czech Republic	253
18	Turkmenistan	243
19	Finland	240

Maternal mortality rate
Deaths per 100,000 live births, estimates, 2000

1	Sierra Leone	2,000
2	Afghanistan	1,900
3	Malawi	1,800
4	Angola	1,700
5	Niger	1,600
6	Tanzania	1,500
7	Rwanda	1,400
8	Mali	1,200
9	Central African Rep	1,100
	Chad	1,100
	Guinea-Bissau	1,100
	Somalia	1,100
	Zimbabwe	1,100
14	Burkina Faso	1,000
	Burundi	1,000
	Kenya	1,000
	Mauritania	1,000
	Mozambique	1,000
19	Congo-Kinshasa	990
20	Equatorial Guinea	880
	Uganda	880
22	Benin	850
	Ethiopia	850

Tuberculosis
Incidence per 100,000 population, 2004

1	Swaziland	1,226
2	South Africa	718
3	Namibia	717
4	Lesotho	696
5	Zambia	680
6	Zimbabwe	674
7	Botswana	670
8	Kenya	619
9	Cambodia	510
10	Mozambique	460
11	Sierra Leone	443
12	Malawi	413
13	Somalia	411
14	Uganda	402
15	Côte d'Ivoire	393
16	Congo-Brazzaville	377
17	Rwanda	371
18	Congo-Kinshasa	366
19	Togo	355
20	Ethiopia	353
21	Tanzania	347
22	Burundi	343
23	Afghanistan	333

Note: Statistics are not available for all countries. The number of cases diagnosed and reported depends on the quality of medical practice and administration and can be under-reported in a number of countries.

Measles immunisation

Lowest % of children aged
12-23 months, 2004

1	Central African Rep	35
	Nigeria	35
3	Laos	36
4	Somalia	40
5	Liberia	42
6	Papua New Guinea	44
7	Côte d'Ivoire	49
8	Haiti	54
9	Gabon	55
10	Chad	56
	India	56
12	Senegal	57
13	Madagascar	59
	Sudan	59
15	Afghanistan	61
16	Angola	64
	Bolivia	64
	Cameroon	64
	Congo-Kinshasa	64
	Mauritania	64
	Sierra Leone	64

DPTa immunisation

Lowest % of children aged
12-23 months, 2004

1	Nigeria	25
2	Somalia	30
3	Liberia	31
4	Gabon	38
5	Central African Rep	40
6	Haiti	43
7	Laos	45
8	Papua New Guinea	46
9	Chad	50
	Côte d'Ivoire	50
11	Sudan	55
12	Angola	59
13	Madagascar	61
	Sierra Leone	61
15	Niger	62
16	Congo-Kinshasa	64
	India	64
18	Pakistan	65
19	Afghanistan	66
20	Congo-Brazzaville	67
21	Guinea	69

HIV/AIDS

Prevalence among population
aged 15-49, %, 2005

1	Swaziland	33.4
2	Botswana	24.1
3	Lesotho	23.2
4	Zimbabwe	20.1
5	Namibia	19.6
6	South Africa	18.8
7	Zambia	17.0
8	Mozambique	16.1
9	Malawi	14.1
10	Central African Rep	10.7
11	Gabon	7.9
12	Côte d'Ivoire	7.1
13	Uganda	6.7
14	Tanzania	6.5
15	Kenya	6.1
16	Cameroon	5.4
17	Congo-Brazzaville	5.3
18	Nigeria	3.9
19	Guinea-Bissau	3.8
	Haiti	3.8
21	Angola	3.7
22	Chad	3.5

AIDS

Estimated deaths per 100,000
pop., 2005

1	Swaziland	1,455
2	Zimbabwe	1,395
3	Lesotho	1,278
4	Botswana	1,000
5	Zambia	899
6	Namibia	850
7	Mozambique	729
8	South Africa	708
9	Malawi	634
10	Central African Rep	615
11	Kenya	432
12	Côte d'Ivoire	385
13	Tanzania	371
14	Uganda	341
15	Gabon	336
16	Congo-Brazzaville	289
17	Cameroon	282
18	Rwanda	247
19	Angola	213
20	Equatorial Guinea	197
21	Belize	192
22	Haiti	190

a Diptheria, pertussis and tetanus

Health

Highest health spending
As % of GDP

1	United States	15.2
2	Switzerland	11.5
3	Germany	11.1
4	Cambodia	10.9
5	Iceland	10.5
6	Norway	10.3
7	Lebanon	10.2
8	France	10.1
9	Canada	9.9
	Greece	9.9
11	Netherlands	9.8
	Uruguay	9.8
13	Portugal	9.6
	Serbia	9.6
15	Australia	9.5
	Bosnia	9.5
17	Belgium	9.4
	Jordan	9.4
	Sweden	9.4
20	Malawi	9.3
	Malta	9.3
22	Denmark	9.0
23	Argentina	8.9
	Israel	8.9
25	Slovenia	8.8
26	Hungary	8.4
	Italy	8.4
	South Africa	8.4
29	El Salvador	8.1
	Gambia, The	8.1
	New Zealand	8.1

Lowest health spending
As % of GDP

1	Congo-Kinshasa	2.0
2	Pakistan	2.4
3	Somalia	2.6
4	Iraq	2.7
	Madagascar	2.7
	Qatar	2.7
7	Angola	2.8
	Myanmar	2.8
9	Bhutan	3.1
	Burundi	3.1
	Indonesia	3.1
12	Laos	3.2
	Oman	3.2
	Philippines	3.2
15	Thailand	3.3
	United Arab Emirates	3.3
17	Bangladesh	3.4
	Papua New Guinea	3.4
19	Bermuda	3.5
	Brunei	3.5
	Kazakhstan	3.5
	Kuwait	3.5
	Sierra Leone	3.5
	Sri Lanka	3.5
25	Azerbaijan	3.6
	Côte d'Ivoire	3.6
27	Fiji	3.7
	Mauritius	3.7
29	Malaysia	3.8
30	Trinidad & Tobago	3.9
	Turkmenistan	3.9

Highest pop. per doctor

1	Congo-Kinshasa	71,958
2	Malawi	46,241
3	Tanzania	45,864
4	Ethiopia	37,397
5	Mozambique	37,354
6	Burundi	35,500
7	Liberia	33,981
8	Niger	32,891
9	Sierra Leone	30,952
10	Chad	25,797
11	Togo	22,222
12	Benin	22,186
13	Rwanda	21,197
14	Papua New Guinea	21,091
15	Lesotho	20,225
16	Eritrea	20,000
17	Bhutan	19,492

Lowest pop. per doctor

1	Cuba	170
2	Estonia	212
3	Belarus	220
4	Belgium	223
5	Greece	229
6	Russia	234
7	Italy	238
8	Georgia	243
9	Turkmenistan	245
10	Lithuania	249
11	Israel	269
12	Uruguay	275
13	Bulgaria	277
	Iceland	277
15	Switzerland	278
16	Armenia	282
	Kazakhstan	282

Most hospital beds

Beds per 1,000 pop.

1	Japan	14.3	16	Finland	7.2
2	Belarus	11.3		Slovakia	7.2
3	Russia	10.5	18	South Korea	7.1
4	Germany	8.9	19	Belgium	6.9
5	Czech Republic	8.8	20	Moldova	6.7
	Ukraine	8.8	21	Romania	6.6
7	Lithuania	8.7	22	Bulgaria	6.3
8	Austria	8.3		Taiwan	6.3
	Azerbaijan	8.3	24	Israel	6.1
10	Luxembourg	8.0		New Zealand	6.1
11	Hungary	7.8		Tajikistan	6.1
	Latvia	7.8	27	Croatia	6.0
13	France	7.7		Estonia	6.0
	Kazakhstan	7.7		Serbia	6.0
15	Australia	7.4		Switzerland	6.0

Obesity[a]

Men, % of total population			*Women, % of total population*		
1	Lebanon	36.3	1	Qatar	45.3
2	Qatar	34.6	2	Saudi Arabia	44.0
3	Kuwait	32.8	3	West Bank and Gaza	42.5
4	Panama	27.9	4	Lebanon	38.3
5	United States	27.7	5	Panama	36.1
6	Cyprus	26.6	6	Albania	35.6
7	Saudi Arabia	26.4	7	Bahrain	34.1
8	West Bank and Gaza	23.9	8	United States	34.0
9	Bahrain	23.3	9	Egypt	32.4
10	Albania	22.8	10	United Arab Emirates	31.4
11	England	22.7	11	Iran	30.0
12	Germany	22.5	12	Kuwait	29.9
13	Scotland	22.3	13	Turkey	29.4
14	Ireland	20.1	14	Mexico	29.0
15	Israel	19.9	15	Scotland	26.0
16	Mexico	19.4	16	Israel	25.7
17	Australia	19.3	17	Mongolia	24.6
18	United Arab Emirates	17.1	18	Jamaica	23.9
19	Wales	17.0	19	England	23.8
20	Oman	16.7	20	Cyprus	23.7
21	Slovenia	16.5	21	Germany	23.3
	Turkey	16.5	22	Oman	23.1
23	Lithuania	16.2	23	Peru	23.0
24	Canada	16.0	24	Australia	22.2
	Peru	16.0	25	Morocco	21.7
26	Luxembourg	15.3	26	Russia	21.6
27	Sweden	14.8	27	Trinidad & Tobago	21.1
28	Portugal	14.5	28	Fiji	19.3
29	Switzerland	14.1	29	Mauritania	19.2
30	Mongolia	13.8	30	Wales	18.0

Note: Data for these health rankings refer to the latest year available, 1999–2003.

a   Defined as body mass index of 30 or more – see Glossary, page 246.

Marriage and divorce

Highest marriage rates
Number of marriages per 1,000 population

1	Cyprus	15.0	31	Portugal	6.4
2	Bermuda	13.8	32	Singapore	6.3
3	Barbados	13.1		South Korea	6.3
4	Vietnam	12.1	34	Belize	6.2
5	Bangladesh	11.2		China	6.2
6	Egypt	11.0	36	Brunei	6.1
7	Iran	10.2		Croatia	6.1
8	Fiji	9.9	38	Costa Rica	6.0
9	Cayman Islands	9.6		Denmark	6.0
10	Sri Lanka	9.3		Tajikistan	6.0
11	Albania	8.8	41	Malta	5.9
	Mauritius	8.8	42	Bahamas	5.8
13	Jamaica	8.5		Greece	5.8
	Turkey	8.5		Mongolia	5.8
15	Guam	8.2	45	Bahrain	5.7
	United States	8.2		Channel Islands[a]	5.7
17	West Bank and Gaza	7.5		Japan	5.7
18	Iraq	7.3		Ukraine	5.7
19	Taiwan	7.2	49	Algeria	5.6
20	Macedonia	7.1		Serbia	5.6
21	Aruba	6.9	51	Guatemala	5.5
	Belarus	6.9	52	Bosnia	5.4
	Moldova	6.9	53	Ireland	5.3
24	Kyrkyzstan	6.8		Romania	5.3
	Uzbekistan	6.8		Trinidad & Tobago	5.3
26	Australia	6.7		Turkmenistan	5.3
27	Philippines	6.6	57	France	5.2
28	Mexico	6.5		Netherlands	5.2
	Puerto Rico	6.5		Norway	5.2
	Thailand	6.5		United Kingdom	5.2

Lowest marriage rates
Number of marriages per 1,000 population

1	Andorra	2.8		Slovenia	3.5
	Dominican Republic	2.8	14	Argentina	3.6
3	Georgia	2.9		Bulgaria	3.6
	Macau	2.9		Martinique	3.6
	Saudi Arabia	2.9	17	El Salvador	3.8
6	Latvia	3.0		Hong Kong	3.8
7	Panama	3.1	19	Czech Republic	3.9
	United Arab Emirates	3.1		Guadeloupe	3.9
9	Estonia	3.2		Nicaragua	3.9
	Poland	3.2	22	New Caledonia	4.0
11	Belgium	3.5		Peru	4.0
	Qatar	3.5	24	Sweden	4.1

a Guernsey only
Note: The data are based on latest available figures and hence will be affected by the population age structure at the time. Marriage rates refer to registered marriages only and, therefore, reflect the customs surrounding registry and efficiency of administration.

Highest divorce rates
Number of divorces per 1,000 population

1	Aruba	5.3		Kazakhstan	2.3
2	United States	4.8		Luxembourg	2.3
3	Belarus	4.5	32	Austria	2.2
4	Guam	4.3		Japan	2.2
5	Uruguay	4.2	34	Guadeloupe	2.1
6	Moldova	4.1		Israel	2.1
7	Puerto Rico	3.7		Romania	2.1
8	South Korea	3.5		Sweden	2.1
9	Ukraine	3.4	38	Netherlands	1.9
10	Czech Republic	3.3		Taiwan	1.9
	Lithuania	3.3	40	France	1.8
	New Zealand	3.3		Hong Kong	1.8
13	Estonia	3.2		Iceland	1.8
14	Bermuda	3.0		Singapore	1.8
	Cuba	3.0	44	Bahamas	1.7
	Netherlands Antilles	3.0		Portugal	1.7
	Russia	3.0		Slovakia	1.7
	United Kingdom	3.0		Suriname	1.7
19	Channel Islands[a]	2.9	48	Cayman Islands	1.6
20	Australia	2.8	49	Egypt	1.5
	Denmark	2.8	50	Barbados	1.4
	Switzerland	2.8		Kuwait	1.4
23	Finland	2.7	52	Bulgaria	1.3
24	Hungary	2.6	53	Albania	1.2
25	Latvia	2.5		Jordan	1.2
26	Belgium	2.4		Martinique	1.2
	Germany	2.4		Tunisia	1.2
	Norway	2.4		Turkmenistan	1.2
29	Canada	2.3			

Lowest divorce rates
Number of divorces per 1,000 population

1	Belize	0.2		Nicaragua	0.6
	Colombia	0.2		Panama	0.6
3	Libya	0.3		Turkey	0.6
4	Georgia	0.4		Uzbekistan	0.6
	Mongolia	0.4	19	Azerbaijan	0.7
	Tajikistan	0.4		Ecuador	0.7
7	Bosnia	0.5		Ireland	0.7
	Brazil	0.5		Macedonia	0.7
	Chile	0.5	23	China	0.8
	Mexico	0.5		Italy	0.8
	Vietnam	0.5		Spain	0.8
12	Armenia	0.6	26	Greece	0.9
	El Salvador	0.6		Venezuela	0.9
	Jamaica	0.6			

a Guernsey only

Households and prices

Biggest number of households[a]
m

1	China	378.09	15	Italy	23.03
2	India	202.88	16	Pakistan	21.53
3	United States	110.24	17	Ukraine	19.76
4	Indonesia	57.41	18	South Korea	17.04
5	Russia	52.88	19	Congo	16.92
6	Brazil	51.61	20	Thailand	16.90
7	Japan	48.48	21	Philippines	16.76
8	Germany	39.17	22	Egypt	15.54
9	Nigeria	26.10	23	Turkey	15.13
10	United Kingdom	25.26	24	Spain	15.04
11	Bangladesh	25.11	25	Ethiopia	14.44
12	France	24.88	26	Poland	13.51
13	Vietnam	24.67	27	Myanmar	13.33
14	Mexico	24.16	28	Iran	12.67

Biggest households[a]
Population per dwelling

1	Congo-Brazzaville	8.1		Sudan	6.1
2	Pakistan	7.2	11	Bangladesh	5.9
3	Kuwait	6.4		Saudi Arabia	5.9
	United Arab Emirates	6.4	13	French Polynesia	5.8
5	Gabon	6.3		Uzbekistan	5.8
	Guinea	6.3	15	Jordan	5.7
7	Cambodia	6.2		Kyrgyzstan	5.7
	Réunion	6.2	17	Guinea-Bissau	5.6
9	Algeria	6.1			

Highest cost of living[b]
Autumn 2005, USA=100

1	Norway	140		Sweden	105
2	Japan	136	17	Netherlands	104
3	Iceland	135	18	Singapore	103
4	France	130	19	United States	100
5	Denmark	127	20	Russia	98
6	United Kingdom	125	21	Italy	97
7	Switzerland	116	22	New Zealand	96
8	Finland	115	23	Spain	95
9	Austria	113	24	Côte d'Ivoire	94
10	South Korea	110		Luxembourg	94
11	Hong Kong	109	26	Canada	92
12	Australia	108	27	Taiwan	88
	Ireland	108		Turkey	88
14	Germany	106	29	Israel	86
15	Belgium	105			

a Latest available year.
b The cost of living index shown is compiled by the Economist Intelligence Unit for use by companies in determining expatriate compensation: it is a comparison of the cost of maintaining a typical international lifestyle in the country rather than a comparison of the purchasing power of a citizen of the country. The index is based on typical urban prices an international executive and family will face abroad. The prices

Smallest number of households[a]

m

1	Virgin Islands	0.01	16	Equatorial Guinea	0.12
2	Bermuda	0.02		Malta	0.12
3	Aruba	0.03		Réunion	0.12
	Guam	0.03	19	Iceland	0.13
5	French Polynesia	0.04	20	Macau	0.15
	New Caledonia	0.04	21	Fiji	0.16
7	Netherlands Antilles	0.05		Luxembourg	0.16
8	Barbados	0.06		Qatar	0.16
9	Bahamas	0.07	24	Bahrain	0.19
	Brunei	0.07	25	Swaziland	0.20
11	Suriname	0.08	26	Gabon	0.21
12	Cayman Islands	0.09	27	Mauritius	0.22
13	Martinique	0.10	28	Cyprus	0.27
14	Belize	0.11		Guinea-Bissau	0.27
	Guadeloupe	0.11		Trinidad & Tobago	0.27

Smallest households[a]

Population per dwelling

1	Germany	2.1		Norway	2.3
	Sweden	2.1	9	Austria	2.4
3	Denmark	2.2		Belgium	2.4
	Finland	2.2		Estonia	2.4
	Switzerland	2.2		France	2.4
6	Iceland	2.3		Ukraine	2.4
	Netherlands	2.3		United Kingdom	2.4

Lowest cost of living[b]

Autumn 2005, USA=100

1	Iran	33	17	Cambodia	59
2	Philippines	39	18	Bulgaria	60
3	Pakistan	43	19	Peru	61
4	Paraguay	45		Serbia	61
5	India	47		Thailand	61
	Libya	47	22	Brunei	62
7	Bangladesh	48	23	Ecuador	64
8	Costa Rica	53		Indonesia	64
9	Argentina	54		Uraguay	64
	Kazakhstan	54	26	Kuwait	65
	Uzbekistan	54		Malaysia	65
12	Algeria	55		Panama	65
	Syria	55		Romania	65
14	Egypt	56	30	Kenya	66
	Sri Lanka	56		Oman	66
16	Venezuela	58			

are for products of international comparable quality found in a supermarket or department store. Prices found in local markets and bazaars are not used unless the available merchandise is of the specified quality and the shopping area itself is safe for executive and family members. New York City prices are used as the base, so United States = 100.

Consumer goods ownership

TV

Colour TVs per 100 households

1	Belgium	99.6	26	Norway	93.5
	United States	99.6	27	Jordan	93.0
3	Taiwan	99.4	28	Slovenia	92.6
4	Finland	99.3	29	Denmark	92.5
	Ireland	99.3	30	Australia	92.0
6	Hong Kong	99.1	31	Czech Republic	91.9
7	Japan	99.0	32	Greece	91.7
8	Saudi Arabia	98.9	33	Kuwait	91.4
9	Canada	98.8	34	Argentina	91.2
10	Netherlands	98.7	35	Tunisia	90.7
	Singapore	98.7	36	Mexico	90.5
12	Spain	98.5	37	Malaysia	90.3
13	United Kingdom	98.2	38	Hungary	89.2
14	Portugal	98.1	39	Croatia	89.0
15	New Zealand	98.0	40	Brazil	87.5
16	Austria	97.6	41	Colombia	86.7
17	Germany	97.3	42	Estonia	86.2
18	Sweden	97.1	43	Poland	85.6
19	United Arab Emirates	97.0	44	Slovakia	84.0
20	Switzerland	96.9	45	Thailand	83.9
21	Israel	96.6	46	Belarus	80.4
22	Italy	96.0	47	Ukraine	76.9
23	France	95.9	48	Lithuania	76.7
24	Venezuela	95.1	49	Russia	75.2
25	South Korea	93.6	50	Algeria	74.3

Telephone

Telephone lines per 100 people

1	Bermuda	86.2	23	Faroe Islands	49.8
2	Luxembourg	79.8	24	Guadeloupe	48.7
3	Sweden	71.5	25	Netherlands	48.4
4	Switzerland	71.0	26	Norway	47.2
5	Iceland	66.4	27	Belgium	46.4
6	Germany	66.2		Ireland	46.4
7	Denmark	64.5	29	Austria	46.2
8	Canada	64.3		Italy	46.2
9	Virgin Islands	63.9	31	New Zealand	46.1
10	United States	60.6	32	Japan	46.0
11	Taiwan	59.6	33	Greenland	45.7
12	Australia	58.6	34	Finland	45.4
13	Greece	57.8	35	Martinique	44.5
14	United Kingdom	56.4	36	Bahamas	44.1
15	France	56.0	37	Israel	43.7
16	South Korea	55.3	38	Singapore	43.2
17	Hong Kong	54.4	39	Croatia	42.7
18	Andorra	52.3	40	Spain	41.5
19	Cyprus	51.8	41	Réunion	41.0
20	Malta	51.6	42	Slovenia	40.7
21	Guam	50.9	43	Portugal	40.3
22	Barbados	50.1	44	Macau	37.4

CD player
CD players per 100 households

1	Norway	90.1	13 Belgium	68.0
2	Denmark	90.0	14 Finland	64.8
3	Netherlands	87.8	15 Switzerland	59.8
4	New Zealand	87.6	16 United States	59.6
5	Germany	87.1	17 Hong Kong	57.7
6	United Kingdom	86.8	18 Singapore	56.6
7	Australia	85.0	19 Portugal	44.7
8	Sweden	84.3	20 Ireland	42.1
9	Canada	81.1	21 Spain	41.7
10	Taiwan	70.6	22 Peru	35.1
11	Austria	70.5	23 Saudi Arabia	33.1
12	Japan	68.5	24 United Arab Emirates	31.1

Computer
Computers per 100 people

1	Switzerland	82.3	18 Bermuda	52.3
2	United States	76.2	19 Ireland	49.7
3	Sweden	76.1	20 New Zealand	49.3
4	Israel	73.4	21 France	48.7
5	Canada	69.8	22 Germany	48.5
6	Australia	68.9	23 Finland	48.2
7	Netherlands	68.5	24 Estonia	47.4
8	Denmark	65.5	25 Iceland	47.1
9	Singapore	62.2	26 Réunion	36.3
10	Luxembourg	62.1	27 Slovenia	35.5
11	Hong Kong	60.5	28 Belgium	35.1
12	United Kingdom	60.0	29 Saudi Arabia	34.0
13	Norway	57.8	30 Malta	31.5
14	Austria	57.6	31 Italy	31.3
15	South Korea	54.5	32 Cyprus	30.9
16	Japan	54.2	33 Slovakia	29.6
17	Taiwan	52.8	34 Macau	29.0

Mobile telephone
Subscribers per 100 people

1	Luxembourg	138.2	16 Finland	95.6
2	Hong Kong	118.8	17 Denmark	95.5
3	Sweden	108.5	18 Ireland	93.5
4	Italy	108.2	19 Andorra	93.4
5	Czech Republic	105.6	20 Macau	92.9
6	Israel	105.3	21 Netherlands	91.2
7	Norway	103.6	22 Bahrain	90.6
8	United Kingdom	102.2	23 Netherlands Antilles	90.1
9	Slovenia	100.5	24 Singapore	89.5
10	Taiwan	100.3		Spain	89.5
11	Lithuania	99.3	26 Aruba	89.4
12	Iceland	99.0	27 Belgium	88.3
13	Portugal	98.4	28 Germany	86.4
14	Austria	97.4		Hungary	86.4
15	Estonia	96.0	30 Faroe Islands	85.8

Books and newspapers

Cultural goods[a]

Exports, 2002, $m			*Imports, 2002, $m*		
1	United Kingdom	8,548.8	1	United States	15,338.6
2	United States	7,648.4	2	United Kingdom	7,871.9
3	Germany	5,788.9	3	Germany	4,162.1
4	China	5,274.9	4	Canada	3,829.9
5	France	2,521.3	5	France	3,406.8
6	Ireland	2,276.9	6	Switzerland	2,466.0
7	Singapore	2,001.0	7	China	2,189.2
8	Japan	1,805.1	8	Japan	2,014.2
9	Canada	1,577.2	9	Italy	1,819.4
10	Austria	1,561.1	10	Belgium	1,510.7
11	Netherlands	1,546.4	11	Spain	1,484.6
12	Spain	1,532.7	12	Netherlands	1,425.5
13	Switzerland	1,383.9	13	Australia	1,210.0
14	Italy	1,380.7	14	Mexico	1,149.4
15	Mexico	1,244.4	15	Austria	1,078.0
16	Belgium	1,130.0	16	South Korea	1,021.0
17	Sweden	875.3	17	Sweden	830.1
18	Hungary	719.5	18	India	803.6
19	Hong Kong	577.9	19	Singapore	639.5
20	Denmark	498.8	20	Ireland	574.8
21	South Korea	388.4	21	Norway	552.4
22	Russia	347.1	22	Denmark	514.4
23	Australia	317.7	23	Portugal	394.0
24	Finland	290.2	24	Russia	372.9
25	India	284.4	25	Finland	344.4
26	Czech Republic	218.6	26	South Africa	309.4
27	Malaysia	215.9	27	New Zealand	301.7
28	Poland	209.3	28	Czech Republic	287.4
29	Portugal	158.0	29	Poland	260.9
30	Israel	155.0	30	Brazil	235.5

Daily newspapers

Copies per '000 population, latest year

1	Iceland	548	16	Turkmenistan	200
2	Norway	528	17	Estonia	192
3	Sweden	492	18	New Zealand	190
4	Finland	428	19	Slovenia	174
5	Bulgaria	390	20	South Africa	166
6	United States	381	21	Latvia	165
7	Denmark	369	22	Czech Republic	163
8	Switzerland	346	23	Hungary	151
9	Austria	316	24	Italy	142
10	United Kingdom	311	25	China	141
11	Germany	269	26	Belgium	140
12	Netherlands	257	27	Ireland	132
13	Singapore	249	28	France	129
14	Luxembourg	246	29	Australia	126
15	Hong Kong	213	30	Croatia	116

Music and the internet

Music sales: Total
$m, 2005

1	United States	12,269		11	Mexico	412
2	Japan	5,448		12	Brazil	394
3	United Kingdom	3,446		13	Russia	388
4	Germany	2,211		14	Austria	285
5	France	1,990		15	Switzerland	267
6	Canada	732		16	Belgium	262
7	Australia	674		17	South Africa	254
8	Italy	669		18	Norway	253
9	Spain	555		19	Sweden	240
10	Netherlands	431		20	Denmark	180

Music sales: Digital downloads
Trade revenues, $m, 2005

1	United States	636		6	Italy	16
2	Japan	278		7	Canada	15
3	United Kingdom	69		8	South Korea	12
4	Germany	39		9	Australia	7
5	France	28		10	Netherlands	5

Internet hosts

	By country, January 2006				*Per 1,000 pop., January 2006*	
1	United States[b]	246,745,030		1	United States	830.8
2	Japan	24,903,795		2	Iceland	660.4
3	Argentina	14,664,719		3	Finland	481.9
4	Italy	11,222,960		4	Norway	458.5
5	Germany	9,852,798		5	Netherlands	448.0
6	Netherlands	7,258,159		6	Denmark	429.0
7	France	6,863,156		7	Argentina	377.0
8	Australia	6,039,486		8	Sweden	316.5
9	United Kingdom	5,778,422		9	Australia	303.5
10	Brazil	5,094,730		10	Switzerland	295.2
11	Taiwan	3,943,555		11	Estonia	273.1
12	Poland	3,941,769		12	New Zealand	249.2
13	Canada	3,622,706		13	Belgium	247.2
14	Sweden	2,817,010		14	Austria	241.6
15	Mexico	2,555,047		15	Italy	195.9
16	Belgium	2,546,148		16	Japan	194.9
17	Finland	2,505,805		17	Cayman Islands	190.3
18	Spain	2,459,614		18	Singapore	187.0
19	Denmark	2,316,370		19	Israel	183.7
20	Switzerland	2,125,269		20	Luxembourg	183.2
21	Norway	2,109,283		21	Taiwan	173.7
22	Austria	1,957,154		22	Bermuda	156.0
23	Russia	1,628,987		23	Andorra	151.2
24	Portugal	1,378,817		24	Portugal	136.5
25	Israel	1,212,264		25	Aruba	135.8

a Includes art, antiques, books, newspapers, music and cultural services.
b Includes all hosts ending ".com", ".net" and ".org", which exaggerates the numbers.

Nobel prize winners: 1901–2005

Peace

1	United States	17
2	United Kingdom	11
3	France	9
4	Sweden	5
5	Belgium	4
	Germany	4
7	Austria	3
	Norway	3
	South Africa	3
10	Argentina	2
	Egypt	2
	Israel	2
	Russia	2
	Switzerland	2

Economics[a]

1	United States	29
2	United Kingdom	8
3	Norway	2
	Sweden	2
5	France	1
	Germany	1
	Israel	1
	Netherlands	1
	Russia	1

Literature

1	France	14
2	United States	12
3	United Kingdom	10
4	Germany	7
5	Sweden	6
6	Italy	5
	Spain	5
8	Norway	3
	Poland	3
	Russia	3

Physiology or medicine

1	United States	49
2	United Kingdom	21
3	Germany	14
4	Sweden	7
5	France	6
	Switzerland	6
7	Austria	5
	Denmark	5
9	Australia	3
	Belgium	3
	Italy	3

Physics

1	United States	47
2	United Kingdom	19
3	Germany	18
4	France	8
5	Netherlands	6
	Russia	6
7	Japan	4
	Sweden	4
	Switzerland	4
10	Austria	3
	Italy	3
12	Canada	2
	Denmark	2
14	Colombia	1
	India	1
	Ireland	1
	Pakistan	1
	Poland	1

Chemistry

1	United States	41
2	United Kingdom	22
3	Germany	14
4	France	7
5	Switzerland	6
6	Sweden	5
7	Canada	4
	Japan	4
9	Argentina	1
	Austria	1
	Belgium	1
	Czech Republic	1
	Denmark	1
	Finland	1
	Israel	1
	Italy	1
	Netherlands	1
	Norway	1
	Russia	1

a Since 1969.
Notes: Prizes by country of residence at time awarded. When prizes have been shared in the same field, one credit given to each country. Only top rankings in each field are included.

Olympic medal winners

Summer games, 1896–2004

		Gold	Silver	Bronze
1	United States	895	690	604
2	Soviet Union[a]	440	357	325
3	United Kingdom	180	233	225
4	France	173	187	203
5	Italy	172	136	153
6	Germany[b]	162	191	205
7	Germany (East)	153	129	127
8	Hungary	148	130	154
9	Sweden	138	154	171
10	China	112	96	78
11	Australia	100	106	131
12	Finland	100	80	113
13	Japan	98	97	103
14	Romania	74	86	106
15	Netherlands	60	65	84
16	Russia[c]	59	53	47
17	Poland	56	72	113
18	Germany (West)	56	67	81
19	Cuba	56	46	41
20	Canada	52	79	99

Winter games, 1924–2006

		Gold	Silver	Bronze
1	Germany[b]	129	117	93
2	Norway	96	102	75
3	Soviet Union[a]	87	63	67
4	United States	78	81	59
5	Austria	50	64	70
6	Sweden	46	32	34
7	Finland	42	57	52
8	Canada	38	38	44
9	Switzerland	37	37	43
10	Italy	36	31	33
11	Russia	35	26	21
12	France	25	24	32
13	Netherlands	25	30	23
14	South Korea	17	8	6
15	Japan	9	10	13
16	United Kingdom	8	5	15
17	China	4	16	13
18	Croatia	4	3	0
19	Estonia	4	1	1
20	Australia	3	0	2

a 1952-1992.
b Germany 1896-1936, unified teams in 1956-64, then since 1992.
c Russia 1896-1912, then since 1996.
Note: Figures exclude mixed teams in 1896, 1900 and 1904 and Australasia teams in 1908 and 1912.

Drinking and smoking

Beer drinkers
Off-trade sales, litres per head of pop.

1	Czech Republic	81.7
2	Germany	69.2
3	Venezuela	67.7
4	Denmark	66.6
5	Austria	66.3
6	Australia	66.1
7	Finland	63.3
8	United States	62.7
9	Slovakia	56.6
10	New Zealand	54.6
11	Netherlands	54.2
12	Canada	52.4
13	Russia	51.8
14	Hungary	51.4
15	Poland	48.9
16	Belgium	45.0
17	Bulgaria	42.0
18	Romania	41.1
19	Mexico	39.9
20	Sweden	39.7
21	South Africa	39.2
22	Norway	37.9
23	Japan	37.2

Wine drinkers
Off-trade sales, litres per head of pop.

1	Portugal	31.5
2	Switzerland	30.1
3	Italy	29.1
4	Argentina	28.2
5	France	28.0
6	Denmark	24.9
7	Hungary	24.0
8	Germany	21.9
9	Belgium	19.1
	Netherlands	19.1
11	United Kingdom	16.9
12	Australia	16.7
	New Zealand	16.7
14	Austria	16.5
15	Chile	15.2
	Sweden	15.2
17	Spain	12.8
18	Iraq	12.4
19	Norway	11.2
20	Finland	10.1
21	Czech Republic	10.0
22	Greece	9.0

Alcoholic drinks
Off-trade sales, litres per head of pop.

1	Germany	99.0
2	Czech Republic	96.4
3	Denmark	95.6
4	Australia	93.9
5	Finland	90.5
6	Austria	87.3
7	Hungary	79.3
8	New Zealand	78.0
9	Russia	77.6
10	Netherlands	77.3
11	United States	74.9
12	Venezuela	70.8
13	Slovakia	67.5
14	Belgium	67.2
	Canada	67.2
16	Portugal	65.8
17	United Kingdom	64.9
18	Poland	63.6
19	Argentina	63.0
20	Sweden	62.9
21	Switzerland	61.9
22	France	57.0
23	Norway	53.7
24	Japan	53.4

Smokers
Av. ann. consumption of cigarettes per head per day

1	Greece	8.5
2	Bulgaria	6.8
3	Macedonia	6.3
4	Japan	6.2
	Spain	6.2
6	Bosnia	6.0
	Russian	6.0
8	Czech Republic	5.6
	Ukraine	5.6
10	Serbia	5.5
11	Cyprus	5.2
	Moldova	5.2
	Poland	5.2
	Slovenia	5.2
	Switzerland	5.2
16	Belgium	5.1
	Taiwan	5.1
18	Belarus	4.7
	Kazakhstan	4.7
20	South Korea	4.6

Crime and punishment

Police

Total police personnel per 100,000 pop.

1	Mauritius	756
2	Italy	560
3	Barbados	516
4	Portugal	491
5	Hong Kong	487
6	Macedonia	482
7	Kazakhstan	464
8	Czech Republic	445
9	Latvia	436
10	Thailand	355
11	Malaysia	354
12	Slovakia	347
13	Lithuania	345
14	Singapore	324
15	Slovenia	318
16	Moldova	314
17	Ireland	307
18	Spain	293
19	Germany	292
20	Hungary	289

Crime[a]

Tot. recorded crimes per 100,000 pop.

1	New Zealand	11,152
2	Finland	10,243
3	United Kingdom	9,767
4	Denmark	9,450
5	Chile	9,276
6	Netherlands	8,212
7	Canada	8,041
8	South Africa	7,997
9	Germany	7,621
10	Norway	7,350
11	France	6,404
12	Swaziland	4,803
13	Hungary	4,501
14	Estonia	4,222
15	Barbados	4,085
16	Italy	3,823
17	Czech Republic	3,801
18	Switzerland	3,774
19	Portugal	3,634
20	Slovenia	3,401

Prisoners

Total prison pop., latest available year

1	United States	2,135,901
2	China	1,548,498
3	Russia	828,900
4	Brazil	336,358
5	India	322,357
6	Mexico	201,931
7	Ukraine	170,057
8	Thailand	168,264
9	South Africa	156,175
10	Iran	135,132
11	Rwanda	87,000
12	Pakistan	86,000
13	Poland	85,048
14	United Kingdom	84,945
15	Indonesia	84,357
16	Germany	80,413
17	Japan	76,413
18	Bangladesh	74,170
19	Colombia	68,545
20	Philippines	67,968
21	Ethiopia	65,000
22	Egypt	61,845
23	Spain	61,333

Per 100,000 pop., latest available year

1	Rwanda	1,024
2	United States	719
3	Russia	582
4	Belarus	530
5	Virgin Islands	524
6	Belize	495
7	Bermuda	490
8	Cuba	487
9	Cayman Islands	468
10	Turkmenistan	449
11	Suriname	439
12	Bahamas	417
13	Barbados	369
	Puerto Rico	369
15	Panama	362
16	Netherlands Antilles	355
17	Ukraine	353
18	Singapore	350
19	South Africa	346
20	Estonia	343
21	Kazakhstan	342
22	Botswana	339
23	Aruba	330

a Including attempted crimes. The definition of offences, the proportion of crimes reported and the efficiency of police administration systems differ so numbers may not be strictly comparable.

Stars...

Space missions
Firsts and selected events

1957 Man-made satellite Dog in space, Laika
1961 Human in space, Yuri Gagarin
Entire day in space, Gherman Titov
1963 Woman in space, Valentina Tereshkova
1964 Space crew, one pilot and two passengers
1965 Space walk, Alexei Leonov
Computer guidance system
Eight days in space achieved (needed to travel to moon and back)
1966 Docking between space craft and target vehicle
Autopilot re-entry and landing
1968 Live television broadcast from space
Moon orbit
1969 Astronaut transfer from one craft to another in space
Moon landing
1971 Space station, Salyut
Drive on the moon
1973 Space laboratory, Skylab
1978 Non-Amercian, non-Soviet, Vladimir Remek (Czechoslovakia)
1982 Space shuttle, Columbia (first craft to carry four crew members)
1983 Five crew mission
1984 Space walk, untethered
Capture, repair and redeployment of satellite in space
Seven crew mission
1985 Classified US Defence Department mission
1986 Space shuttle explosion, Challenger
Mir space station activated
1990 Hubble telescope deployed
2001 Dennis Tito, first paying space tourist
2003 Space shuttle explosion, Columbia. Shuttle programme suspended
China's first manned space flight, Yang Liwei
2004 SpaceShipOne, first successful private manned space flight
2005 Space shuttle, resumption of flights

Space vehicle launches
By host country

2002

1	Russia	23
2	United States	18
3	France	11
4	China	3
5	Japan	2
6	India	1
	Israel	1

2003

1	United States	24
2	Russia	19
3	China	6
4	France	4
5	India	2
	Japan	2

2004

1	United States	21
2	Russia	17
3	China	2
	France	2
5	India	1
	Sweden	1

2005

1	Russia	21
2	United States	15
3	France	5
4	China	3
5	Japan	2
6	India	1
	Sweden	1

...and Wars

Defence spending
As % of GDP

1	North Korea	25.0		16	Brunei	5.6
2	Oman	10.0		17	Uzbekistan	4.9
3	Eritrea	9.2		18	Singapore	4.7
4	Myanmar	9.0		19	Egypt	4.6
5	Saudi Arabia	8.8		20	Angola	4.3
6	Israel	8.2			Bahrain	4.3
7	Jordan	7.9			Russia	4.3
8	Kuwait	7.8		23	Botswana	4.0
9	Syria	7.4			Colombia	4.0
10	Qatar	7.2			Cuba	4.0
11	Vietnam	6.9		26	Belarus	3.9
12	Burundi	6.4			Ethiopia	3.9
13	Armenia	6.3		28	Tanzania	3.8
14	Yemen	6.2			United States	3.8
15	Zimbabwe	5.9				

Armed forces
'000

		Regulars	Reserves			Regulars	Reserves
1	China	2,255	800	12	Iran	420	0
2	United States	1,433	1,140	13	Syria	307	354
3	India	1,325	1,155	14	Thailand	306	200
4	North Korea	1,106	4,700	15	Brazil	302	1,340
5	Russia	1,037	20,000	16	Indonesia	302	400
6	South Korea	687	4,500	17	Taiwan	290	1,657
7	Pakistan	619	513	18	Germany	284	358
8	Turkey	514	378	19	France	254	21
9	Vietnam	484	4,000	20	Japan	239	44
10	Myanmar	482		21	Colombia	207	60
11	Egypt	468	479	22	UK	205	272

Current UN peacekeeping missions[a]

	Military	Civilian police	Staff	Fatalities
Middle East (May 1948)	152	0	222	44
India/Pakistan (January 1949)	44	0	69	11
Cyprus (March 1964)	854	69	143	176
Syria (May 1974)	1,123	0	141	43
Lebanon (March 1978)	2,030	0	401	256
Western Sahara (April 1991)	225	0	224	14
Georgia (August 1993)	122	12	290	10
Kosovo (June 1999)	36	3,303	3,434	32
Congo-Kinshasa (November 1999)	15,748	1,072	2,275	83
Ethiopia and Eritrea (July 2000)	3,359	0	409	13
Liberia (September 2003)	15,037	1,028	1,393	68
Côte d'Ivoire (April 2004)	6,897	697	786	15
Burundi (June 2004)	5,323	87	707	20
Haiti (June 2004)	7,519	1,776	971	17
Sudan (March 2005)	10,000	715	3,641	1

a March 2006. Dates in brackets refer to missions' start dates.

Environment

Environmental performance index[a]

Highest			Lowest		
1	New Zealand	88.0	1	Niger	25.7
2	Sweden	87.8	2	Chad	30.5
3	Finland	87.0	3	Mauritania	32.0
4	Czech Republic	86.0	4	Mali	33.9
5	United Kingdom	85.6	5	Ethiopia	36.7
6	Austria	85.2	6	Angola	39.3
7	Denmark	84.2	7	Pakistan	41.1
8	Canada	84.0	8	Burkina Faso	43.2
9	Ireland	83.3	9	Bangladesh	43.5
	Malaysia	83.3	10	Sudan	44.0
11	Portugal	82.9	11	Nigeria	44.5
12	France	82.5	12	Yemen	45.2
13	Iceland	82.1	13	Mozambique	45.7
14	Japan	81.9	14	Guinea-Bissau	46.1
15	Costa Rica	81.6	15	Congo-Kinshasa	46.3
16	Switzerland	81.4	16	India	47.7
17	Colombia	80.4	17	Tajikistan	48.2
18	Greece	80.2	18	Madagascar	48.5
	Norway	80.2	19	Mongolia	48.8
20	Australia	80.1	20	Haiti	48.9
21	Italy	79.8	21	Guinea	49.2
22	Germany	79.4	22	Congo-Brazzaville	49.4
23	Spain	79.2	23	Sierra Leone	49.5
24	Slovakia	79.1	24	Cambodia	49.7
	Taiwan	79.1	25	Liberia	51.0
26	Chile	78.9	26	Burundi	51.6
27	Netherlands	78.7	27	Senegal	52.1
28	United States	78.5	28	Gambia, The	52.3
29	Cyprus	78.4		Turkmenistan	52.3
30	Argentina	77.7		Uzbekistan	52.3
31	Russia	77.5	31	Togo	52.8
	Slovenia	77.5	32	Laos	52.9
33	Brazil	77.0	33	Swaziland	53.9
	Hungary	77.0	34	Cameroon	54.1
35	Trinidad & Tobago	76.9	35	Vietnam	54.3
36	Lebanon	76.7	36	Zambia	54.4
37	Panama	76.5	37	Syria	55.3
38	Poland	76.2	38	Papua New Guinea	55.5
39	Belgium	75.9	39	Azerbaijan	55.7
40	Ecuador	75.5	40	China	56.2

a Score ranges from 0–100 based on six policy categories: environmental health; air quality; water resources; biodiversity and habitat; productive natural resources; sustainable energy.

Environmental health scores[a]

Highest			Lowest		
1	Sweden	99.4	1	Chad	0.0
2	France	99.2	2	Niger	1.0
3	Australia	99.0	3	Angola	7.8
4	United Kingdom	98.9	4	Mali	8.6
5	Finland	98.8	5	Burkina Faso	9.9
	Iceland	98.8	6	Ethiopia	10.4
	Norway	98.8	7	Congo-Kinshasa	12.8
8	Germany	98.7	8	Mozambique	16.7
9	Canada	98.6	9	Guinea-Bissau	17.1
	Ireland	98.6	10	Guinea	17.2
11	Denmark	98.5	11	Cambodia	18.3
12	Switzerland	98.3	12	Congo-Brazzaville	19.4
	United States	98.3	13	Sierra Leone	20.4
14	New Zealand	97.9	14	Laos	21.4
15	Austria	97.7	15	Nigeria	23.0
16	Japan	97.6	16	Liberia	23.3
17	Portugal	97.4		Madagascar	23.3
18	Czech Republic	97.3	18	Zambia	24.0
	Slovenia	97.3	19	Sudan	24.5
20	Netherlands	97.1	20	Central African Rep	26.6
21	Spain	97.0	21	Togo	28.3
22	Belgium	96.6	22	Mauritania	28.4
23	Slovakia	96.4	23	Malawi	29.6
24	Greece	96.3	24	Swaziland	30.0
25	Israel	95.9	25	Burundi	30.6
26	Italy	95.3	26	Rwanda	31.1
27	Poland	95.0	27	Cameroon	31.5
28	Hungary	94.2	28	Uganda	31.7
29	Trinidad & Tobago	94.1	29	Benin	33.1
30	Ukraine	93.8	30	Papua New Guinea	34.2

Population with access to improved water source

Lowest, %

1	Afghanistan	13	15	Burkina Faso	51
2	Ethiopia	22		Guinea	51
3	Somalia	29		Togo	51
4	Cambodia	34	18	Swaziland	52
5	Papua New Guinea	39	19	Zambia	55
6	Mozambique	42	20	Mauritania	56
7	Laos	43		Uganda	56
8	Equatorial Guinea	44	22	Eritrea	57
9	Madagascar	45		Romania	57
10	Congo-Brazzaville	46		Sierra Leone	57
	Congo-Kinshasa	46	25	Tajikistan	58
	Niger	46	26	Guinea-Bissau	59
13	Mali	48	27	Nigeria	60
14	Angola	50			

a A score ranging from 0–100 based on: child mortality; indoor air pollution; drinking
  water; sanitation; urban air particulates.

Air quality scores[a]

Highest			Lowest		
1	Uganda	98.0	1	Bangladesh	6.9
2	Gabon	96.1	2	Pakistan	8.2
3	Rwanda	91.1	3	Albania	14.4
4	Burundi	90.9	4	Egypt	14.8
5	Ghana	87.3	5	Mali	21.2
6	Kenya	87.0	6	China	22.3
7	Liberia	86.5	7	Niger	22.9
8	Tanzania	86.2	8	Chad	24.4
9	New Zealand	83.7	9	Sudan	24.9
10	Congo-Kinshasa	82.3	10	Indonesia	25.1
	Togo	82.3	11	Myanmar	27.4
12	Central African Rep	80.1	12	Oman	28.1
13	Malaysia	79.8	13	India	28.4
14	Malawi	79.2	14	Mongolia	28.5
15	Benin	78.9	15	Saudi Arabia	30.2
16	South Africa	78.6	16	Mauritania	30.9
17	Ecuador	78.3	17	Iran	31.1
18	Venezuela	76.9	18	Syria	31.8
19	Côte d'Ivoire	76.2	19	Turkmenistan	32.4
20	Sierra Leone	75.5	20	Guatemala	32.6
21	Mozambique	74.6	21	Azerbaijan	32.7
22	Trinidad & Tobago	74.4	22	Georgia	33.2
23	Swaziland	74.3	23	Mexico	34.6
24	Madagascar	74.2	24	Nepal	35.9
25	Papua New Guinea	73.7	25	Uzbekistan	36.4
	Suriname	73.7	26	Armenia	37.8

Highest concentration of ozone

Parts per billion

1	Belize	64.5	20	Bangladesh	52.7
2	Guatemala	64.4	21	French Polynesia	52.6
3	Mexico	64.2	22	India	52.1
4	China	63.4	23	Indonesia	51.0
5	Mongolia	60.9	24	Pakistan	50.6
6	Australia	60.6	25	North Korea	50.3
7	Bhutan	58.9	26	Portugal	50.2
8	Nepal	58.6	27	South Korea	50.1
9	United States	57.5	28	Puerto Rico	49.8
10	Afghanistan	57.3	29	Tajikistan	49.2
11	Iran	55.1	30	Spain	49.0
12	Turkmenistan	55.0	31	Cayman Islands	48.7
13	Honduras	54.8	32	Canada	48.5
14	Bahamas	54.2	33	Virgin Islands	48.4
15	El Salvador	53.9	34	Japan	48.3
16	Haiti	53.4	35	Russia	48.0
17	Cuba	52.8	36	Bermuda	47.9
	Dominican Republic	52.8		Morocco	47.9
	Myanmar	52.8	38	Kyrgyzstan	47.6

a A score ranging from 0–100 based on particulate concentration in urban areas and regional ozone levels.

Forests

Hectares, m

1	Russia	808.8	23	Japan	24.9
2	Brazil	477.7	24	Central African Rep	22.8
3	Canada	310.1	25	Congo-Brazzaville	22.5
4	United States	303.1		Finland	22.5
5	China	197.3	27	Gabon	21.8
6	Australia	163.7	28	Cameroon	21.2
7	Congo-Kinshasa	133.6	29	Malaysia	20.9
8	Indonesia	88.5	30	Mozambique	19.3
9	Peru	68.7	31	Paraguay	18.5
10	India	67.7	32	Spain	17.9
11	Sudan	67.5	33	Zimbabwe	17.5
12	Mexico	64.2	34	Chile	16.1
13	Colombia	60.7		Laos	16.1
14	Angola	59.1	36	France	15.6
15	Bolivia	58.7	37	Suriname	14.8
16	Venezuela	47.7	38	Thailand	14.5
17	Zambia	42.5	39	Ethiopia	13.0
18	Tanzania	35.3	40	Vietnam	12.9
19	Argentina	33.0	41	Madagascar	12.8
20	Myanmar	32.2	42	Mali	12.6
21	Papua	29.4	43	Botswana	11.9
22	Sweden	27.5		Chad	11.9

Forests

As % of total land

1	Suriname	94.7	26	Brunei	52.8
2	Gabon	84.5	27	Fiji	51.7
3	Finland	73.9	28	Bahamas	51.5
4	Guinea-Bissau	73.7	29	North Korea	51.4
5	Belize	72.5	30	Myanmar	49.0
6	Laos	69.9	31	Indonesia	48.8
7	Japan	68.2	32	Cayman Islands	48.4
8	Bhutan	68.0	33	Russia	47.9
9	Sweden	66.9	34	Angola	47.4
10	Congo-Brazzaville	65.8		Latvia	47.4
11	Papua New Guinea	65.0	36	Guadeloupe	47.2
12	Malaysia	63.6	37	Guam	47.1
13	South Korea	63.5	38	Costa Rica	46.8
14	Slovenia	62.8	39	Austria	46.7
15	Cambodia	59.2	40	Paraguay	46.5
16	Congo-Kinshasa	58.9	41	Puerto Rico	46.0
17	Colombia	58.5	42	Cameroon	45.6
18	Equatorial Guinea	58.2	43	Zimbabwe	45.3
19	Panama	57.7	44	Senegal	45.0
20	Brazil	57.2	45	Martinique	43.9
21	Zambia	57.1	46	Bosnia	43.1
22	Bolivia	54.2	47	Nicaragua	42.7
23	Venezuela	54.1	48	Gambia, The	41.7
24	Estonia	53.9	49	Honduras	41.5
25	Peru	53.7	50	Portugal	41.3

Biggest loss of forested land
Average annual change 2000–05, hectares '000

1	Brazil	-3,103	15	Ecuador		-198
2	Indonesia	-1,871	16	Australia		-193
3	Sudan	-589	17	Paraguay		-179
4	Myanmar	-466	18	Philippines		-157
5	Zambia	-445	19	Honduras		-156
6	Tanzania	-412	20	Argentina		-150
7	Nigeria	-410	21	Ethiopia		-141
8	Congo	-319	22	Malaysia		-140
9	Zimbabwe	-313	23	Papua		-139
10	Venezuela	-288	24	North Korea		-127
11	Bolivia	-270	25	Angola		-125
12	Mexico	-260	26	Botswana		-118
13	Cameroon	-220	27	Ghana		-115
14	Cambodia	-219	28	Mali		-100

Biggest loss of forested land
Average annual change 2000–05, %

1	Burundi	-5.2	15	Liberia	-1.8
2	Togo	-4.5		Virgin Islands	-1.8
3	Mauritania	-3.4	17	Ecuador	-1.7
4	Nigeria	-3.3		El Salvador	-1.7
5	Afghanistan	-3.1		Zimbabwe	-1.7
	Honduras	-3.1	20	Armenia	-1.5
7	Benin	-2.5		Sri Lanka	-1.5
8	Uganda	-2.2	22	Myanmar	-1.4
9	Pakistan	-2.1		Nepal	-1.4
	Philippines	-2.1	24	Guatemala	-1.3
11	Cambodia	-2.0		Nicaragua	-1.3
	Ghana	-2.0	26	Ethiopia	-1.1
	Indonesia	-2.0		Tanzania	-1.1
14	North Korea	-1.9			

Biggest gain in forested land
Average annual change 2000–05, hectares '000

1	China	4,058	17	Tunisia	19
2	Spain	296		Uruguay	19
3	Vietnam	241	19	New Zealand	17
4	United States	159		Norway	17
5	Italy	106		Uzbekistan	17
6	Chile	57	22	Lithuania	16
7	Cuba	56	23	Côte d'Ivoire	15
8	Bulgaria	50	24	Hungary	14
9	France	41	25	Ukraine	13
10	Portugal	40	26	Ireland	12
11	Greece	30	27	Bhutan	11
12	India	29		Latvia	11
13	Algeria	27		Sweden	11
	Poland	27	30	United Kingdom	10
	Rwanda	27	31	Belarus	9
16	Turkey	25		Serbia	9

Country
profiles

ALGERIA

Area	2,381,741 sq km	Capital	Algiers
Arable as % of total land	3	Currency	Algerian dinar (AD)

People

Population	32.3m	Life expectancy: men	70.9 yrs
Pop. per sq km	13.6	women	73.7 yrs
Av. ann. growth		Adult literacy	69.9%
in pop. 2000–05	1.51%	Fertility rate (per woman)	2.5
Pop. under 15	29.6%	Urban population	60.0%
Pop. over 60	6.5%		per 1,000 pop.
No. of men per 100 women	102	Crude birth rate	22.8
Human Development Index	72.2	Crude death rate	4.9

The economy

GDP	AD6,100bn	GDP per head	$2,620
GDP	$84.6bn	GDP per head in purchasing	
Av. ann. growth in real		power parity (USA=100)	16.6
GDP 1994–2004	3.8%	Economic freedom index	3.46

Origins of GDP

Components of GDP[a]

	% of total		% of total
Agriculture	10	Private consumption	41.2
Industry, of which:	57	Public consumption	14.8
manufacturing	7	Investment	29.8
Services	34	Exports	38.8
		Imports	-24.6

Structure of employment

	% of total		% of labour force
Agriculture	21	Unemployed 2004	17.7
Industry	24	Av. ann. rate 1995–2004	26.7
Services	55		

Energy

	m TOE		
Total output	163.3	Net energy imports as %	
Total consumption	33.0	of energy use	-395
Consumption per head,			
kg oil equivalent	1,036		

Inflation and finance

Consumer price		av. ann. increase 1999–2004	
inflation 2005	1.6%	Narrow money (M1)	19.6%
Av. ann. inflation 2000–05	2.7%	Broad money	20.0%
Money market rate, 2005	2.01%		

Exchange rates

	end 2005		December 2005
AD per $	73.38	Effective rates	2000 = 100
AD per SDR	104.88	– nominal	89.10
AD per €	86.33	– real	85.15

Trade

Principal exports[a]		**Principal imports**[a]	
	$bn fob		*$bn cif*
Crude oil	11.6	Capital goods	4.1
Natural gas	4.4	Food	2.6
Condensate	4.2	Semi-finished goods	2.2
Total incl. others	**32.2**	Total incl. others	**19.4**

Main export destinations		**Main origins of imports**	
	% of total		*% of total*
Italy	21.4	France	32.3
United States	16.3	Italy	8.8
France	10.8	Spain	6.9
Spain	9.5	Germany	5.8

Balance of payments[b], reserves and debt, $bn

Visible exports fob	18.7	Change in reserves	10.2
Visible imports fob	-12.0	Level of reserves	
Trade balance	6.7	end Dec.	45.7
Invisibles inflows	2.2	No. months of import cover	20.8
Invisibles outflows	-5.4	Official gold holdings, m oz	5.6
Net transfers	1.1	Foreign debt	22.0
Current account balance	4.6	– as % of GDP	33
– as % of GDP	8.2	– as % of total exports	83
Capital balance[c]	-2.0	Debt service ratio	22
Overall balance[c]	5.0		

Health and education

Health spending, % of GDP	4.1	Education spending, % of GDP	...
Doctors per 1,000 pop.	1.1	Enrolment, %: primary	109
Hospital beds per 1,000 pop.	2.1	secondary	80
Improved-water source access,		tertiary	21
% of pop.	87		

Society

No. of households	5.3m	Colour TVs per 100 households	74.3
Av. no. per household	6.1	Telephone lines per 100 pop.	7.1
Marriages per 1,000 pop.	5.6	Mobile telephone subscribers	
Divorces per 1,000 pop.	...	per 100 pop.	14.5
Cost of living, Dec. 2005		Computers per 100 pop.	0.9
New York = 100	55	Internet hosts per 1,000 pop.	...

a   2003
b   2002
c   2001

ARGENTINA

Area	2,766,889 sq km	Capital	Buenos Aires
Arable as % of total land	10	Currency	Peso (P)

People

Population	38.9m	Life expectancy: men	71.6 yrs
Pop. per sq km	14.1	women	79.1 yrs
Av. ann. growth		Adult literacy	97.2%
in pop. 2000–05	0.98%	Fertility rate (per woman)	2.4
Pop. under 15	26.4%	Urban population	90.6%
Pop. over 60	13.9%		per 1,000 pop.
No. of men per 100 women	96	Crude birth rate	19.0
Human Development Index	86.3	Crude death rate	7.7

The economy

GDP	P447bn	GDP per head	$3,930
GDP	$153bn	GDP per head in purchasing	
Av. ann. growth in real		power parity (USA=100)	33.5
GDP 1994–2004	1.1%	Economic freedom index	3.30

Origins of GDP		Components of GDP	
	% of total		% of total
Agriculture	10.5	Private consumption	62.8
Industry, of which:	35.8	Public consumption	11.1
manufacturing	24.2	Investment	19.0
Services	53.7	Exports	25.3
		Imports	-18.2

Structure of employment

	% of total		% of labour force
Agricultural	1	Unemployed 2003	15.6
Industry	21	Av. ann. rate 1995–2003	16.2
Services	78		

Energy

	m TOE		
Total output	84.3	Net energy imports as %	
Total consumption	59.9	of energy use	-41
Consumption per head			
kg oil equivalent	1,575		

Inflation and finance

Consumer price		av. ann. increase 1999–2004	
inflation 2005	9.6%	Narrow money (M1)	20.7%
Av. ann. inflation 2000–05	10.1%	Broad money	9.0%
Money market rate, 2005	3.23%		

Exchange rates

	end 2005		December 2005
P per $	3.01	Effective rates	2000 = 100
P per SDR	4.30	– nominal	...
P per €	3.54	– real	...

Trade

Principal exports		Principal imports	
	$bn fob		*$bn cif*
Agricultural products	11.9	Intermediate goods	8.6
Manufactures	9.5	Capital goods	5.4
Primary products	6.8	Consumer goods	2.5
Fuels	6.2	Fuels	1.0
Total incl. others	**34.6**	Total incl. others	**22.4**

Main export destinations		Main origins of imports	
	% of total		*% of total*
Brazil	17.7	Brazil	27.7
Chile	11.3	United States	16.7
United States	10.7	Germany	5.5
China	8.8	Italy	4.1

Balance of payments, reserves and debt, $bn

Visible exports fob	34.6	Change in reserves	5.5
Visible imports fob	-21.3	Level of reserves	
Trade balance	13.2	end Dec.	19.7
Invisibles inflows	8.6	No. months of import cover	5.8
Invisibles outflows	-19.2	Official gold holdings, m oz	1.8
Net transfers	0.7	Foreign debt	169.3
Current account balance	3.4	– as % of GDP	141
– as % of GDP	2.2	– as % of total exports	451
Capital balance	-10.4	Debt service ratio	33
Overall balance	-7.0		

Health and education

Health spending, % of GDP	8.9	Education spending, % of GDP	4.0
Doctors per 1,000 pop.	2.8	Enrolment, %: primary	119
Hospital beds per 1,000 pop.	4.1	secondary	100
Improved-water source access,		tertiary	60
% of pop.	...		

Society

No. of households	10.4m	Colour TVs per 100 households	91.2
Av. no. per household	3.6	Telephone lines per 100 pop.	22.8
Marriages per 1,000 pop.	3.6	Mobile telephone subscribers	
Divorces per 1,000 pop.	...	per 100 pop.	35.4
Cost of living, Dec. 2005		Computers per 100 pop.	8.0
New York = 100	54	Internet hosts per 1,000 pop.	37.6

AUSTRALIA

Area	7,682,300 sq km	Capital	Canberra
Arable as % of total land	6	Currency	Australian dollar (A$)

People

Population	19.9m	Life expectancy: men	78.5 yrs
Pop. per sq km	2.6	women	83.4 yrs
Av. ann. growth		Adult literacy	99.0%
in pop. 2000–05	1.11%	Fertility rate (per woman)	1.8
Pop. under 15	19.6%	Urban population	92.7%
Pop. over 60	17.3%		per 1,000 pop.
No. of men per 100 women	98	Crude birth rate	12.3
Human Development Index	95.5	Crude death rate	7.0

The economy

GDP	A$867bn	GDP per head	$32,030
GDP	$637bn	GDP per head in purchasing	
Av. ann. growth in real		power parity (USA=100)	76.4
GDP 1994–2004	3.7%	Economic freedom index	1.84

Origins of GDP		Components of GDP	
	% of total		% of total
Agriculture & mining	8.3	Private consumption	61.4
Manufacturing	11.4	Public consumption	18.2
Other	80.3	Investment	25.0
		Exports	19.1
		Imports	-25.0

Structure of employment

	% of total		% of labour force
Agriculture	4	Unemployed 2004	5.6
Industry	21	Av. ann. rate 1995–2004	7.1
Services	75		

Energy

	m TOE		
Total output	253.5	Net energy imports as %	
Total consumption	112.6	of energy use	-125
Consumption per head,			
kg oil equivalent	5,668		

Inflation and finance

Consumer price		av. ann. increase 1999–2004	
inflation 2005	2.7%	Narrow money (M1)	14.1%
Av. ann. inflation 2000–05	3.0%	Broad money	9.4%
Money market, 2005	5.50%	Household saving rate, 2004	-3.0%

Exchange rates

	end 2005		December 2005
A$ per $	1.36	Effective rates	2000 = 100
A$ per SDR	1.95	– nominal	118.0
A$ per €	1.60	– real	125.3

Trade

Principal exports	$bn fob	Principal imports	$bn cif
Minerals & metals	39.5	Intermediate & other goods	37.1
Rural goods	19.8	Consumption goods	33.3
Manufacturing goods	18.9	Capital goods	25.2
Other goods	8.8	Fuels and lubricants	9.3
Total incl. others	**86.6**	Total incl. others	**109.5**

Main export destinations	% of total	Main origins of imports	% of total
Japan	18.9	Asean[a]	16.4
Asean[a]	11.7	United States	14.5
China	9.3	China	12.6
United States	8.1	Japan	11.8
EU25	11.2	EU25	23.7

Balance of payments, reserves and aid, $bn

Visible exports fob	87.1	Overall balance	1.2
Visible imports fob	-105.2	Change in reserves	3.7
Trade balance	-18.1	Level of reserves	
Invisibles inflows	39.5	end Dec.	36.9
Invisibles outflows	-60.7	No. months of import cover	2.7
Net transfers	-0.3	Official gold holdings, m oz	2.6
Current account balance	-39.7	Aid given	1.46
– as % of GDP	-6.2	– as % of GDP	0.25
Capital balance	41.0		

Health and education

Health spending, % of GDP	9.5	Education spending, % of GDP	4.9
Doctors per 1,000 pop.	2.4	Enrolment, %: primary	104
Hospital beds per 1,000 pop.	7.4	secondary	156
Improved-water source access,		tertiary	73
% of pop.	100		

Society

No. of households	7.4m	Colour TVs per 100 households	92.0
Av. no. per household	2.7	Telephone lines per 100 pop.	58.6
Marriages per 1,000 pop.	6.7	Mobile telephone subscribers	
Divorces per 1,000 pop.	2.8	per 100 pop.	82.8
Cost of living, Dec. 2005		Computers per 100 pop.	68.9
New York = 100	108	Internet hosts per 1,000 pop.	303.5

a Brunei, Indonesia, Laos, Malaysia, Myanmar, Philippines, Singapore, Thailand, Vietnam.

AUSTRIA

Area	83,855 sq km	Capital	Vienna
Arable as % of total land	17	Currency	Euro (€)

People

Population	8.1m	Life expectancy: men	76.9 yrs
Pop. per sq km	96.6	women	82.4 yrs
Av. ann. growth		Adult literacy	99.0%
in pop. 2000–05	0.23%	Fertility rate (per woman)	1.4
Pop. under 15	15.5%	Urban population	65.8%
Pop. over 60	22.7%		per 1,000 pop.
No. of men per 100 women	96	Crude birth rate	8.6
Human Development Index	93.6	Crude death rate	9.8

The economy

GDP	€235bn	GDP per head	$36,090
GDP	$292bn	GDP per head in purchasing	
Av. ann. growth in real		power parity (USA=100)	81.3
GDP 1994–2004	2.1%	Economic freedom index	1.95

Origins of GDP		**Components of GDP**	
	% of total		% of total
Agriculture	2.2	Private consumption	55.8
Industry, of which:	31.8	Public consumption	17.8
manufacturing	...	Investment	21.2
Services	66.0	Exports	50.6
		Imports	-45.3

Structure of employment

	% of total		% of labour force
Agriculture	5	Unemployed 2004	4.9
Industry	30	Av. ann. rate 1995–2004	4.0
Services	65		

Energy

	m TOE		
Total output	10.0	Net energy imports as %	
Total consumption	33.2	of energy use	70
Consumption per head,			
kg oil equivalent	4,086		

Inflation and finance

Consumer price		av. ann. increase 1999–2004	
inflation 2005	2.3%	Euro area:	
Av. ann. inflation 2000–05	2.0%	Narrow money (M1)	8.4%
Deposit rate, h'holds, 2005	1.70%	Broad money	6.9%
		Household saving rate, 2004	8.3%

Exchange rates

	end 2005		December 2005
€ per $	0.85	Effective rates	2000 = 100
€ per SDR	1.21	– nominal	104.7
		– real	99.9

Trade

Principal exports		Principal imports	
	$bn fob		*$bn cif*
Consumer goods	51.6	Consumer goods	48.7
Investment goods	31.3	Investment goods	28.0
Intermediate goods	14.5	Raw materials (incl. fuels)	14.5
Raw materials (incl. fuels)	7.1	Intermediate goods	13.8
Food & beverages	6.1		
Total incl. others	**112**	Total incl. others	**113**

Main export destinations		Main origins of imports	
	% of total		*% of total*
Germany	32.3	Germany	42.9
Eastern Europe	18.7	Eastern Europe	14.5
Italy	8.6	Italy	6.8
United States	5.9	France	4.0
EU25	71.8	United States	3.3
		EU25	77.1

Balance of payments, reserves and aid, $bn

Visible exports fob	112.1	Overall balance	-1.8
Visible imports fob	-109.0	Change in reserves	-0.5
Trade balance	3.0	Level of reserves	
Invisibles inflows	67.7	end Dec.	12.2
Invisibles outflows	-67.2	No. months of import cover	0.8
Net transfers	-2.8	Official gold holdings, m oz	9.9
Current account balance	0.8	Aid given	0.68
– as % of GDP	0.3	– as % of GDP	0.23
Capital balance	-2.2		

Health and education

Health spending, % of GDP	7.5	Education spending, % of GDP	5.7
Doctors per 1,000 pop.	3.4	Enrolment, %: primary	103
Hospital beds per 1,000 pop.	8.3	secondary	100
Improved-water source access,		tertiary	49
% of pop.	100		

Society

No. of households	3.4m	Colour TVs per 100 households	97.6
Av. no. per household	2.4	Telephone lines per 100 pop.	46.2
Marriages per 1,000 pop.	4.5	Mobile telephone subscribers	
Divorces per 1,000 pop.	2.2	per 100 pop.	97.4
Cost of living, Dec. 2005		Computers per 100 pop.	57.6
New York = 100	113	Internet hosts per 1,000 pop.	241.6

BANGLADESH

Area	143,998 sq km	Capital	Dhaka
Arable as % of total land	61	Currency	Taka (Tk)

People

Population	149.7m	Life expectancy: men	63.8 yrs
Pop. per sq km	1,039.6	women	65.8 yrs
Av. ann. growth		Adult literacy	41.1%
in pop. 2000–05	1.91%	Fertility rate (per woman)	3.3
Pop. under 15	35.5%	Urban population	25.0%
Pop. over 60	5.7%		per 1,000 pop.
No. of men per 100 women	104	Crude birth rate	28.9
Human Development Index	52.0	Crude death rate	7.2

The economy

GDP	Tk3,330bn	GDP per head	$380
GDP	$56.6bn	GDP per head in purchasing	
Av. ann. growth in real		power parity (USA=100)	4.7
GDP 1994–2004	5.2%	Economic freedom index	3.88

Origins of GDP		Components of GDP[a]	
	% of total		% of total
Agriculture	21	Private consumption	76.5
Industry, of which:	27	Public consumption	5.0
manufacturing	16	Investment	23.2
Services	52	Exports	13.3
		Imports	-18.8

Structure of employment

	% of total		% of labour force
Agriculture	66	Unemployed 2003	4.3
Industry	10	Av. ann. rate 1995–2003	2.7
Services	24		

Energy

			m TOE
Total output	17.5	Net energy imports as %	
Total consumption	21.7	of energy use	19
Consumption per head,			
kg oil equivalent	159		

Inflation and finance

Consumer price		av. ann. increase 1999–2004	
inflation 2004	3.2%	Narrow money (M1)	11.8%
Av. ann. inflation 2000–04	3.5%	Broad money	15.3%
Deposit rate, 2005	8.81%		

Exchange rates

	end 2005		December 2005
Tk per $	66.21	Effective rates	2000 = 100
Tk per SDR	94.63	– nominal	...
Tk per €	77.89	– real	...

Trade

Principal exports[b]		**Principal imports**[b]	
	$bn fob		*$bn cif*
Clothing	4.4	Capital goods	2.7
Fish & fish products	0.4	Textiles & yarn	2.4
Jute goods	0.2	Fuels	1.0
Leather	0.2	Cereal & dairy products	0.5
Total incl. others	**5.9**	Total incl. others	**10.0**

Main export destinations		**Main origins of imports**	
	% of total		*% of total*
United States	25.7	India	15.5
Germany	16.7	China	12.8
United Kingdom	12.9	Singapore	7.8
France	8.0	Kuwait	5.7
Italy	4.6	Japan	5.4

Balance of payments, reserves and debt, $bn

Visible exports fob	8.2	Change in reserves	0.6
Visible imports fob	-11.2	Level of reserves	
Trade balance	-3.0	end Dec.	3.2
Invisibles inflows	1.2	No. months of import cover	2.9
Invisibles outflows	-2.4	Official gold holdings, m oz	0.1
Net transfers	4.0	Foreign debt	20.3
Current account balance	-0.3	– as % of GDP	37
– as % of GDP	-0.5	– as % of total exports	179
Capital balance	0.8	Debt service ratio	6
Overall balance	0.5		

Health and education

Health spending, % of GDP	3.4	Education spending, % of GDP	2.4
Doctors per 1,000 pop.	0.3	Enrolment, %: primary	96
Hospital beds per 1,000 pop.	...	secondary	47
Improved-water source access,		tertiary	6
% of pop.	75		

Society

No. of households	25.1m	Colour TVs per 100 households	2.7
Av. no. per household	5.9	Telephone lines per 100 pop.	0.6
Marriages per 1,000 pop.	11.2	Mobile telephone subscribers	
Divorces per 1,000 pop.	...	per 100 pop.	2.0
Cost of living, Dec. 2005		Computers per 100 pop.	1.2
New York = 100	48	Internet hosts per 1,000 pop.	...

a Fiscal year ending June 30 2003.
b Fiscal year ending June 30 2004.

BELGIUM

Area	30,520 sq km	Capital	Brussels
Arable as % of total land	27	Currency	Euro (€)

People

Population	10.3m	Life expectancy:	men	76.5 yrs
Pop. per sq km	337.5		women	82.7 yrs
Av. ann. growth		Adult literacy		99.0%
in pop. 2000–05	0.22%	Fertility rate (per woman)		1.7
Pop. under 15	16.8%	Urban population		97.3%
Pop. over 60	22.4%			*per 1,000 pop.*
No. of men per 100 women	96	Crude birth rate		10.8
Human Development Index	94.5	Crude death rate		10.2

The economy

GDP	€284bn	GDP per head	$34,210
GDP	$352bn	GDP per head in purchasing	
Av. ann. growth in real		power parity (USA=100)	78.4
GDP 1994–2004	2.2%	Economic freedom index	2.11

Origins of GDP		**Components of GDP**	
	% of total		*% of total*
Agriculture	1.0	Private consumption	54.0
Industry, of which:	24.8	Public consumption	22.7
manufacturing	...	Investment	16.7
Services	74.2	Exports	83.7
		Imports	-80.7

Structure of employment

	% of total		*% of labour force*
Agriculture	2	Unemployed 2003	8.2
Industry	25	Av. ann. rate 1995–2003	8.3
Services	73		

Energy

	m TOE		
Total output	13.4	Net energy imports as %	
Total consumption	59.2	of energy use	77
Consumption per head,			
kg oil equivalent	5,701		

Inflation and finance

		av. ann. increase 1999–2004	
Consumer price			
inflation 2005	2.8%	Euro area:	
Av. ann. inflation 2000–05	2.1%	Narrow money (M1)	8.4%
Treasury bill rate, 2005	2.02%	Broad money	6.9%
		Household saving rate, 2004	10.7%

Exchange rates

	end 2005		*December 2005*
€ per $	0.85	Effective rates	*2000 = 100*
€ per SDR	1.21	– nominal	106.2
		– real	112.5

Trade

Principal exports		Principal imports	
	$bn fob		*$bn cif*
Chemicals	69.4	Chemicals	60.6
Transport equipment	42.2	Machinery	38.6
Machinery	39.6	Transport equipment	30.6
Food, drink & tobacco	26.0	Food, drink & tobacco	23.1
Total incl. others	**306.9**	Total incl. others	**285.7**

Main export destinations		Main origins of imports	
	% of total		*% of total*
Germany	20.0	Germany	18.5
France	17.3	Netherlands	17.0
Netherlands	11.9	France	12.5
United Kingdom	8.7	United Kingdom	6.8
EU25	77.3	EU25	73.6

Balance of payments, reserves and aid, $bn

Visible exports fob	245.5	Overall balance	-1.0
Visible imports fob	-235.7	Change in reserves	-0.5
Trade balance	9.7	Level of reserves	
Invisibles inflows	95.5	end Dec.	14.0
Invisibles outflows	-84.5	No. months of import cover	0.5
Net transfers	-6.6	Official gold holdings, m oz	8.3
Current account balance	14.0	Aid given	1.46
– as % of GDP	4.0	– as % of GDP	0.41
Capital balance	-2.1		

Health and education

Health spending, % of GDP	9.4	Education spending, % of GDP	6.3
Doctors per 1,000 pop.	4.5	Enrolment, %: primary	105
Hospital beds per 1,000 pop.	6.9	secondary	161
Improved-water source access, % of pop.	...	tertiary	61

Society

No. of households	4.4m	Colour TVs per 100 households	99.6
Av. no. per household	2.4	Telephone lines per 100 pop.	46.4
Marriages per 1,000 pop.	3.5	Mobile telephone subscribers	
Divorces per 1,000 pop.	2.4	per 100 pop.	88.3
Cost of living, Dec. 2005		Computers per 100 pop.	35.1
New York = 100	105	Internet hosts per 1,000 pop.	247.2

BRAZIL

Area	8,511,965 sq km	Capital	Brasilia
Arable as % of total land	7	Currency	Real (R)

People

Population	180.7m	Life expectancy: men	68.2 yrs
Pop. per sq km	21.2	women	75.7 yrs
Av. ann. growth		Adult literacy	88.6%
in pop. 2000–05	1.39%	Fertility rate (per woman)	2.4
Pop. under 15	27.9%	Urban population	84.2%
Pop. over 60	8.8%		per 1,000 pop.
No. of men per 100 women	97	Crude birth rate	19.7
Human Development Index	79.2	Crude death rate	6.5

The economy

GDP	R1,767n	GDP per head	$3,340
GDP	$604bn	GDP per head in purchasing	
Av. ann. growth in real		power parity (USA=100)	20.7
GDP 1994–2004	2.4%	Economic freedom index	3.08

Origins of GDP		Components of GDP	
	% of total		% of total
Agriculture	10.1	Private consumption	56.7
Industry, of which:	38.9	Public consumption	19.9
manufacturing	...	Investment	19.8
Services	51.0	Exports	16.4
		Imports	-12.8

Structure of employment

	% of total		% of labour force
Agriculture	20	Unemployed 2002	9.7
Industry	22	Av. ann. rate 1995–2002	8.3
Services	58		

Energy

			m TOE
Total output	171.1	Net energy imports as %	
Total consumption	193.2	of energy use	11
Consumption per head,			
kg oil equivalent	1,065		

Inflation and finance

Consumer price		av. ann. increase 1999–2004	
inflation 2005	6.9%	Narrow money (M1)	16.1%
Av. ann. inflation 2000–05	8.7%	Broad money	12.4%
Money market rate, 2005	19.12%		

Exchange rates

	end 2005		December 2005
R per $	2.34	Effective rates	2000 = 100
R per sdr	3.34	– nominal	...
R per €	2.75	– real	...

Trade

Principal exports		Principal imports	
	$bn fob		*$bn cif*
Transport equipment & parts	14.3	Machines & electrical	
Metal goods	9.8	equipment	14.4
Soyabeans etc.	9.8	Chemical products	11.1
Chemical products	1.7	Oil & derivatives	10.3
		Transport equipment & parts	6.5
Total incl. others	**96.5**	Total incl. others	**62.8**

Main export destinations		Main origins of imports	
	% of total		*% of total*
United States	21.1	United States	18.3
Argentina	7.6	Argentina	8.9
Netherlands	6.1	Germany	8.1
China	5.6	China	5.9

Balance of payments, reserves and debt, $bn

Visible exports fob	96.5	Change in reserves	3.6
Visible imports fob	-62.8	Level of reserves	
Trade balance	33.7	end Dec.	52.9
Invisibles inflows	15.8	No. months of import cover	6.1
Invisibles outflows	-41.0	Official gold holdings, m oz	0.5
Net transfers	3.3	Foreign debt	222.0
Current account balance	11.7	– as % of GDP	44
– as % of GDP	1.9	– as % of total exports	239
Capital balance	-3.0	Debt service ratio	58
Overall balance	6.6		

Health and education

Health spending, % of GDP	7.6	Education spending, % of GDP	4.2
Doctors per 1,000 pop.	1.1	Enrolment, %: primary	147
Hospital beds per 1,000 pop.	2.7	secondary	110
Improved-water source access,		tertiary	21
% of pop.	89		

Society

No. of households	51.6m	Colour TVs per 100 households	87.5
Av. no. per household	3.5	Telephone lines per 100 pop.	23.5
Marriages per 1,000 pop.	4.3	Mobile telephone subscribers	
Divorces per 1,000 pop.	0.5	per 100 pop.	36.3
Cost of living, Dec. 2005		Computers per 100 pop.	10.7
New York = 100	68	Internet hosts per 1,000 pop.	28.2

BULGARIA

Area	110,994 sq km	Capital	Sofia
Arable as % of total land	30	Currency	Lev (BGL)

People

Population	7.8m	Life expectancy:	men	69.8 yrs
Pop. per sq km	70.3		women	76.3 yrs
Av. ann. growth		Adult literacy		98.2%
in pop. 2000–05	-0.69%	Fertility rate (per woman)		1.2
Pop. under 15	13.8%	Urban population		70.5%
Pop. over 60	22.4%			per 1,000 pop.
No. of men per 100 women	94	Crude birth rate		7.9
Human Development Index	80.8	Crude death rate		14.5

The economy

GDP	BGL38.0bn	GDP per head	$3,090
GDP	$24.1bn	GDP per head in purchasing	
Av. ann. growth in real		power parity (USA=100)	20.4
GDP 1994–2004	1.7%	Economic freedom index	2.88

Origins of GDP		**Components of GDP**	
	% of total		% of total
Agriculture	10.9	Private consumption	68.1
Industry, of which:	30.0	Public consumption	18.7
manufacturing	...	Investment	23.5
Services	59.1	Exports	58.4
		Imports	-68.7

Structure of employment

	% of total		% of labour force
Agriculture	10	Unemployed 2004	12.0
Industry	33	Av. ann. rate 1995–2004	15.2
Services	57		

Energy

		m TOE	
Total output	10.1	Net energy imports as %	
Total consumption	19.5	of energy use	48
Consumption per head,			
kg oil equivalent	2,494		

Inflation and finance

Consumer price		av. ann change 1999–2004	
inflation 2005	5.0%	Narrow money (M1)	20.6%
Av. ann. inflation 2000–05	5.3%	Broad money	22.5%
Money market rate 2005	2.03%		

Exchange rates

	end 2005		December 2005
BGL per $	1.66	Effective rates	2000 = 100
BGL per SDR	2.37	– nominal	110.51
BGL per €	1.95	– real	121.29

Trade

Principal exports		Principal imports	
	$bn fob		*$bn cif*
Clothing	1.9	Mineral fuels	1.8
Iron & steel	1.0	Textiles	1.7
Other metals	0.9	Machinery & equipment	1.3
Chemicals	0.6	Chemicals	1.0
Total incl. others	**9.8**	Total incl. others	**14.4**

Main export destinations		Main origins of imports	
	% of total		*% of total*
Italy	13.1	Germany	14.7
Germany	10.3	Italy	12.7
Greece	10.0	Russia	9.9
Turkey	9.9	Greece	5.8

Balance of payments, reserves and debt, $bn

Visible exports fob	9.8	Change in reserves	2.5
Visible imports fob	-13.2	Level of reserves	
Trade balance	-3.4	end Dec.	9.3
Invisibles inflows	4.5	No. months of import cover	6.4
Invisibles outflows	-4.3	Official gold holdings, m oz	1.3
Net transfers	1.1	Foreign debt	15.7
Current account balance	-2.1	– as % of GDP	81
– as % of GDP	-8.5	– as % of total exports	139
Capital balance	3.1	Debt service ratio	22
Overall balance	1.7		

Health and education

Health spending, % of GDP	7.5	Education spending, % of GDP	3.6
Doctors per 1,000 pop.	3.6	Enrolment, %: primary	100
Hospital beds per 1,000 pop.	6.3	secondary	98
Improved-water source access,		tertiary	39
% of pop.	100		

Society

No. of households	2.9m	Colour TVs per 100 households	64.3
Av. no. per household	2.7	Telephone lines per 100 pop.	35.1
Marriages per 1,000 pop.	3.6	Mobile telephone subscribers	
Divorces per 1,000 pop.	1.3	per 100 pop.	60.9
Cost of living, Dec. 2005		Computers per 100 pop.	5.9
New York = 100	60	Internet hosts per 1,000 pop.	20.7

CAMEROON

Area	475,442 sq km	Capital	Yaoundé
Arable as % of total land	13	Currency	CFA franc (CFAfr)

People

Population	16.3m	Life expectancy:	men	45.8 yrs
Pop. per sq km	34.3		women	46.7 yrs
Av. ann. growth		Adult literacy		67.9%
in pop. 2000–05	1.88%	Fertility rate (per woman)		4.7
Pop. under 15	41.2%	Urban population		52.9%
Pop. over 60	5.6%			per 1,000 pop.
No. of men per 100 women	99	Crude birth rate		35.4
Human Development Index	49.7	Crude death rate		16.8

The economy

GDP	CFAfr7,602bn	GDP per head	$880
GDP	$14.4bn	GDP per head in purchasing	
Av. ann. growth in real		power parity (USA=100)	5.5
GDP 1994–2004	4.5%	Economic freedom index	3.46

Origins of GDP		Components of GDP	
	% of total		% of total
Agriculture	41.5	Private consumption	67.8
Industry, of which:	28.6	Public consumption	8.0
manufacturing	...	Investment	27.1
Services	29.9	Exports	20.7
		Imports	-23.7

Structure of employment

	% of total		% of labour force
Agriculture	70	Unemployed 2004	...
Industry	13	Av. ann. rate 1995–2004	...
Services	17		

Energy

	m TOE		
Total output	12.1	Net energy imports as %	
Total consumption	6.8	of energy use	-80
Consumption per head,			
kg oil equivalent	429		

Inflation and finance

		av. ann. change 1999–2004	
Consumer price			
inflation 2002	2.8%	Narrow money (M1)	9.1%
Av. ann. inflation 2000–02	3.7%	Broad money	11.4%
Deposit rate, 2005	4.92%		

Exchange rates

	end 2005		December 2005
CFAfr per $	556.04	Effective rates	2000 = 100
CFAfr per SDR	794.73	– nominal	108.6
CFAfr per €	654.16	– real	109.6

Trade

Principal exports		Principal imports	
	$bn fob		*$bn cif*
Crude oil	1.3	Capital goods	0.4
Cocoa	0.2	Intermediate goods	0.4
Cotton	0.2	Minerals & raw materials	0.3
Total incl. others	**2.6**	Total incl. others	**2.4**

Main export destinations		Main origins of imports	
	% of total		*% of total*
Spain	16.5	France	27.1
Italy	13.5	Nigeria	9.6
France	10.0	Belgium	7.3
United Kingdom	9.8	United States	4.7

Balance of payments[a], reserves and debt, $bn

Visible exports fob	2.4	Change in reserves	0.2
Visible imports fob	-2.1	Level of reserves	
Trade balance	0.2	end Dec.	0.8
Invisibles inflows	0.4	No. months of import cover	2.9
Invisibles outflows	-1.1	Official gold holdings, m oz	0.0
Net transfers	0.2	Foreign debt	9.5
Current account balance	-0.3	– as % of GDP	81
– as % of GDP	-2.4	– as % of total exports	296
Capital balance	0.2	Debt service ratio	20
Overall balance	0.0		

Health and education

Health spending, % of GDP	4.2	Education spending, % of GDP	3.8
Doctors per 1,000 pop.	0.2	Enrolment, %: primary	108
Hospital beds per 1,000 pop.	…	secondary	31
Improved-water source access,		tertiary	5
% of pop.	63		

Society

No. of households	4.3m	Colour TVs per 100 households	2.3
Av. no. per household	3.8	Telephone lines per 100 pop.	0.6
Marriages per 1,000 pop.	…	Mobile telephone subscribers	
Divorces per 1,000 pop.	…	per 100 pop.	9.4
Cost of living, Dec. 2005		Computers per 100 pop.	1.0
New York = 100	…	Internet hosts per 1,000 pop.	…

a 2003

CANADA

Area[a]	9,970,610 sq km	Capital	Ottawa
Arable as % of total land	5	Currency	Canadian dollar (C$)

People

Population	31.7m	Life expectancy: men	78.2 yrs
Pop. per sq km	3.2	women	83.1 yrs
Av. ann. growth		Adult literacy	99.0%
in pop. 2000–05	1.00%	Fertility rate (per woman)	1.5
Pop. under 15	17.6%	Urban population	81.1%
Pop. over 60	17.9%		per 1,000 pop.
No. of men per 100 women	98	Crude birth rate	10.3
Human Development Index	94.9	Crude death rate	7.4

The economy

GDP	C$1,272bn	GDP per head	$30,850
GDP	$978bn	GDP per head in purchasing	
Av. ann. growth in real		power parity (USA=100)	78.8
GDP 1994–2004	3.4%	Economic freedom index	1.85

Origins of GDP

	% of total
Agriculture	2.2
Industry, of which:	29.1
manufacturing & mining	21.0
Services	68.7

Components of GDP

	% of total
Private consumption	55.9
Public consumption	19.3
Investment	19.3
Exports	38.2
Imports	-33.8

Structure of employment

	% of total		% of labour force
Agriculture	3	Unemployed 2004	7.2
Industry	22	Av. ann. rate 1995–2004	8.1
Services	75		

Energy

	m TOE		
Total output	385.3	Net energy imports as %	
Total consumption	260.6	of energy use	-48
Consumption per head,			
kg oil equivalent	8,240		

Inflation and finance

Consumer price		av. ann. increase 1999–2004	
inflation 2005	2.2%	Narrow money (M1)	9.4%
Av. ann. inflation 2000–05	2.3%	Broad money	8.6%
Money market rate, 2005	2.66%	Household saving rate, 2004	2.4%

Exchange rates

	end 2005		December 2005
C$ per $	1.16	Effective rates	2000 = 100
C$ per SDR	1.66	– nominal	123.7
C$ per €	1.36	– real	107.5

Trade

Principal exports	$bn fob	Principal imports	$bn fob
Machinery & equipment	70.6	Machinery & equipment	79.8
Motor vehicles and parts	69.5	Motor vehicles & parts	59.5
Industrial goods	59.7	Industrial goods	56.5
Energy products	53.2	Consumer goods	36.7
Forest products	30.2	Energy products	19.2
Total incl. others	**304.5**	Total incl. others	**273.1**

Main export destinations	% of total	Main origins of imports	% of total
United States	85.1	United States	58.9
Japan	2.1	China	6.8
China	1.6	Japan	3.8
United Kingdom	1.6	Mexico	3.8
EU25	5.1	EU25	11.8

Balance of payments, reserves and aid, $bn

Visible exports fob	330.1	Overall balance	-2.8
Visible imports fob	-279.4	Change in reserves	-1.8
Trade balance	50.7	Level of reserves	
Invisibles inflows	77.1	end Dec.	34.5
Invisibles outflows	-106.0	No. months of import cover	1.1
Net transfers	0.3	Official gold holdings, m oz	0.1
Current account balance	22.0	Aid given	2.60
– as % of GDP	2.2	– as % of GDP	0.27
Capital balance	-20.2		

Health and education

Health spending, % of GDP	9.9	Education spending, % of GDP	5.2
Doctors per 1,000 pop.	2.1	Enrolment, %: primary	101
Hospital beds per 1,000 pop.	3.7	secondary	105
Improved-water source access,		tertiary	58
% of pop.	100		

Society

No. of households	11.9m	Colour TVs per 100 households	98.8
Av. no. per household	2.7	Telephone lines per 100 pop.	64.3
Marriages per 1,000 pop.	4.6	Mobile telephone subscribers	
Divorces per 1,000 pop.	2.3	per 100 pop.	46.7
Cost of living, Dec. 2005		Computers per 100 pop.	69.8
New York = 100	92	Internet hosts per 1,000 pop.	114.3

a Including freshwater.

CHILE

Area	756,945 sq km	Capital	Santiago
Arable as % of total land	3	Currency	Chilean peso (Ps)

People

Population	16.0m	Life expectancy: men	75.5 yrs
Pop. per sq km	21.1	women	81.5 yrs
Av. ann. growth		Adult literacy	95.7%
in pop. 2000–05	1.12%	Fertility rate (per woman)	2.0
Pop. under 15	24.9%	Urban population	87.7%
Pop. over 60	11.6%		per 1,000 pop.
No. of men per 100 women	98	Crude birth rate	18.2
Human Development Index	85.4	Crude death rate	5.4

The economy

GDP	57,357bn pesos	GDP per head	$5,880
GDP	$94.1bn	GDP per head in purchasing	
Av. ann. growth in real		power parity (USA=100)	27.4
GDP 1994–2004	4.7%	Economic freedom index	1.88

Origins of GDP		**Components of GDP**	
	% of total		% of total
Agriculture	6.3	Private consumption	57.7
Industry, of which:	46.6	Public consumption	11.6
manufacturing	32.4	Investment	19.5
Services	47.1	Exports	41.0
		Imports	-31.9

Structure of employment

	% of total		% of labour force
Agriculture	14	Unemployed 2004	7.8
Industry	23	Av. ann. rate 1995–2004	7.1
Services	63		

Energy

	m TOE		
Total output	8.3	Net energy imports as %	
Total consumption	26.3	of energy use	68
Consumption per head,			
kg oil equivalent	1,647		

Inflation and finance

Consumer price		av. ann. increase 1999–2004	
inflation 2005	3.1%	Narrow money (M1)	11.0%
Av. ann. inflation 2000–05	2.6%	Broad money	4.8%
Money market rate, 2005	3.48%		

Exchange rates

	end 2005		December 2005
Ps per $	514.21	Effective rates	2000 = 100
Ps per SDR	734.94	– nominal	104.3
Ps per €	604.55	– real	102.2

Trade

Principal exports		Principal imports	
	$bn fob		*$bn cif*
Copper	14.4	Intermediate goods	14.4
Fruit	2.0	Capital goods	4.7
Paper products	1.6	Consumer goods	4.0
Total incl. others	**32.0**	Total incl. others	**24.9**

Main export destinations		Main origins of imports	
	% of total		*% of total*
United States	14.3	Argentina	17.7
Japan	11.5	United States	14.1
China	10.0	Brazil	11.2
South Korea	5.6	China	7.1
Netherlands	5.2	Germany	3.3

Balance of payments, reserves and debt, $bn

Visible exports fob	32.0	Change in reserves	0.2
Visible imports fob	-23.0	Level of reserves	
Trade balance	9.0	end Dec.	16.0
Invisibles inflows	7.5	No. months of import cover	4.9
Invisibles outflows	-16.1	Official gold holdings, m oz	0.0
Net transfers	1.1	Foreign debt	44.1
Current account balance	1.4	– as % of GDP	58
– as % of GDP	1.5	– as % of total exports	145
Capital balance	-0.5	Debt service ratio	32
Overall balance	-0.2		

Health and education

Health spending, % of GDP	6.1	Education spending, % of GDP	4.1
Doctors per 1,000 pop.	1.1	Enrolment, %: primary	98
Hospital beds per 1,000 pop.	2.6	secondary	91
Improved-water source access,		tertiary	45
% of pop.	95		

Society

No. of households	4.3m	Colour TVs per 100 households	62.6
Av. no. per household	3.7	Telephone lines per 100 pop.	21.5
Marriages per 1,000 pop.	4.8	Mobile telephone subscribers	
Divorces per 1,000 pop.	0.5	per 100 pop.	62.1
Cost of living, Dec. 2005		Computers per 100 pop.	13.9
New York = 100	70	Internet hosts per 1,000 pop.	28.9

CHINA

Area	9,560,900 sq km	Capital	Beijing
Arable as % of total land	15	Currency	Yuan

People

Population	1,313.3m	Life expectancy: men	70.8 yrs
Pop. per sq km	137.4	women	74.6 yrs
Av. ann. growth		Adult literacy	90.9%
in pop. 2000–05	0.65%	Fertility rate (per woman)	1.7
Pop. under 15	21.4%	Urban population	40.5%
Pop. over 60	10.9%		per 1,000 pop.
No. of men per 100 women	106	Crude birth rate	14.5
Human Development Index	75.5	Crude death rate	7.1

The economy

GDP	Yuan15,988bn	GDP per head	$1,470
GDP	$1,932bn	GDP per head in purchasing	
Av. ann. growth in real		power parity (USA=100)	14.9
GDP 1994–2004	9.1%	Economic freedom index	3.34

Origins of GDP		Components of GDP	
	% of total		% of total
Agriculture	15.2	Private consumption	41.4
Industry, of which:	52.9	Public consumption	11.6
manufacturing	46.0	Investment	44.2
Services	31.8	Exports	38.1
		Imports	-35.3

Structure of employment

	% of total		% of labour force
Agriculture	49	Unemployed 2004	4.2
Industry	22	Av. ann. rate 1995–2004	3.3
Services	29		

Energy

	m TOE		
Total output	1,380.8	Net energy imports as %	
Total consumption	1,409.4	of energy use	2
Consumption per head,			
kg oil equivalent	1,094		

Inflation and finance

		av. ann. increase 1999–2004	
Consumer price			
inflation 2005	1.9%	Narrow money (M1)	16.2%
Av. ann. inflation 2000–05	1.4%	Broad money	16.2%
Deposit rate, 2005	2.25%		

Exchange rates

	end 2005		December 2005
			2000 = 100
Yuan per $	8.07	Effective rates	
Yuan per SDR	11.53	– nominal	98.23
Yuan per €	9.49	– real	95.83

Trade

Principal exports		Principal imports	
	$bn fob		$bn cif
Office equipment	87.1	Electrical machinery	110.5
Telecoms equipment	68.5	Petroleum products	44.5
Apparel & clothing	61.9	Professional &	
Electrical machinery	59.5	scientific instruments	33.3
Textiles	33.4	Office equipment	29.6
		Other machinery	26.3
Total incl. others	**593**	Total incl. others	**561**

Main export destinations		Main origins of imports	
	% of total		% of total
United States	21.0	Japan	16.8
Hong Kong	17.0	Taiwan	11.5
Japan	12.4	South Korea	11.1
South Korea	4.7	United States	8.0
Germany	4.0	Germany	5.4

Balance of payments, reserves and debt, $bn

Visible exports fob	593.4	Change in reserves	206.7
Visible imports fob	-534.4	Level of reserves	
Trade balance	59.0	end Dec.	623.0
Invisibles inflows	83.0	No. months of import cover	11.9
Invisibles outflows	-96.2	Official gold holdings, m oz	19.3
Net transfers	22.9	Foreign debt	248.9
Current account balance	68.7	– as % of GDP	15
– as % of GDP	3.6	– as % of total exports	48
Capital balance	110.7	Debt service ratio	5
Overall balance	206.2		

Health and education

Health spending, % of GDP	5.6	Education spending, % of GDP	...
Doctors per 1,000 pop.	1.0	Enrolment, %: primary	115
Hospital beds per 1,000 pop.	2.5	secondary	70
Improved-water source access,		tertiary	16
% of pop.	77		

Society

No. of households	378.1m	Colour TVs per 100 households	46.4
Av. no. per household	3.5	Telephone lines per 100 pop.	24.0
Marriages per 1,000 pop.	6.2	Mobile telephone subscribers	
Divorces per 1,000 pop.	0.8	per 100 pop.	25.8
Cost of living, Dec. 2005		Computers per 100 pop.	4.1
New York = 100	83	Internet hosts per 1,000 pop.	0.2

Note: Data excludes Special Administrative Regions ie, Hong Kong and Macau.

COLOMBIA

Area	1,141,748 sq km	Capital	Bogota
Arable as % of total land	2	Currency	Colombian peso (peso)

People

Population	44.9m	Life expectancy: men	70.3 yrs
Pop. per sq km	39.3	women	76.3 yrs
Av. ann. growth		Adult literacy	92.8%
in pop. 2000–05	1.59%	Fertility rate (per woman)	2.6
Pop. under 15	31.0%	Urban population	77.4%
Pop. over 60	7.5%		per 1,000 pop.
No. of men per 100 women	98	Crude birth rate	22.2
Human Development Index	78.5	Crude death rate	5.4

The economy

GDP	256,862bn pesos	GDP per head	$2,180
GDP	$97.7bn	GDP per head in purchasing	
Av. ann. growth in real		power parity (USA=100)	18.3
GDP 1994–2004	2.1%	Economic freedom index	3.16

Origins of GDP		Components of GDP	
	% of total		% of total
Agriculture	12.5	Private consumption	63.0
Industry, of which:	33.8	Public consumption	19.9
manufacturing	15.9	Investment	18.2
Services	53.7	Exports	21.2
		Imports	-22.3

Structure of employment

	% of total		% of labour force
Agriculture	22	Unemployed 2004	13.6
Industry	19	Av. ann. rate 1995–2004	14.7
Services	59		

Energy

	m TOE		
Total output	74.4	Net energy imports as %	
Total consumption	28.4	of energy use	-162
Consumption per head, kg oil equivalent	642		

Inflation and finance

Consumer price		av. ann. increase 1999–2004	
inflation 2005	5.1%	Narrow money (M1)	16.7%
Av. ann. inflation 2000–05	6.5%	Broad money	14.4%
Money market rate, 2005	6.18%		

Exchange rates

	end 2005		December 2005
Peso per $	2,282	Effective rates	2000 = 100
Peso per SDR	3,262	– nominal	101.2
Peso per €	2,685	– real	109.3

Trade

Principal exports		Principal imports	
	$bn fob		*$bn cif*
Oil	4.2	Intermediate goods &	
Coal	1.8	raw materials	8.0
Coffee	0.9	Capital goods	5.5
		Consumer goods	3.2
Total incl. others	**16.7**	Total	**16.7**

Main export destinations		Main origins of imports	
	% of total		*% of total*
United States	42.2	United States	29.6
Ecuador	6.1	Brazil	6.0
Venezuela	5.4	Mexico	5.8
Peru	3.1	Venezuela	5.7

Balance of payments, reserves and debt, $bn

Visible exports fob	17.2	Change in reserves	2.6
Visible imports fob	-15.9	Level of reserves	
Trade balance	1.4	end Dec.	13.5
Invisibles inflows	2.9	No. months of import cover	6.6
Invisibles outflows	-8.9	Official gold holdings, m oz	0.3
Net transfers	3.7	Foreign debt	37.7
Current account balance	-1.0	– as % of GDP	45
– as % of GDP	-1.0	– as % of total exports	189
Capital balance	3.1	Debt service ratio	38
Overall balance	2.5		

Health and education

Health spending, % of GDP	7.6	Education spending, % of GDP	5.2
Doctors per 1,000 pop.	1.3	Enrolment, %: primary	110
Hospital beds per 1,000 pop.	1.1	secondary	71
Improved-water source access,		tertiary	24
% of pop.	92		

Society

No. of households	11.6m	Colour TVs per 100 households	86.7
Av. no. per household	3.8	Telephone lines per 100 pop.	17.1
Marriages per 1,000 pop.	...	Mobile telephone subscribers	
Divorces per 1,000 pop.	0.2	per 100 pop.	23.0
Cost of living, Dec. 2005		Computers per 100 pop.	5.5
New York = 100	70	Internet hosts per 1,000 pop.	9.8

CÔTE D'IVOIRE

Area	322,463 sq km	Capital	Abidjan/Yamoussoukro
Arable as % of total land	10	Currency	CFA franc (CFAfr)

People

Population	16.9m	Life expectancy: men	45.6 yrs
Pop. per sq km	52.4	women	47.0 yrs
Av. ann. growth		Adult literacy	48.7%
in pop. 2000–05	1.63%	Fertility rate (per woman)	5.1
Pop. under 15	41.9%	Urban population	45.8%
Pop. over 60	5.3%		per 1,000 pop.
No. of men per 100 women	103	Crude birth rate	35.5
Human Development Index	42.0	Crude death rate	16.7

The economy

GDP	CFAfr8,175bn	GDP per head	$920
GDP	$15.5bn	GDP per head in purchasing	
Av. ann. growth in real		power parity (USA=100)	3.9
GDP 1994–2004	2.1%	Economic freedom index	3.14

Origins of GDP		Components of GDP	
	% of total		% of total
Agriculture	23	Private consumption	65.3
Industry, of which:	23	Public consumption	14.5
manufacturing	...	Investment	10.7
Services	54	Exports	49.4
		Imports	-39.9

Structure of employment

	% of total		% of labour force
Agriculture	...	Unemployed 2004	...
Industry	...	Av. ann. rate 1995–2004	...
Services	...		

Energy

	m TOE		
Total output	6.7	Net energy imports as %	
Total consumption	6.6	of energy use	-2
Consumption per head,			
kg oil equivalent	374		

Inflation and finance

Consumer price		av. ann. change 1999-2004	
inflation 2005	3.9%	Narrow money (M1)	1.7%
Av. ann. inflation 2000–05	3.2%	Broad money	2.9%
Money market rate, 2005	4.95%		

Exchange rates

	end 2005		December 2005
			2000 = 100
CFAfr per $	556.0	Effective rates	
CFAfr per SDR	794.7	– nominal	111.6
CFAfr per €	654.2	– real	114.2

Trade

Principal exports		Principal imports	
	$bn fob		*$bn cif*
Cocoa beans & products	2.2	Capital equipment	1.2
Petroleum products	1.0	Foodstuffs	0.9
Timber	0.3	Fuel & lubricants	0.9
Coffee & products	0.2		
Total incl. others	**6.9**	Total incl. others	**5.7**

Main export destinations		Main origins of imports	
	% of total		*% of total*
United States	11.1	France	23.6
Netherlands	9.8	Nigeria	18.7
France	9.1	China	4.0
Italy	5.3	Italy	3.7
Belgium	4.5	Belgium	3.6

Balance of payments, reserves and debt, $bn

Visible exports fob	6.9	Change in reserves	0.4
Visible imports fob	-4.2	Level of reserves	
Trade balance	2.7	end Dec.	1.7
Invisibles inflows	0.9	No. months of import cover	2.9
Invisibles outflows	-2.9	Official gold holdings, m oz	0.0
Net transfers	-0.5	Foreign debt	11.7
Current account balance	0.3	– as % of GDP	91
– as % of GDP	2.0	– as % of total exports	172
Capital balance	-1.1	Debt service ratio	8
Overall balance	-0.8		

Health and education

Health spending, % of GDP	3.6	Education spending, % of GDP	4.6
Doctors per 1,000 pop.	0.1	Enrolment, %: primary	78
Hospital beds per 1,000 pop.	...	secondary	26
Improved-water source access,		tertiary	7
% of pop.	84		

Society

No. of households	3.5m	Colour TVs per 100 households	28.0
Av. no. per household	4.8	Telephone lines per 100 pop.	1.4
Marriages per 1,000 pop.	...	Mobile telephone subscribers	
Divorces per 1,000 pop.	...	per 100 pop.	9.1
Cost of living, Dec. 2005		Computers per 100 pop.	1.6
New York = 100	94	Internet hosts per 1,000 pop.	0.1

CZECH REPUBLIC

Area	78,864 sq km	Capital	Prague
Arable as % of total land	40	Currency	Koruna (Kc)

People

Population	10.2m	Life expectancy: men	73.1 yrs
Pop. per sq km	129.3	women	79.4 yrs
Av. ann. growth		Adult literacy	99.0%
in pop. 2000–05	-0.09	Fertility rate (per woman)	1.2
Pop. under 15	14.6%	Urban population	74.5%
Pop. over 60	20.0%		per 1,000 pop.
No. of men per 100 women	95	Crude birth rate	8.8
Human Development Index	87.4	Crude death rate	11.1

The economy

GDP	Kc2,750bn	GDP per head	$10,490
GDP	$107bn	GDP per head in purchasing	
Av. ann. growth in real		power parity (USA=100)	48.9
GDP 1994–2004	2.5%	Economic freedom index	2.10

Origins of GDP		Components of GDP	
	% of total		% of total
Agriculture	3.1	Private consumption	50.1
Industry, of which:	38.1	Public consumption	22.7
manufacturing	...	Investment	27.0
Services	58.8	Exports	71.7
		Imports	-72.1

Structure of employment

	% of total		% of labour force
Agriculture	4	Unemployed 2004	8.3
Industry	40	Av. ann. rate 1995–2004	6.7
Services	56		

Energy

	m TOE		
Total output	33.0	Net energy imports as %	
Total consumption	44.1	of energy use	25
Consumption per head,			
kg oil equivalent	4,324		

Inflation and finance

		av. ann. increase 1999–2004	
Consumer price			
inflation 2005	1.8%	Narrow money (M1)	18.0%
Av. ann. inflation 2000–05	2.2%	Broad money	9.1%
Money market rate, 2005	2.17%		

Exchange rates

	end 2005		December 2005
Kc per $	24.59	Effective rates	2000 = 100
Kc per SDR	35.14	– nominal	127.96
Kc per €	28.93	– real	127.69

Trade

Principal exports		Principal imports	
	$bn fob		*$bn cif*
Machinery & transport		Machinery & transport	
equipment	33.9	equipment	28.4
Semi-manufactures	15.4	Semi-manufactures	14.3
Chemicals	4.2	Chemicals	7.6
Raw materials & fuels	3.8	Raw materials & fuels	6.9
Total incl. others	**67.2**	Total incl. others	**68.2**

Main export destinations		Main origins of imports	
	% of total		*% of total*
Germany	36.3	Germany	31.4
Slovakia	8.5	Slovakia	5.4
Austria	6.0	Italy	5.3
Poland	5.2	China	5.1
United Kingdom	4.7	Austria	4.1
EU25	86.0	EU25	72.2

Balance of payments, reserves and debt, $bn

Visible exports fob	66.9	Change in reserves	1.5
Visible imports fob	-67.8	Level of reserves	
Trade balance	-0.9	end Dec.	28.5
Invisibles inflows	12.4	No. months of import cover	4.0
Invisibles outflows	-17.4	Official gold holdings, m oz	0.4
Net transfers	0.2	Foreign debt	45.6
Current account balance	5.6	– as % of GDP	53
– as % of GDP	-5.2	– as % of total exports	73
Capital balance	6.6	Debt service ratio	13
Overall balance	0.3		

Health and education

Health spending, % of GDP	7.5	Education spending, % of GDP	4.4
Doctors per 1,000 pop.	3.5	Enrolment, %: primary	102
Hospital beds per 1,000 pop.	8.8	secondary	97
Improved-water source access,		tertiary	36
% of pop.	...		

Society

No. of households	3.8m	Colour TVs per 100 households	91.9
Av. no. per household	2.7	Telephone lines per 100 pop.	33.6
Marriages per 1,000 pop.	3.9	Mobile telephone subscribers	
Divorces per 1,000 pop.	3.3	per 100 pop.	105.6
Cost of living, Dec. 2005		Computers per 100 pop.	21.6
New York = 100	83	Internet hosts per 1,000 pop.	97.4

DENMARK

Area	43,075 sq km	Capital	Copenhagen
Arable as % of total land	53	Currency	Danish krone (DKr)

People

Population	5.4m	Life expectancy: men	75.5 yrs
Pop. per sq km	125.4	women	80.1 yrs
Av. ann. growth		Adult literacy	99.0%
in pop. 2000–05	0.34	Fertility rate (per woman)	1.8
Pop. under 15	18.8%	Urban population	85.5%
Pop. over 60	21.1%		per 1,000 pop.
No. of men per 100 women	98	Crude birth rate	11.8
Human Development Index	94.1	Crude death rate	10.6

The economy

GDP	DKr1,447bn	GDP per head	$44,710
GDP	$241bn	GDP per head in purchasing	
Av. ann. growth in real		power parity (USA=100)	48.9
GDP 1994–2004	2.1%	Economic freedom index	1.78

Origins of GDP		**Components of GDP**	
	% of total		% of total
Agriculture	2.3	Private consumption	47.9
Industry, of which:	24.9	Public consumption	26.5
manufacturing	...	Investment	20.0
Services	71.5	Exports	43.4
		Imports	-38.4

Structure of employment

	% of total		% of labour force
Agriculture	3	Unemployed 2004	5.6
Industry	24	Av. ann. rate 1995–2004	5.6
Services	73		

Energy

	m TOE		
Total output	28.5	Net energy imports as %	
Total consumption	20.8	of energy use	-37
Consumption per head,			
kg oil equivalent	3,853		

Inflation and finance

Consumer price		av. ann. increase 1999–2004	
inflation 2005	1.8%	Narrow money (M1)	7.0%
Av. ann. inflation 2000–05	2.0%	Broad money	3.8%
Money market rate, 2005	2.20%	Household saving rate, 2004	2.9%

Exchange rates

	end 2005		December 2005
DKr per $	6.32	Effective rates	2000 = 100
DKr per SDR	9.04	– nominal	106.7
DKr per €	7.44	– real	111.0

Trade

Principal exports	$bn fob	Principal imports	$bn cif
Manufactured goods	56.8	Intermediate goods	28.3
Agric. products	7.4	Consumer goods	19.4
Energy & products	6.3	Capital goods	9.1
Total incl. others	**75.6**	**Total incl. others**	**66.9**

Main export destinations	% of total	Main origins of imports	% of total
Germany	18.0	Germany	22.2
Sweden	13.3	Sweden	13.4
United Kingdom	8.7	United Kingdom	6.1
United States	5.7	Netherlands	6.0
Norway	5.4	France	4.8
Netherlands	5.1	Norway	4.5
EU25	69.8	EU25	72.5

Balance of payments, reserves and aid, $bn

Visible exports fob	75.1	Overall balance	11.6
Visible imports fob	-65.5	Change in reserves	2.0
Trade balance	9.5	Level of reserves	
Invisibles inflows	49.1	end Dec.	40.0
Invisibles outflows	-48.5	No. months of import cover	4.2
Net transfers	-4.2	Official gold holdings, m oz	2.0
Current account balance	5.9	Aid given	2.04
– as % of GDP	2.5	– as % of GDP	0.85
Capital balance	-19.0		

Health and education

Health spending, % of GDP	9.0	Education spending, % of GDP	8.5
Doctors per 1,000 pop.	2.9	Enrolment, %: primary	104
Hospital beds per 1,000 pop.	4.0	secondary	129
Improved-water source access,		tertiary	67
% of pop.	100		

Society

No. of households	2.5m	Colour TVs per 100 households	92.5
Av. no. per household	2.2	Telephone lines per 100 pop.	64.5
Marriages per 1,000 pop.	6.0	Mobile telephone subscribers	
Divorces per 1,000 pop.	2.8	per 100 pop.	95.5
Cost of living, Dec. 2005		Computers per 100 pop.	65.5
New York = 100	127	Internet hosts per 1,000 pop.	429.0

EGYPT

Area	1,000,250 sq km	Capital	Cairo
Arable as % of total land	3	Currency	Egyptian pound (£E)

People

Population	73.4m	Life expectancy: men		68.9 yrs
Pop. per sq km	73.4	women		73.5 yrs
Av. ann. growth		Adult literacy		55.6%
in pop. 2000–05	1.91%	Fertility rate (per woman)		3.3
Pop. under 15	33.6%	Urban population		42.3%
Pop. over 60	7.1%			per 1,000 pop.
No. of men per 100 women	101	Crude birth rate		26.6
Human Development Index	65.9	Crude death rate		5.7

The economy

GDP	£E485bn	GDP per head	$1,070
GDP	$78.8bn	GDP per head in purchasing	
Av. ann. growth in real		power parity (USA=100)	10.6
GDP 1994–2004	4.7%	Economic freedom index	3.59

Origins of GDP		Components of GDP[a]	
	% of total		% of total
Agriculture	13.9	Private consumption	71.3
Industry, of which:	33.0	Public consumption	12.2
manufacturing	18.2	Investment	16.5
Services	53.1	Exports	30.5
		Imports	-30.6

Structure of employment

	% of total		% of labour force
Agriculture	27	Unemployed 2004	11.0
Industry	21	Av. ann. rate 1995–2004	9.6
Services	52		

Energy

	m TOE		
Total output	61.0	Net energy imports as %	
Total consumption	52.4	of energy use	-17
Consumption per head,			
kg oil equivalent	735		

Inflation and finance

		av. ann. increase 1999–2004	
Consumer price			
inflation 2005	4.9%	Narrow money (M1)	12.9%
Av. ann. inflation 2000–05	5.1%	Broad money	14.6%
Treasury bill rate, 2005	8.57%		

Exchange rates

	end 2005		December 2005
£E per $	5.73	Effective rates	2000 = 100
£E per SDR	8.19	– nominal	...
£E per €	6.74	– real	...

Trade

Principal exports[b]	$bn fob	Principal imports[b]	$bn fob
Petroleum & products	5.3	Intermediate goods	6.8
Cotton yarn & textiles	0.9	Investment goods	4.9
Metals	0.9	Fuels	4.0
Agricultural products	0.2	Consumer goods	3.2
Pharmaceuticals	0.2		
Total incl. others	**6.3**	Total incl. others	**11.1**

Main export destinations	% of total	Main origins of imports	% of total
Italy	12.8	United States	12.5
United States	11.6	Germany	6.8
United Kingdom	7.3	Italy	6.8
France	4.9	France	5.8

Balance of payments, reserves and debt, $bn

Visible exports fob	12.3	Change in reserves	0.7
Visible imports fob	-18.9	Level of reserves	
Trade balance	-6.6	end Dec.	15.3
Invisibles inflows	14.8	No. months of import cover	6.6
Invisibles outflows	-8.8	Official gold holdings, m oz	2.4
Net transfers	4.6	Foreign debt	30.3
Current account balance	3.9	– as % of GDP	36
– as % of GDP	5.0	– as % of total exports	123
Capital balance	-4.5	Debt service ratio	9
Overall balance	-0.6		

Health and education

Health spending, % of GDP	5.8	Education spending, % of GDP	...
Doctors per 1,000 pop.	0.5	Enrolment, %: primary	97
Hospital beds per 1,000 pop.	2.2	secondary	85
Improved-water source access, % of pop.	98	tertiary	29

Society

No. of households	15.5m	Colour TVs per 100 households	51.1
Av. no. per household	4.4	Telephone lines per 100 pop.	13.5
Marriages per 1,000 pop.	11.0	Mobile telephone subscribers	
Divorces per 1,000 pop.	1.5	per 100 pop.	10.9
Cost of living, Dec. 2005		Computers per 100 pop.	3.3
New York = 100	56	Internet hosts per 1,000 pop.	1.2

a Year ending June 30, 2005.
b Year ending June 30, 2004.

ESTONIA

Area	45,200 sq km	Capital	Tallinn
Arable as % of total land	13	Currency	Kroon (EEK)

People

Population	1.3m	Life expectancy:	men	67.0 yrs
Pop. per sq km	28.8		women	78.0 yrs
Av. ann. growth		Adult literacy[a]		99.8%
in pop. 2000–05	-0.55%	Fertility rate (per woman)		1.4
Pop. under 15	15.2%	Urban population		69.6%
Pop. over 60	21.6%			per 1,000 pop.
No. of men per 100 women	85	Crude birth rate		8.7
Human Development Index	85.3	Crude death rate		13.6

The economy

GDP	EEK142bn	GDP per head	$8,650
GDP	$11.2bn	GDP per head in purchasing	
Av. ann. growth in real		power parity (USA=100)	36.7
GDP 1994–2004	6.0%	Economic freedom index	1.75

Origins of GDP

	% of total
Agriculture	4.3
Industry, of which:	28.9
manufacturing	...
Services	66.8

Components of GDP

	% of total
Private consumption	56.0
Public consumption	19.0
Investment	31.2
Exports	78.4
Imports	-86.1

Structure of employment

	% of total		% of labour force
Agriculture	6	Unemployed 2004	9.7
Industry	33	Av. ann. rate 1995–2004	10.7
Services	61		

Energy

	m TOE		
Total output	3.7	Net energy imports as %	
Total consumption	4.9	of energy use	26
Consumption per head,			
kg oil equivalent	3,631		

Inflation and finance

		av. ann. increase 1999–2004	
Consumer price			
inflation 2005	4.1%	Narrow money (M1)	15.9%
Av. ann. inflation 2000–05	3.5%	Broad money	17.2%
Money market rate, 2005	2.38%		

Exchange rates

	end 2005		December 2005
EEK per $	13.22	Effective rates	2000 = 100
EEK per SDR	18.90	– nominal	...
EEK per €	15.55	– real	...

Trade

Principal exports	$bn fob	Principal imports	$bn cif
Machinery & equipment	1.6	Machinery & equipment	2.4
Wood & paper	0.9	Transport equipment	1.0
Clothing & footwear	0.6	Metals	0.9
Food	0.5	Chemicals	0.8
Furniture	0.5	Food	0.8
Total incl. others	**5.9**	Total incl. others	**8.4**

Main export destinations	% of total	Main origins of imports	% of total
Finland	23.1	Finland	22.2
Sweden	15.3	Germany	12.9
Germany	8.4	Sweden	9.7
Latvia	7.9	Russia	9.2
Russia	5.6	Lithuania	5.3
EU25	80.0	EU25	77.7

Balance of payments, reserves and debt, $bn

Visible exports fob	6.0	Change in reserves	0.4
Visible imports fob	-7.9	Level of reserves	
Trade balance	-2.0	end Dec.	1.8
Invisibles inflows	3.3	No. months of import cover	2.0
Invisibles outflows	-2.9	Official gold holdings, m oz	0.0
Net transfers	0.2	Foreign debt	10.0
Current account balance	-1.4	– as % of GDP	116
– as % of GDP	-12.7	– as % of total exports	138
Capital balance	1.8	Debt service ratio	20
Overall balance	0.3		

Health and education

Health spending, % of GDP	5.3	Education spending, % of GDP	5.7
Doctors per 1,000 pop.	4.7	Enrolment, %: primary	101
Hospital beds per 1,000 pop.	6.0	secondary	96
Improved-water source access,		tertiary	66
% of pop.	...		

Society

No. of households	0.6m	Colour TVs per 100 households	86.2
Av. no. per household	2.4	Telephone lines per 100 pop.	34.0
Marriages per 1,000 pop.	3.2	Mobile telephone subscribers	
Divorces per 1,000 pop.	3.2	per 100 pop.	96.0
Cost of living, Dec. 2005		Computers per 100 pop.	47.4
New York = 100	...	Internet hosts per 1,000 pop.	273.1

FINLAND

Area	338,145 sq km	Capital	Helsinki
Arable as % of total land	7	Currency	Euro (€)

People

Population	5.2m	Life expectancy: men	76.0 yrs
Pop. per sq km	15.4	women	82.4 yrs
Av. ann. growth		Adult literacy	99.0%
in pop. 2000–05	0.28%	Fertility rate (per woman)	1.7
Pop. under 15	17.3%	Urban population	60.9%
Pop. over 60	21.3%		per 1,000 pop.
No. of men per 100 women	96	Crude birth rate	10.8
Human Development Index	94.1	Crude death rate	9.8

The economy

GDP	€150bn	GDP per head	$35,750
GDP	$186bn	GDP per head in purchasing	
Av. ann. growth in real		power parity (USA=100)	75.5
GDP 1994–2004	3.6%	Economic freedom index	1.85

Origins of GDP		Components of GDP	
	% of total		% of total
Agriculture	3.2	Private consumption	52.4
Industry, of which:	29.1	Public consumption	22.3
manufacturing & mining	22.7	Investment	18.5
Services	67.7	Exports	37.3
		Imports	-30.7

Structure of employment

	% of total		% of labour force
Agriculture	6	Unemployed 2004	8.8
Industry	26	Av. ann. rate 1995–2004	10.9
Services	68		

Energy

	m TOE		
Total output	16.0	Net energy imports as %	
Total consumption	37.6	of energy use	57
Consumption per head,			
kg oil equivalent	7,204		

Inflation and finance

Consumer price		av. ann. increase 1999–2004	
inflation 2005	0.9%	Euro area:	
Av. ann. inflation 2000–05	1.2%	Narrow money (M1)	8.4%
Money market rate, 2005	2.18%	Broad money	6.9%
		Household saving rate, 2004	2.7%

Exchange rates

	end 2005		December 2005
€ per $	0.85	Effective rates	2000 = 100
€ per SDR	1.21	– nominal	107.8
		– real	109.7

Trade

Principal exports		Principal imports	
	$bn fob		*$bn cif*
Electrical & optical equipment	22.1	Raw materials	15.7
Metals, machinery &		Consumer goods	5.1
transport equipment	16.5	Capital goods	5.0
Paper & products	3.8	Energy	4.9
Chemicals	3.5		
Total incl. others	**60.9**	Total incl. others	**50.7**

Main export destinations		Main origins of imports	
	% of total		*% of total*
Sweden	11.0	Germany	14.7
Germany	10.7	Sweden	13.2
Russia	8.9	Russia	10.9
United Kingdom	7.1	China	4.9
United States	6.4	France	4.6
Netherlands	5.1	United Kingdom	4.5
EU25	57.9	EU25	67.3

Balance of payments, reserves and aid, $bn

Visible exports fob	61.1	Overall balance	0.9
Visible imports fob	-48.3	Change in reserves	1.8
Trade balance	12.8	Level of reserves	
Invisibles inflows	20.1	end Dec.	13.0
Invisibles outflows	-24.4	No. months of import cover	2.1
Net transfers	-1.0	Official gold holdings, m oz	1.6
Current account balance	7.5	Aid given	0.66
– as % of GDP	4.0	– as % of GDP	0.35
Capital balance	-6.6		

Health and education

Health spending, % of GDP	7.4	Education spending, % of GDP	6.4
Doctors per 1,000 pop.	3.2	Enrolment, %: primary	102
Hospital beds per 1,000 pop.	7.2	secondary	128
Improved-water source access,		tertiary	88
% of pop.	100		

Society

No. of households	2.4m	Colour TVs per 100 households	99.3
Av. no. per household	2.2	Telephone lines per 100 pop.	45.4
Marriages per 1,000 pop.	4.6	Mobile telephone subscribers	
Divorces per 1,000 pop.	2.7	per 100 pop.	95.6
Cost of living, Dec. 2005		Computers per 100 pop.	48.2
New York = 100	115	Internet hosts per 1,000 pop.	481.9

FRANCE

Area	543,965 sq km	Capital	Paris
Arable as % of total land	34	Currency	Euro (€)

People

Population	60.4m	Life expectancy:	men	76.6 yrs
Pop. per sq km	111.0		women	83.5 yrs
Av. ann. growth		Adult literacy		99.0%
in pop. 2000–05	0.41%	Fertility rate (per woman)		1.9
Pop. under 15	18.2%	Urban population		76.7%
Pop. over 60	21.1%			per 1,000 pop.
No. of men per 100 women	95	Crude birth rate		12.8
Human Development Index	93.8	Crude death rate		9.6

The economy

GDP	€1,648bn	GDP per head	$33,890
GDP	$2,047bn	GDP per head in purchasing	
Av. ann. growth in real		power parity (USA=100)	73.8
GDP 1994–2004	2.3%	Economic freedom index	2.51

Origins of GDP		Components of GDP	
	% of total		% of total
Agriculture	2.5	Private consumption	55.3
Industry, of which:	21.7	Public consumption	24.2
manufacturing	...	Investment	19.5
Services	75.8	Exports	25.9
		Imports	-25.4

Structure of employment

	% of total		% of labour force
Agriculture	2	Unemployed 2004	9.9
Industry	24	Av. ann. rate 1995–2004	10.7
Services	74		

Energy

	m TOE		
Total output	136.0	Net energy imports as %	
Total consumption	271.3	of energy use	50
Consumption per head,			
kg oil equivalent	4,519		

Inflation and finance

Consumer price		av. ann. increase 1999–2004	
inflation 2005	1.8%	Euro area:	
Av. ann. inflation 2000–05	1.9%	Narrow money (M1)	8.4%
Deposit rate, households, 2005	2.47%	Broad money	6.9%
		Household saving rate, 2004	11.8%

Exchange rates

	end 2005		December 2005
€ per $	0.85	Effective rates	2000 = 100
€ per SDR	1.21	– nominal	106.9
		– real	104.4

Trade

Principal exports		Principal imports	
	$bn fob		*$bn cif*
Intermediate goods	126.9	Intermediate goods	131.9
Capital goods	94.7	Capital goods	91.4
Motor vehicles & other		Consumer goods	73.3
transport equipment	65.8	Motor vehicles & other	
Consumer goods	63.2	transport equipment	51.0
Food & drink	36.5	Energy	49.6
Total incl. others	**416.7**	Total incl. others	**439.6**

Main export destinations		Main origins of imports	
	% of total		*% of total*
Germany	15.0	Germany	17.4
Spain	10.0	Italy	9.0
United Kingdom	9.4	Belgium-Luxembourg	7.8
Italy	9.3	Spain	7.4
Belgium-Luxembourg	8.2	United Kingdom	6.5
EU25	65.0	EU25	69.0

Balance of payments, reserves and aid, $bn

Visible exports fob	421.1	Overall balance	4.1
Visible imports fob	-429.1	Change in reserves	6.6
Trade balance	-7.9	Level of reserves	
Invisibles inflows	223.3	end Dec.	77.4
Invisibles outflows	-198.4	No. months of import cover	1.5
Net transfers	-21.8	Official gold holdings, m oz	96.0
Current account balance	-4.8	Aid given	8.47
– as % of GDP	-0.2	– as % of GDP	0.41
Capital balance	7.6		

Health and education

Health spending, % of GDP	10.1	Education spending, % of GDP	5.6
Doctors per 1,000 pop.	3.4	Enrolment, %: primary	104
Hospital beds per 1,000 pop.	7.7	secondary	109
Improved-water source access,		tertiary	56
% of pop.	...		

Society

No. of households	24.9m	Colour TVs per 100 households	95.9
Av. no. per household	2.4	Telephone lines per 100 pop.	56.0
Marriages per 1,000 pop.	5.2	Mobile telephone subscribers	
Divorces per 1,000 pop.	1.8	per 100 pop.	73.7
Cost of living, Dec. 2005		Computers per 100 pop.	48.7
New York = 100	130	Internet hosts per 1,000 pop.	113.6

GERMANY

Area	357,868 sq km	Capital	Berlin
Arable as % of total land	34	Currency	Euro (€)

People

Population	82.5m	Life expectancy: men	76.4 yrs
Pop. per sq km	230.5	women	82.1 yrs
Av. ann. growth		Adult literacy	99.0%
in pop. 2000–05	0.08%	Fertility rate (per woman)	1.3
Pop. under 15	14.3%	Urban population	88.5%
Pop. over 60	25.1%		per 1,000 pop.
No. of men per 100 women	95	Crude birth rate	8.7
Human Development Index	93.0	Crude death rate	10.7

The economy

GDP	€2,207bn	GDP per head	$33,220
GDP	$2,741bn	GDP per head in purchasing	
Av. ann. growth in real		power parity (USA=100)	73.8
GDP 1994–2004	1.5%	Economic freedom index	1.96

Origins of GDP		**Components of GDP**	
	% of total		% of total
Agriculture	1.1	Private consumption	59.2
Industry, of which:	29.0	Public consumption	18.6
manufacturing	...	Investment	17.2
Services	69.9	Exports	38.0
		Imports	-33.1

Structure of employment

	% of total		% of labour force
Agriculture	2	Unemployed 2004	11.0
Industry	32	Av. ann. rate 1995–2004	9.3
Services	66		

Energy

	m TOE		
Total output	134.5	Net energy imports as %	
Total consumption	347.1	of energy use	61
Consumption per head,			
kg oil equivalent	4,205		

Inflation and finance

Consumer price		av. ann. increase 1999–2004	
inflation 2005	2.0%	Euro area:	
Av. ann. inflation 2000–05	1.6%	Narrow money (M1)	8.4%
Deposit rate, households, 2005	1.98%	Broad money	6.9%
		Household saving rate, 2004	10.5%

Exchange rates

	end 2005		December 2005
€ per $	0.85	Effective rates	2000 = 100
€ per SDR	1.21	– nominal	108.3
		– real	97.5

Trade

Principal exports	
	$bn fob
Road vehicles	167.3
Machinery	127.1
Chemicals	117.4
Telecoms technology	45.0
Electricity devices	44.8
Total incl. others	**911.6**

Principal imports	
	$bn cif
Chemicals	78.7
Road vehicles	73.9
Fuels	48.7
Machinery	48.1
Computer technology	34.5
Total incl. others	**718.0**

Main export destinations	
	% of total
France	10.3
United States	8.9
United Kingdom	8.3
Italy	7.2
Netherlands	6.2
Belgium	5.6
EU25	63.9

Main origins of imports	
	% of total
France	9.0
Netherlands	7.8
United States	7.3
Italy	6.1
United Kingdom	6.1
China	4.9
EU25	60.0

Balance of payments, reserves and aid, $bn

Visible exports fob	909.5	Overall balance	-1.8
Visible imports fob	-719.5	Change in reserves	0.3
Trade balance	190.0	Level of reserves	
Invisibles inflows	274.7	end Dec.	97.2
Invisibles outflows	-325.7	No. months of import cover	1.1
Net transfers	-35.2	Official gold holdings, m oz	110.4
Current account balance	103.8	Aid given	7.53
– as % of GDP	3.8	– as % of GDP	0.28
Capital balance	-138.0		

Health and education

Health spending, % of GDP	11.1	Education spending, % of GDP	4.8
Doctors per 1,000 pop.	3.4	Enrolment, %: primary	99
Hospital beds per 1,000 pop.	8.9	secondary	100
Improved-water source access,		tertiary	51
% of pop.	100		

Society

No. of households	39.2m	Colour TVs per 100 households	97.3
Av. no. per household	2.1	Telephone lines per 100 pop.	66.2
Marriages per 1,000 pop.	5.0	Mobile telephone subscribers	
Divorces per 1,000 pop.	2.4	per 100 pop.	86.4
Cost of living, Dec. 2005		Computers per 100 pop.	48.5
New York = 100	106	Internet hosts per 1,000 pop.	119.4

GREECE

Area	131,957 sq km	Capital	Athens
Arable as % of total land	21	Currency	Euro (€)

People

Population	11.0m	Life expectancy: men	76.1 yrs
Pop. per sq km	83.4	women	81.3 yrs
Av. ann. growth		Adult literacy	99.0%
in pop. 2000–05	0.26%	Fertility rate (per woman)	1.3
Pop. under 15	14.3%	Urban population	61.4%
Pop. over 60	23.0%		per 1,000 pop.
No. of men per 100 women	98	Crude birth rate	9.1
Human Development Index	91.2	Crude death rate	10.5

The economy

GDP	€165bn	GDP per head	$18,660
GDP	$205bn	GDP per head in purchasing	
Av. ann. growth in real		power parity (USA=100)	56.0
GDP 1994–2004	3.6%	Economic freedom index	2.80

Origins of GDP		Components of GDP	
	% of total		% of total
Agriculture	7	Private consumption	66.8
Industry, of which:	23	Public consumption	16.4
manufacturing	12	Investment	25.8
Services	70	Exports	20.5
		Imports	-29.4

Structure of employment

	% of total		% of labour force
Agriculture	15	Unemployed 2003	8.9
Industry	23	Av. ann. rate 1995–2003	10.3
Services	62		

Energy

	m TOE		
Total output	9.9	Net energy imports as %	
Total consumption	29.9	of energy use	67
Consumption per head,			
kg oil equivalent	2,709		

Inflation and finance

Consumer price		av. ann. increase 1999–2004	
inflation 2005	3.6%	Euro area:	
Av. ann. inflation 2000–05	3.4%	Narrow money (M1)	8.4%
Treasury bill rate, 2005	2.3%	Broad money	6.9%

Exchange rates

	end 2005		December 2005
€ per $	0.85	Effective rates	2000 = 100
€ per SDR	1.21	– nominal	104.0
		– real	116.3

Trade

Principal exports		Principal imports	
	$bn fob		*$bn cif*
Machinery	2.9	Machinery	10.7
Food	2.6	Chemicals & plastics	7.3
Transport equipment	2.1	Food	7.1
Total incl. others	**15.0**	Total incl. others	**51.6**

Main export destinations		Main origins of imports	
	% of total		*% of total*
Germany	12.6	Germany	12.3
Italy	10.5	Italy	12.0
United Kingdom	7.0	France	6.5
France	4.2	Netherlands	5.1
EU25	54.8	EU25	57.8

Balance of payments, reserves and debt, $bn

Visible exports fob	15.7	Overall balance	-3.3
Visible imports fob	-47.4	Change in reserves	-3.1
Trade balance	-31.6	Level of reserves	
Invisibles inflows	36.2	end Dec.	2.7
Invisibles outflows	-22.2	No. months of import cover	0.5
Net transfers	4.5	Official gold holdings, m oz	3.5
Current account balance	-13.1	Aid given	0.46
– as % of GDP	-6.4	– as % of GDP	0.23
Capital balance	9.5		

Health and education

Health spending, % of GDP	9.9	Education spending, % of GDP	4.0
Doctors per 1,000 pop.	4.4	Enrolment, %: primary	101
Hospital beds per 1,000 pop.	4.7	secondary	97
Improved-water source access,		tertiary	74
% of pop.	...		

Society

No. of households	3.8m	Colour TVs per 100 households	91.7
Av. no. per household	2.8	Telephone lines per 100 pop.	57.8
Marriages per 1,000 pop.	5.8	Mobile telephone subscribers	
Divorces per 1,000 pop.	0.9	per 100 pop.	84.7
Cost of living, Dec. 2005		Computers per 100 pop.	9.0
New York = 100	85	Internet hosts per 1,000 pop.	45.8

HONG KONG

Area	1,075 sq km	Capital	Victoria
Arable as % of total land	5	Currency	Hong Kong dollar (HK$)

People

Population	7.1m	Life expectancy: men	79.3 yrs
Pop. per sq km	6,604.7	women	85.1 yrs
Av. ann. growth		Adult literacy	93.5%
in pop. 2000–05	1.18%	Fertility rate (per woman)	0.9
Pop. under 15	14.4%	Urban population	100.0%
Pop. over 60	15.4%		per 1,000 pop.
No. of men per 100 women	89	Crude birth rate	8.5
Human Development Index	91.6	Crude death rate	5.9

The economy

GDP	HK$1,270bn	GDP per head	$22,960
GDP	$163bn	GDP per head in purchasing	
Av. ann. growth in real		power parity (USA=100)	77.7
GDP 1994–2004	3.5%	Economic freedom index	1.28

Origins of GDP		Components of GDP	
	% of total		% of total
Agriculture	0	Private consumption	59.1
Industry, of which:	11	Public consumption	9.8
manufacturing	4	Investment	22.1
Services	89	Exports	189.7
		Imports	-180.7

Structure of employment

	% of total		% of labour force
Agriculture	0	Unemployed 2004	6.8
Industry	17	Av. ann. rate 1995–2004	5.1
Services	83		

Energy

	m TOE		
Total output	0.05	Net energy imports as %	
Total consumption	16.5	of energy use	100
Consumption per head,			
kg oil equivalent	2,428		

Inflation and finance

Consumer price		av. ann. increase 1999–2004	
inflation 2005	1.1%	Narrow money (M1)	15.1%
Av. ann. inflation 2000–05	-1.3%	Broad money	4.6%
Money market rate, 2005	4.25%		

Exchange rates

	end 2005		December 2005
HK$ per $	7.75	Effective rates	2000 = 100
HK$ per SDR	11.24	– nominal	...
HK$ per €	9.12	– real	...

Trade

Principal exports[a]	$bn fob	Principal imports	$bn cif
Clothing	8.1	Raw materials &	
Electrical machinery		semi-manufactures	103.4
& apparatus	1.7	Consumer goods	81.1
Jewellery	0.8	Capital goods	72.6
Textiles	0.7	Food	7.7
Printed matter	0.4	Fuel	6.2
Total incl. others	**20.0**	Total incl. others	**271.0**

Main export destinations	% of total	Main origins of imports	% of total
China	44.9	China	43.5
United States	16.0	Japan	12.1
Japan	5.5	Taiwan	7.3
Germany	3.1	United States	5.3

Balance of payments, reserves and debt, $bn

Visible exports fob	260.3	Change in reserves	5.2
Visible imports fob	-269.6	Level of reserves	
Trade balance	-9.3	end Dec.	123.6
Invisibles inflows	104.2	No. months of import cover	4.3
Invisibles outflows	-76.6	Official gold holdings, m oz	0.1
Net transfers	-2.0	Foreign debt	67.9
Current account balance	16.4	– as % of GDP	41
– as % of GDP	10.0	– as % of total exports	19
Capital balance	-14.2	Debt service ratio	2
Overall balance	3.3		

Health and education

Health spending, % of GDP	...	Education spending, % of GDP	4.4
Doctors per 1,000 pop.	...	Enrolment, %: primary	107
Hospital beds per 1,000 pop.	...	secondary	80
Improved-water source access,		tertiary	31
% of pop.	...		

Society

No. of households	2.2m	Colour TVs per 100 households	99.1
Av. no. per household	3.2	Telephone lines per 100 pop.	54.4
Marriages per 1,000 pop.	3.8	Mobile telephone subscribers	
Divorces per 1,000 pop.	1.8	per 100 pop.	118.8
Cost of living, Dec. 2005		Computers per 100 pop.	60.5
New York = 100	109	Internet hosts per 1,000 pop.	112.8

a Domestic, excluding re-exports.
Note: Hong Kong became a Special Administrative Region of China on July 1 1997.

HUNGARY

Area	93,030 sq km	Capital	Budapest
Arable as % of total land	50	Currency	Forint (Ft)

People

Population	9.8m	Life expectancy: men	69.8 yrs
Pop. per sq km	105.3	women	77.7 yrs
Av. ann. growth		Adult literacy	99.1%
in pop. 2000–05	-0.25%	Fertility rate (per woman)	1.3
Pop. under 15	15.7%	Urban population	65.9%
Pop. over 60	20.8%		per 1,000 pop.
No. of men per 100 women	91	Crude birth rate	8.8
Human Development Index	86.2	Crude death rate	12.9

The economy

GDP	Ft20,414bn	GDP per head	$10,270
GDP	$101bn	GDP per head in purchasing	
Av. ann. growth in real		power parity (USA=100)	42.4
GDP 1994–2004	3.8%	Economic freedom index	2.44

Origins of GDP[a]		Components of GDP	
	% of total		% of total
Agriculture	3.3	Private consumption	68.4
Industry, of which:	27.5	Public consumption	10.4
manufacturing	...	Investment	23.9
Services	69.2	Exports	64.3
		Imports	-68.0

Structure of employment

	% of total		% of labour force
Agriculture	5	Unemployed 2004	6.1
Industry	34	Av. ann. rate 1995–2004	7.3
Services	61		

Energy

	m TOE		
Total output	10.4	Net energy imports as %	
Total consumption	26.3	of energy use	60
Consumption per head,			
kg oil equivalent	2,600		

Inflation and finance

		av. ann. increase 1999–2004	
Consumer price			
inflation 2005	3.6%	Narrow money (M1)	11.3%
Av. ann. inflation 2000–05	5.9%	Broad money	12.8%
Treasury bill rate, 2005	7.0%		

Exchange rates

	end 2005		December 2005
Ft per $	213.58	Effective rates	2000 = 100
Ft per SDR	305.26	– nominal	108.9
Ft per €	251.27	– real	130.0

Trade

Principal exports		Principal imports	
	$bn fob		*$bn cif*
Machinery & equipment	34.1	Machinery & equipment	31.7
Other manufactures	15.1	Other manufactures	20.2
Food, drink & tobacco	3.3	Fuels	4.3
Raw materials	1.2	Food, drink & tobacco	2.1
Total incl. others	**54.9**	Total incl. others	**59.6**

Main export destinations		Main origins of imports	
	% of total		*% of total*
Germany	31.1	Germany	28.8
Austria	6.7	Austria	8.2
France	5.6	Russia	5.6
Italy	5.6	Italy	5.4
EU25	79.4	EU25	71.5

Balance of payments, reserves and debt, $bn

Visible exports fob	55.4	Change in reserves	3.2
Visible imports fob	-58.3	Level of reserves	
Trade balance	-2.9	end Dec.	16.0
Invisibles inflows	11.4	No. months of import cover	2.5
Invisibles outflows	-17.5	Official gold holdings, m oz	0.1
Net transfers	0.2	Foreign debt	63.2
Current account balance	-8.8	– as % of GDP	80
– as % of GDP	-8.8	– as % of total exports	115
Capital balance	10.8	Debt service ratio	31
Overall balance	2.0		

Health and education

Health spending, % of GDP	8.4	Education spending, % of GDP	5.5
Doctors per 1,000 pop.	3.4	Enrolment, %: primary	100
Hospital beds per 1,000 pop.	7.8	secondary	106
Improved-water source access,		tertiary	51
% of pop.	99		

Society

No. of households	3.7m	Colour TVs per 100 households	89.2
Av. no. per household	2.7	Telephone lines per 100 pop.	35.4
Marriages per 1,000 pop.	4.2	Mobile telephone subscribers	
Divorces per 1,000 pop.	2.6	per 100 pop.	86.4
Cost of living, Dec. 2005		Computers per 100 pop.	14.6
New York = 100	74	Internet hosts per 1,000 pop.	91.3

INDIA

Area	3,287,263 sq km	Capital	New Delhi
Arable as % of total land	54	Currency	Indian rupee (Rs)

People

Population	1,081.2m	Life expectancy: men	63.2 yrs
Pop. per sq km	328.9	women	66.7 yrs
Av. ann. growth		Adult literacy	61.0%
in pop. 2000–05	1.55%	Fertility rate (per woman)	3.1
Pop. under 15	32.1%	Urban population	28.7%
Pop. over 60	7.9%		per 1,000 pop.
No. of men per 100 women	105	Crude birth rate	23.8
Human Development Index	60.2	Crude death rate	8.3

The economy

GDP	Rs31,055bn	GDP per head	$640
GDP	$691bn	GDP per head in purchasing	
Av. ann. growth in real		power parity (USA=100)	7.9
GDP 1994–2004	6.1%	Economic freedom index	3.49

Origins of GDP[a]		Components of GDP[a]	
	% of total		% of total
Agriculture	21.5	Private consumption	61.6
Industry, of which:	27.0	Public consumption	10.6
manufacturing	16.0	Investment	24.8
Services	51.5	Exports	19.1
		Imports	-16.3

Structure of employment

	% of total		% of labour force
Agriculture	60	Unemployed 2000	4.3
Industry	17	Av. ann. rate 1995–2000	3.0
Services	23		

Energy

	m TOE		
Total output	453.1	Net energy imports as %	
Total consumption	553.4	of energy use	18
Consumption per head,			
kg oil equivalent	520		

Inflation and finance

		av. ann. increase 1999–2004	
Consumer price			
inflation 2005	4.2%	Narrow money (M1)	13.9%
Av. ann. inflation 2000–05	4.0%	Broad money	15.2%
Lending rate, 2005	10.8%		

Exchange rates

	end 2005		December 2005
Rs per $	45.07	Effective rates	2000 = 100
Rs per SDR	64.41	– nominal	...
Rs per €	53.02	– real	...

Trade

Principal exports[a]		Principal imports[a]	
	$bn fob		*$bn cif*
Engineering goods	16.4	Petroleum & products	29.9
Gems & jewellery	13.7	Capital goods	12.8
Textiles	12.6	Gold & silver	10.8
Agricultural goods	7.6	Electronic goods	9.6
Chemicals	6.0	Gems	9.4
Total incl. others	**79.6**	Total incl. others	**107.3**

Main export destinations		Main origins of imports	
	% of total		*% of total*
United States	19.8	United States	6.9
China	8.3	Belgium	6.0
United Arab Emirates	8.0	China	6.0
United Kingdom	5.1	Singapore	4.7

Balance of payments[a], reserves and debt, $bn

Visible exports fob	82.2	Change in reserves	27.9
Visible imports fob	-118.8	Level of reserves	
Trade balance	-36.6	end Dec.	131.6
Invisibles inflows	56.0	No. months of import cover	12.5
Invisibles outflows	-45.4	Official gold holdings, m oz	11.5
Net transfers	20.8	Foreign debt	122.7
Current account balance	-5.4	– as % of GDP	21
– as % of GDP	-1.9	– as % of total exports	106
Capital balance	16.7	Debt service ratio	16
Overall balance	31.4		

Health and education

Health spending, % of GDP	4.8	Education spending, % of GDP	4.1
Doctors per 1,000 pop.	0.6	Enrolment, %: primary	108
Hospital beds per 1,000 pop.	0.9	secondary	53
Improved-water source access,		tertiary	12
% of pop.	86		

Society

No. of households	202.9m	Colour TVs per 100 households	35.1
Av. no. per household	5.3	Telephone lines per 100 pop.	4.1
Marriages per 1,000 pop.	...	Mobile telephone subscribers	
Divorces per 1,000 pop.	...	per 100 pop.	4.4
Cost of living, Dec. 2005		Computers per 100 pop.	1.2
New York = 100	47	Internet hosts per 1,000 pop.	0.8

a   Year ending March 31, 2005.

INDONESIA

Area	1,904,443 sq km	Capital	Jakarta
Arable as % of total land	12	Currency	Rupiah (Rp)

People

Population	222.6m	Life expectancy: men	67.0 yrs
Pop. per sq km	116.9	women	70.5 yrs
Av. ann. growth		Adult literacy	90.4%
in pop. 2000–05	1.26%	Fertility rate (per woman)	2.4
Pop. under 15	28.3%	Urban population	47.9%
Pop. over 60	8.4%		per 1,000 pop.
No. of men per 100 women	100	Crude birth rate	20.7
Human Development Index	69.7	Crude death rate	7.1

The economy

GDP	Rp2,303trn	GDP per head	$1,160
GDP	$258bn	GDP per head in purchasing	
Av. ann. growth in real		power parity (USA=100)	9.1
GDP 1994–2004	3.0%	Economic freedom index	3.71

Origins of GDP		Components of GDP	
	% of total		% of total
Agriculture	16.2	Private consumption	66.5
Industry, of which:	46.1	Public consumption	8.2
manufacturing	29.9	Investment	22.8
Services	37.7	Exports	30.9
		Imports	-26.9

Structure of employment

	% of total		% of total
Agriculture	43	Unemployed 2002	9.1
Industry	13	Av. ann. rate 1995–2002	5.9
Services	44		

Energy

	m TOE		
Total output	250.0	Net energy imports as %	
Total consumption	161.6	of energy use	-55
Consumption per head,			
kg oil equivalent	753		

Inflation and finance

Consumer price		av. ann. increase 1999–2004	
inflation 2005	10.5%	Narrow money (M1)	16.5%
Av. ann. inflation 2000–05	9.3%	Broad money	10.0%
Money market rate, 2005	6.78%		

Exchange rates

	end 2005		December 2005
Rp per $	9,830	Effective rates	2000 = 100
Rp per SDR	14,050	– nominal	...
Rp per €	11,565	– real	...

Trade

Principal exports		Principal imports	
	$bn fob		*$bn cif*
Petroleum & products	7.9	Raw materials	36.2
Garments & textiles	7.7	Capital goods	6.5
Natural gas	7.7	Consumer goods	3.8
Total incl. others	**71.6**	Total incl. others	**46.5**

Main export destinations		Main origins of imports	
	% of total		*% of total*
Japan	24.3	Japan	21.6
United States	15.2	China	12.6
Singapore	10.2	Singapore	11.7
China	8.8	Thailand	7.6

Balance of payments, reserves and debt, $bn

Visible exports fob	72.2	Change in reserves	0.1
Visible imports fob	-50.6	Level of reserves	
Trade balance	21.6	end Dec.	36.3
Invisibles inflows	18.9	No. months of import cover	4.9
Invisibles outflows	-38.5	Official gold holdings, m oz	3.1
Net transfers	1.1	Foreign debt	140.6
Current account balance	3.1	– as % of GDP	63
– as % of GDP	1.2	– as % of total exports	181
Capital balance	3.0	Debt service ratio	26
Overall balance	0.3		

Health and education

Health spending, % of GDP	3.1	Education spending, % of GDP	1.2
Doctors per 1,000 pop.	0.1	Enrolment, %: primary	112
Hospital beds per 1,000 pop.	...	secondary	61
Improved-water source access,		tertiary	16
% of pop.	78		

Society

No. of households	57.4m	Colour TVs per 100 households	51.9
Av. no. per household	3.9	Telephone lines per 100 pop.	4.5
Marriages per 1,000 pop.	...	Mobile telephone subscribers	
Divorces per 1,000 pop.	...	per 100 pop.	13.5
Cost of living, Dec. 2005		Computers per 100 pop.	1.4
New York = 100	64	Internet hosts per 1,000 pop.	0.7

IRAN

Area	1,648,000 sq km	Capital	Tehran
Arable as % of total land	10	Currency	Rial (IR)

People

Population	69.8m	Life expectancy: men		70.1 yrs
Pop. per sq km	42.4	women		73.4 yrs
Av. ann. growth		Adult literacy		77.0%
in pop. 2000–05	0.93%	Fertility rate (per woman)		2.1
Pop. under 15	28.7%	Urban population		68.1%
Pop. over 60	6.4%		per 1,000 pop.	
No. of men per 100 women	103	Crude birth rate		20.3
Human Development Index	73.6	Crude death rate		5.2

The economy

GDP	IR1,408trn	GDP per head	$2,340
GDP	$163bn	GDP per head in purchasing	
Av. ann. growth in real		power parity (USA=100)	19.0
GDP 1994–2004	4.3%	Economic freedom index	4.51

Origins of GDP		Components of GDP[a]	
	% of total		% of total
Agriculture	13.7	Private consumption	45.2
Industry, of which:	46.2	Public consumption	12.5
manufacturing	...	Investment	39.3
Services	51.8	Exports	28.0
		Imports	-25.5

Structure of employment

	% of total		% of labour force
Agriculture	...	Unemployed 2002	12.3
Industry	...	Av. ann. rate 2000–2002	12.4
Services	...		

Energy

	m TOE		
Total output	265.4	Net energy imports as %	
Total consumption	136.4	of energy use	-95
Consumption per head,			
kg oil equivalent	2,055		

Inflation and finance

		av. ann. increase 1999–2004	
Consumer price			
inflation 2005	13.4%	Narrow money (M1)	21.0%
Av. ann. inflation 2000–05	14.0%	Broad money	24.5%

Exchange rates

	end 2005		December 2005
IR per $	9,091	Effective rates	2000 = 100
IR per SDR	12,993	– nominal	80.50
IR per €	10,695	– real	136.16

Trade

Principal exports		Principal imports[b]	
	$bn fob		*$bn cif*
Oil & gas	36.8	Transport, machinery & tools	7.6
Chemicals & petrochemicals	1.4	Chemicals & pharmaceuticals	2.4
Fruits	0.8	Food & animals	2.1
Total incl. others	**44.4**	Total incl. others	**17.6**

Main export destinations		Main origins of imports	
	% of total		*% of total*
Japan	18.5	Germany	12.3
China	9.6	France	8.4
Italy	6.0	Italy	7.8
Netherlands	5.8	China	7.5
South Korea	5.8	United Arab Emirates	7.3

Balance of payments[c], reserves and debt, $bn

Visible exports fob	28.2	Change in reserves	…
Visible imports fob	-23.8	Level of reserves	
Trade balance	4.4	end Dec.	…
Invisibles inflows[d]	1.9	No. months of import cover	…
Invisibles outflows[d]	-2.9	Official gold holdings, m oz	…
Net transfers[d]	0.6	Foreign debt	13.6
Current account balance	4.0	– as % of GDP	10
– as % of GDP	2.4	– as % of total exports	33
Capital balance[d]	-10.2	Debt service ratio	5
Overall balance[d]	1.1		

Health and education

Health spending, % of GDP	6.5	Education spending, % of GDP	4.9
Doctors per 1,000 pop.	0.4	Enrolment, %: primary	92
Hospital beds per 1,000 pop.	1.6	secondary	78
Improved-water source access,		tertiary	21
% of pop.	93		

Society

No. of households	12.7m	Colour TVs per 100 households	9.5
Av. no. per household	5.5	Telephone lines per 100 pop.	22.0
Marriages per 1,000 pop.	10.2	Mobile telephone subscribers	
Divorces per 1,000 pop.	1.1	per 100 pop.	6.2
Cost of living, Dec. 2005		Computers per 100 pop.	10.5
New York = 100	33	Internet hosts per 1,000 pop.	…

a Iranian year ending March 20, 2004.
b 2001
c Iranian year ending March 20, 2003.
d Iranian year ending March 20, 2002.

IRELAND

Area	70,282 sq km	Capital	Dublin
Arable as % of total land	17	Currency	Euro (€)

People

Population	4.0m	Life expectancy: men	75.9 yrs
Pop. per sq km	56.9	women	81.1 yrs
Av. ann. growth		Adult literacy	99.0%
in pop. 2000–05	1.75%	Fertility rate (per woman)	1.9
Pop. under 15	20.2%	Urban population	60.4%
Pop. over 60	15.1%		per 1,000 pop.
No. of men per 100 women	99	Crude birth rate	14.4
Human Development Index	94.6	Crude death rate	7.3

The economy

GDP	€146bn	GDP per head	$45,410
GDP	$182bn	GDP per head in purchasing	
Av. ann. growth in real		power parity (USA=100)	97.9
GDP 1994–2004	7.9%	Economic freedom index	1.58

Origins of GDP		Components of GDP	
	% of total		% of total
Agriculture	4.5	Private consumption	45.4
Industry, of which:	45.6	Public consumption	14.4
manufacturing	...	Investment	25.1
Services	49.9	Exports	80.2
		Imports	-64.7

Structure of employment

	% of total		% of labour force
Agriculture	7	Unemployed 2004	4.4
Industry	28	Av. ann. rate 1995–2004	7.2
Services	65		

Energy

	m TOE		
Total output	1.9	Net energy imports as %	
Total consumption	15.1	of energy use	87
Consumption per head,			
kg oil equivalent	3,777		

Inflation and finance

Consumer price		av. ann. increase 1999–2004	
inflation 2005	2.4%	Euro area:	
Av. ann. inflation 2000–05	3.5%	Narrow money (M1)	8.4%
Money market rate, 2004	2.21%	Broad money	6.9%
Deposit rate, households, 2005	2.00%	Household saving rate, 2004	9.9%

Exchange rates

	end 2005		December 2005
€ per $	0.85	Effective rates	2000 = 100
€ per SDR	1.21	– nominal	111.37
		– real	...

Trade

Principal exports		Principal imports	
	$bn fob		$bn cif
Chemicals	46.5	Machinery & transport	
Machinery & transport		equipment	27.0
equipment	28.1	Chemicals	8.7
Manufactured materials	14.3	Food, drink & tobacco	4.7
Food, drink & tobacco	12.3	Fuels	0.6
Total incl. others	**105**	Total incl. others	**64**

Main export destinations		Main origins of imports	
	% of total		% of total
United States	19.7	United Kingdom	31.1
United Kingdom	17.8	United States	13.8
Germany	7.7	Germany	7.6
France	6.0	Japan	4.3
EU25	62.6	EU25	63.6

Balance of payments, reserves and aid, $bn

Visible exports fob	98.7	Overall balance	-1.4
Visible imports fob	-60.2	Change in reserves	-1.2
Trade balance	39.5	Level of reserves	
Invisibles inflows	94.5	end Dec.	2.9
Invisibles outflows	-135.8	No. months of import cover	0.2
Net transfers	0.4	Official gold holdings, m oz	0.2
Current account balance	-1.4	Aid given	0.61
– as % of GDP	-0.8	– as % of GDP	0.39
Capital balance	4.4		

Health and education

Health spending, % of GDP	7.3	Education spending, % of GDP	4.3
Doctors per 1,000 pop.	2.8	Enrolment, %: primary	106
Hospital beds per 1,000 pop.	4.3	secondary	107
Improved-water source access,		tertiary	52
% of pop.	...		

Society

No. of households	1.3m	Colour TVs per 100 households	99.3
Av. no. per household	3.0	Telephone lines per 100 pop.	49.9
Marriages per 1,000 pop.	5.3	Mobile telephone subscribers	
Divorces per 1,000 pop.	0.1	per 100 pop.	93.5
Cost of living, Dec. 2005		Computers per 100 pop.	49.7
New York = 100	108	Internet hosts per 1,000 pop.	60.2

ISRAEL

Area	20,770 sq km	Capital	Jerusalem
Arable as % of total land	16	Currency	New Shekel (NIS)

People

Population	6.6m	Life expectancy: men	78.4 yrs
Pop. per sq km	317.8	women	82.6 yrs
Av. ann. growth		Adult literacy	97.1%
in pop. 2000–05	2.00%	Fertility rate (per woman)	2.9
Pop. under 15	27.8%	Urban population	91.7%
Pop. over 60	13.3%		per 1,000 pop.
No. of men per 100 women	98	Crude birth rate	19.8
Human Development Index	91.5	Crude death rate	5.6

The economy

GDP	NIS524bn	GDP per head	$17,710
GDP	$117bn	GDP per head in purchasing	
Av. ann. growth in real		power parity (USA=100)	61.5
GDP 1994–2004	3.4%	Economic freedom index	2.36

Origins of GDP		Components of GDP	
	% of total		% of total
Agriculture	2.8	Private consumption	59.2
Industry, of which:	35.3	Public consumption	28.6
manufacturing	24.3	Investment	17.7
Services	59.3	Exports	44.0
		Imports	-49.3

Structure of employment

	% of total		% of labour force
Agriculture	2	Unemployed 2003	10.7
Industry	23	Av. ann. rate 1995–2003	8.7
Services	75		

Energy

	m TOE		
Total output	0.8	Net energy imports as %	
Total consumption	20.6	of energy use	96
Consumption per head,			
kg oil equivalent	3,086		

Inflation and finance

Consumer price		av. ann. increase 1999–2004	
inflation 2005	1.3%	Narrow money (M1)	11.8%
Av. ann. inflation 2000–05	1.7%	Broad money	5.5%
Treasury bill rate, 2005	4.3%		

Exchange rates

	end 2005		December 2005
NIS per $	4.60	Effective rates	2000 = 100
NIS per SDR	6.58	– nominal	81.25
NIS per €	5.41	– real	78.02

Trade

Principal exports	$bn fob	Principal imports	$bn fob
Diamonds	10.6	Diamonds	9.2
Chemicals	5.7	Machinery & equipment	4.9
Communications, medical &		Fuel	4.5
scientific equipment	5.7	Chemicals	2.7
Electronics	2.6		
Total incl. others	**33.8**	Total incl. others	**40.4**

Main export destinations	% of total	Main origins of imports	% of total
United States	41.9	United States	15.2
Belgium	8.6	Belgium	10.2
Hong Kong	5.6	Germany	7.7
United Kingdom	4.3	Switzerland	6.7
Germany	4.0	United Kingdom	6.2

Balance of payments, reserves and debt, $bn

Visible exports fob	36.6	Change in reserves	0.8
Visible imports fob	-38.5	Level of reserves	
Trade balance	-1.9	end Dec.	27.1
Invisibles inflows	17.2	No. months of import cover	5.6
Invisibles outflows	-20.0	Official gold holdings, m oz	0.0
Net transfers	6.2	Foreign debt	75.8
Current account balance	1.5	– as % of GDP	65
– as % of GDP	1.3	– as % of total exports	134
Capital balance	-3.6	Debt service ratio	11
Overall balance	-1.6		

Health and education

Health spending, % of GDP	8.9	Education spending, % of GDP	7.5
Doctors per 1,000 pop.	3.7	Enrolment, %: primary	112
Hospital beds per 1,000 pop.	6.1	secondary	93
Improved-water source access,		tertiary	57
% of pop.	100		

Society

No. of households	2.0m	Colour TVs per 100 households	96.6
Av. no. per household	3.5	Telephone lines per 100 pop.	43.7
Marriages per 1,000 pop.	4.4	Mobile telephone subscribers	
Divorces per 1,000 pop.	2.1	per 100 pop.	105.3
Cost of living, Dec. 2005		Computers per 100 pop.	73.4
New York = 100	86	Internet hosts per 1,000 pop.	183.7

ITALY

Area	301,245 sq km	Capital	Rome
Arable as % of total land	27	Currency	Euro (€)

People

Population	57.3m	Life expectancy: men		77.5 yrs
Pop. per sq km	190.2	women		83.6 yrs
Av. ann. growth		Adult literacy		98.4%
in pop. 2000–05	0.13%	Fertility rate (per woman)		1.3
Pop. under 15	14.0%	Urban population		67.5%
Pop. over 60	25.6%			per 1,000 pop.
No. of men per 100 women	94	Crude birth rate		8.8
Human Development Index	93.4	Crude death rate		10.6

The economy

GDP	€1,351bn	GDP per head	$29,280
GDP	$1,678n	GDP per head in purchasing	
Av. ann. growth in real		power parity (USA=100)	71.0
GDP 1994–2004	1.6%	Economic freedom index	2.50

Origins of GDP		**Components of GDP**	
	% of total		% of total
Agriculture	2.2	Private consumption	59.8
Industry, of which:	28.7	Public consumption	19.7
manufacturing	...	Investment	19.5
Services	69.1	Exports	25.9
		Imports	-25.9

Structure of employment

	% of total		% of labour force
Agriculture	5	Unemployed 2003	8.7
Industry	32	Av. ann. rate 1995–2003	10.6
Services	63		

Energy

	m TOE		
Total output	27.7	Net energy imports as %	
Total consumption	181.0	of energy use	85
Consumption per head,			
kg oil equivalent	3,140		

Inflation and finance

Consumer price		av. ann. increase 1999–2004	
inflation 2005	2.0%	Euro area:	
Av. ann. inflation 2000–05	2.4%	Narrow money (M1)	8.4%
Money market rate, 2005	2.18%	Broad money	6.9%
		Household saving rate, 2004	11.5%

Exchange rates

	end 2005		December 2005
€ per $	0.85	Effective rates	2000 = 100
€ per SDR	1.21	– nominal	106.5
		– real	123.3

Trade

Principal exports		Principal imports	
	$bn fob		$bn cif
Engineering products	89.1	Engineering products	72.2
Textiles & clothing	47.8	Transport equipment	49.9
Transport equipment	39.1	Chemicals	47.4
Chemicals	33.8	Energy products	36.5
Food, drink & tobacco	19.3	Food, drink & tobacco	24.1
Total incl. others	**354**	Total incl. others	**355**

Main export destinations		Main origins of imports	
	% of total		% of total
Germany	14.1	Germany	18.1
France	12.5	France	11.4
United States	8.3	Netherlands	5.8
Spain	7.1	United Kingdom	4.8
United Kingdom	7.1	United States	3.9
EU25	59.3	EU25	59.9

Balance of payments, reserves and aid, $bn

Visible exports fob	352.2	Overall balance	-2.8
Visible imports fob	-341.3	Change in reserves	-0.9
Trade balance	10.9	Level of reserves	
Invisibles inflows	136.9	end Dec.	62.4
Invisibles outflows	-153.4	No. months of import cover	1.5
Net transfers	-9.6	Official gold holdings, m oz	78.8
Current account balance	-15.1	Aid given	2.46
– as % of GDP	-0.9	as % of GDP	0.15
Capital balance	10.8		

Health and education

Health spending, % of GDP	8.4	Education spending, % of GDP	4.7
Doctors per 1,000 pop.	4.2	Enrolment, %: primary	101
Hospital beds per 1,000 pop.	4.4	secondary	99
Improved-water source access,		tertiary	57
% of pop.	...		

Society

No. of households	23.0m	Colour TVs per 100 households	96.0
Av. no. per household	2.5	Telephone lines per 100 pop.	44.8
Marriages per 1,000 pop.	4.5	Mobile telephone subscribers	
Divorces per 1,000 pop.	0.8	per 100 pop.	108.2
Cost of living, Dec. 2005		Computers per 100 pop.	31.3
New York = 100	97	Internet hosts per 1,000 pop.	195.9

JAPAN

Area	377,727 sq km	Capital	Tokyo
Arable as % of total land	12	Currency	Yen (¥)

People

Population	127.8m	Life expectancy:	men	79.1 yrs
Pop. per sq km	338.4		women	86.4 yrs
Av. ann. growth		Adult literacy		99.0%
in pop. 2000–05	0.17%	Fertility rate (per woman)		1.3
Pop. under 15	14.0%	Urban population[a]		65.7%
Pop. over 60	26.3%			per 1,000 pop.
No. of men per 100 women	96	Crude birth rate		9.2
Human Development Index	94.3	Crude death rate		8.8

The economy

GDP	¥500trn	GDP per head	$36,170
GDP	$4,623bn	GDP per head in purchasing	
Av. ann. growth in real		power parity (USA=100)	73.7
GDP 1994–2004	1.2%	Economic freedom index	2.26

Origins of GDP[a]		Components of GDP	
	% of total		% of total
Agriculture	1.3	Private consumption	56.5
Industry, of which:	30.4	Public consumption	17.6
manufacturing	20.8	Investment	23.9
Services	68.3	Exports	13.1
		Imports	-11.2

Structure of employment

	% of total		% of labour force
Agriculture	5	Unemployed 2004	4.7
Industry	29	Av. ann. rate 1995–2004	4.4
Services	66		

Energy

	m TOE		
Total output	84.6	Net energy imports as %	
Total consumption	517.1	of energy use	84
Consumption per head,			
kg oil equivalent	4,053		

Inflation and finance

Consumer price		av. ann. increase 1999–2004	
inflation 2005	-0.3%	Narrow money (M1)	9.6%
Av. ann. inflation 2000–05	-0.4%	Broad money	2.0%
Money market rate, 2005	0.00%	Household saving rate, 2004	6.9%

Exchange rates

	end 2005		December 2005
¥ per $	117.9	Effective rates	2000 = 100
¥ per SDR	186.6	– nominal	80.6
¥ per €	139.0	– real	69.6

Trade

Principal exports		Principal imports	
	$bn fob		*$bn cif*
Electrical machinery	132.8	Machinery & equipment	142.3
Transport equipment	130.4	Mineral fuels	98.5
Non-electrical machinery	116.5	Food	48.9
Chemicals	48.3	Chemicals	35.2
Metals	37.5	Raw materials	28.3
Total incl. others	**566**	Total incl. others	**455**

Main export destinations		Main origins of imports	
	% of total		*% of total*
United States	22.4	China	20.7
China	13.1	United States	13.7
South Korea	7.8	South Korea	4.8
Taiwan	7.4	Australia	4.3
Hong Kong	6.3	Taiwan	3.7

Balance of payments, reserves and aid, $bn

Visible exports fob	539.0	Overall balance	160.9
Visible imports fob	-406.9	Change in reserves	171.1
Trade balance	132.1	Level of reserves	
Invisibles inflows	210.9	end Dec.	844.7
Invisibles outflows	-163.1	No. months of import cover	17.8
Net transfers	-7.9	Official gold holdings, m oz	24.6
Current account balance	172.1	Aid given	8.91
as % of GDP	3.7	as % of GDP	0.19
Capital balance	17.7		

Health and education

Health spending, % of GDP	7.9	Education spending, % of GDP	3.6
Doctors per 1,000 pop.	2.0	Enrolment, %: primary	100
Hospital beds per 1,000 pop.	14.3	secondary	102
Improved-water source access,		tertiary	51
% of pop.	100		

Society

No. of households	48.5m	Colour TVs per 100 households	99.0
Av. no. per household	2.6	Telephone lines per 100 pop.	46.0
Marriages per 1,000 pop.	5.7	Mobile telephone subscribers	
Divorces per 1,000 pop.	2.2	per 100 pop.	71.6
Cost of living, Dec. 2005		Computers per 100 pop.	54.2
New York = 100	136	Internet hosts per 1,000 pop.	194.9

a 2003

KENYA

Area	582,646 sq km	Capital	Nairobi
Arable as % of total land	8	Currency	Kenyan shilling (KSh)

People

Population	32.4m	Life expectancy: men		51.1 yrs
Pop. per sq km	55.6	women		49.4 yrs
Av. ann. growth		Adult literacy		73.6%
in pop. 2000–05	2.20%	Fertility rate (per woman)		5.0
Pop. under 15	42.8%	Urban population		41.6%
Pop. over 60	4.1%			per 1,000 pop.
No. of men per 100 women	100	Crude birth rate		32.5
Human Development Index	47.4	Crude death rate		13.8

The economy

GDP	KSh1,274bn	GDP per head	$500
GDP	$16.1bn	GDP per head in purchasing	
Av. ann. growth in real		power parity (USA=100)	2.9
GDP 1994–2004	2.7%	Economic freedom index	3.20

Origins of GDP		Components of GDP	
	% of total		% of total
Agriculture	27.5	Private consumption	74.7
Industry, of which:	...	Public consumption	17.0
manufacturing	13.3	Investment	17.4
Other	59.2	Exports	28.0
		Imports	-37.1

Structure of employment

	% of total		% of labour force
Agriculture	...	Unemployed 2004	...
Industry	...	Av. ann. rate 1995–2004	...
Services	...		

Energy

	m TOE		
Total output	13.5	Net energy imports as %	
Total consumption	16.2	of energy use	17
Consumption per head,			
kg oil equivalent	494		

Inflation and finance

		av. ann. increase 1999–2004	
Consumer price			
inflation 2005	10.3%	Narrow money (M1)	13.9%
Av. ann. inflation 2000–05	7.8%	Broad money	8.9%
Treasury bill rate, 2005	8.43%		

Exchange rates

	end 2005		December 2005
KSh per $	73.4	Effective rates	2000 = 100
KSh per SDR	103.4	– nominal	...
KSh per €	86.3	– real	...

Trade

Principal exports		Principal imports	
	$m fob		$m cif
Horticultural products	499	Industrial supplies	1,380
Tea	456	Machinery & transport equip.	651
Coffee	88	Consumer goods	331
Fish products	53	Food & drink	182
Total incl. others	**2,685**	Total incl. others	**4,557**

Main export destinations		Main origins of imports	
	% of total		% of total
Uganda	13.1	United Arab Emirates	12.7
United Kingdom	11.3	Saudi Arabia	9.8
United States	10.4	South Africa	6.5
Netherlands	8.0	United States	4.4

Balance of payments, reserves and debt, $bn

Visible exports fob	2.7	Change in reserves	0.0
Visible imports fob	-4.3	Level of reserves	
Trade balance	-1.6	end Dec.	1.5
Invisibles inflows	1.5	No. months of import cover	3.5
Invisibles outflows	-1.0	Official gold holdings, m oz	0.0
Net transfers	0.6	Foreign debt	6.8
Current account balance	-0.4	– as % of GDP	47
– as % of GDP	-2.4	– as % of total exports	185
Capital balance	0.2	Debt service ratio	10
Overall balance	0.0		

Health and education

Health spending, % of GDP	4.3	Education spending, % of GDP	7.0
Doctors per 1,000 pop.	0.1	Enrolment, %: primary	92
Hospital beds per 1,000 pop.	...	secondary	33
Improved-water source access,		tertiary	3
% of pop.	62		

Society

No. of households	7.6m	Colour TVs per 100 households	11.9
Av. no. per household	4.3	Telephone lines per 100 pop.	0.9
Marriages per 1,000 pop.	...	Mobile telephone subscribers	
Divorces per 1,000 pop.	...	per 100 pop.	7.9
Cost of living, Dec. 2005		Computers per 100 pop.	1.4
New York = 100	66	Internet hosts per 1,000 pop.	0.4

LATVIA

Area	63,700 sq km	Capital	Riga
Arable as % of total land	29	Currency	Lats (LVL)

People

Population	2.3m	Life expectancy: men	67.2 yrs
Pop. per sq km	36.1	women	77.8 yrs
Av. ann. growth		Adult literacy	99.7%
in pop. 2000–05	-0.57%	Fertility rate (per woman)	1.3
Pop. under 15	14.7%	Urban population	65.9%
Pop. over 60	22.5%		per 1,000 pop.
No. of men per 100 women	84	Crude birth rate	7.8
Human Development Index	83.6	Crude death rate	13.6

The economy

GDP	LVL7.3bn	GDP per head	$5,900
GDP	$13.6bn	GDP per head in purchasing	
Av. ann. growth in real		power parity (USA=100)	29.4
GDP 1994–2004	5.6%	Economic freedom index	2.43

Origins of GDP		Components of GDP	
	% of total		% of total
Agriculture	4	Private consumption	62.4
Industry, of which:	23	Public consumption	20.0
manufacturing	13	Investment	33.3
Services	73	Exports	44.1
		Imports	-59.7

Structure of employment

	% of total		% of labour force
Agriculture	14	Unemployed 2004	10.4
Industry	27	Av. ann. rate 1996–2004	13.8
Services	59		

Energy

			m TOE
Total output	2.0	Net energy imports as %	
Total consumption	4.4	of energy use	55
Consumption per head,			
kg oil equivalent	1,881		

Inflation and finance

		av. ann. increase 1999–2004	
Consumer price			
inflation 2005	6.7%	Narrow money (M1)	18.7%
Av. ann. inflation 2000–05	4.0%	Broad money	23.1%
Money market rate, 2005	3.49%		

Exchange rates

	end 2005		December 2005
LVL per $	0.59	Effective rates	2000 = 100
LVL per SDR	0.85	– nominal	...
LVL per €	0.69	– real	...

Trade

Principal exports		**Principal imports**	
	$bn fob		*$bn cif*
Wood & wood products	1.2	Machinery & equipment	1.4
Metals	0.7	Mineral products	0.9
Textiles	0.4	Base metals	0.7
Machinery & equipment	0.3	Transport equipment	0.7
Total incl. others	**4.0**	Total incl. others	**7.0**

Main export destinations		**Main origins of imports**	
	% of total		*% of total*
United Kingdom	12.9	Germany	14.5
Germany	12.3	Lithuania	12.4
Sweden	10.3	Russia	8.4
Lithuania	9.5	Estonia	7.1
Estonia	8.5	Finland	6.5
EU25	76.9	EU25	75.1

Balance of payments, reserves and debt, $bn

Visible exports fob	4.2	Change in reserves	0.5
Visible imports fob	-6.9	Level of reserves	
Trade balance	-2.7	end Dec.	2.0
Invisibles inflows	2.3	No. months of import cover	2.7
Invisibles outflows	-1.9	Official gold holdings, m oz	0.2
Net transfers	0.7	Foreign debt	12.7
Current account balance	-1.7	– as % of GDP	112
– as % of GDP	-12.3	– as % of total exports	243
Capital balance	2.1	Debt service ratio	26
Overall balance	0.4		

Health and education

Health spending, % of GDP	6.4	Education spending, % of GDP	5.8
Doctors per 1,000 pop.	3.0	Enrolment, %: primary	94
Hospital beds per 1,000 pop.	7.8	secondary	95
Improved-water source access,		tertiary	73
% of pop.	...		

Society

No. of households	0.8m	Colour TVs per 100 households	74.0
Av. no. per household	2.9	Telephone lines per 100 pop.	28.5
Marriages per 1,000 pop.	3.0	Mobile telephone subscribers	
Divorces per 1,000 pop.	2.5	per 100 pop.	67.2
Cost of living, Dec. 2005		Computers per 100 pop.	21.9
New York = 100	...	Internet hosts per 1,000 pop.	39.3

LITHUANIA

Area	65,200 sq km	Capital	Vilnius
Arable as % of total land	47	Currency	Litas (LTL)

People

Population	3.4m	Life expectancy: men		67.9 yrs
Pop. per sq km	52.1	women		78.6 yrs
Av. ann. growth		Adult literacy		99.6%
in pop. 2000–05	-0.40%	Fertility rate (per woman)		1.3
Pop. under 15	16.7%	Urban population		66.6%
Pop. over 60	20.7%			per 1,000 pop.
No. of men per 100 women	87	Crude birth rate		8.8
Human Development Index	85.2	Crude death rate		12.2

The economy

GDP	LTL61.9bn	GDP per head	$6,550
GDP	$22.3bn	GDP per head in purchasing	
Av. ann. growth in real		power parity (USA=100)	33.0
GDP 1994–2004	5.4%	Economic freedom index	2.14

Origins of GDP		**Components of GDP**	
	% of total		% of total
Agriculture	5.9	Private consumption	64.6
Industry, of which:	32.9	Public consumption	17.5
manufacturing	...	Investment	21.8
Services	61.2	Exports	52.4
		Imports	-58.7

Structure of employment

	% of total		% of labour force
Agriculture	18	Unemployed 2004	12.8
Industry	28	Av. ann. rate 1995–2004	14.8
Services	54		

Energy

		m TOE	
Total output	5.2	Net energy imports as %	
Total consumption	8.9	of energy use	42
Consumption per head,			
kg oil equivalent	2,585		

Inflation and finance

Consumer price		av. ann. increase 1999–2004	
inflation 2005	2.7%	Narrow money (M1)	18.8%
Av. ann. inflation 2000–05	0.8%	Broad money	19.4%
Money market rate, 2005	1.97%		

Exchange rates

	end 2005		December 2005
LTL per $	2.91	Effective rates	2000 = 100
LTL per SDR	4.16	– nominal	...
LTL per €	3.42	– real	...

Trade

Principal exports		Principal imports	
	$bn fob		$bn cif
Mineral products	2.4	Machinery & equipment	2.4
Machinery & equipment	1.2	Mineral products	2.4
Textiles	1.1	Transport equipment	1.6
Transport equipment	0.8	Chemicals	1.0
Total incl. others	**9.3**	Total incl. others	**12.4**

Main export destinations		Main origins of imports	
	% of total		% of total
Germany	10.2	Russia	23.0
Latvia	10.1	Germany	16.9
Russia	9.3	Poland	7.6
France	6.3	Netherlands	4.0
United Kingdom	5.3	Latvia	3.8
EU25	66.4	EU25	63.0

Balance of payments, reserves and debt, $bn

Visible exports fob	9.3	Change in reserves	0.1
Visible imports fob	-11.6	Level of reserves	
Trade balance	-2.3	end Dec.	3.6
Invisibles inflows	2.9	No. months of import cover	3.0
Invisibles outflows	-2.5	Official gold holdings, m oz	0.2
Net transfers	0.3	Foreign debt	9.5
Current account balance	-1.6	– as % of GDP	53
– as % of GDP	-7.1	– as % of total exports	95
Capital balance	1.3	Debt service ratio	18
Overall balance	-0.1		

Health and education

Health spending, % of GDP	6.6	Education spending, % of GDP	5.9
Doctors per 1,000 pop.	4.0	Enrolment, %: primary	98
Hospital beds per 1,000 pop.	8.7	secondary	102
Improved-water source access,		tertiary	72
% of pop.	...		

Society

No. of households	1.4m	Colour TVs per 100 households	76.7
Av. no. per household	2.5	Telephone lines per 100 pop.	23.8
Marriages per 1,000 pop.	4.6	Mobile telephone subscribers	
Divorces per 1,000 pop.	3.3	per 100 pop.	99.3
Cost of living, Dec. 2005		Computers per 100 pop.	15.5
New York = 100	...	Internet hosts per 1,000 pop.	60.8

MALAYSIA

Area	332,665 sq km	Capital	Kuala Lumpur
Arable as % of total land	5	Currency	Malaysian dollar/ringgit (M$)

People

Population	24.9m	Life expectancy: men	71.9 yrs
Pop. per sq km	74.9	women	76.5 yrs
Av. ann. growth		Adult literacy	88.7%
in pop. 2000–05	1.95%	Fertility rate (per woman)	2.9
Pop. under 15	32.4%	Urban population	65.1%
Pop. over 60	7.0%		per 1,000 pop.
No. of men per 100 women	103	Crude birth rate	22.6
Human Development Index	79.6	Crude death rate	4.7

The economy

GDP	M$450bn	GDP per head	$4,750
GDP	$118bn	GDP per head in purchasing	
Av. ann. growth in real		power parity (USA=100)	25.9
GDP 1994–2004	5.1%	Economic freedom index	2.98

Origins of GDP		Components of GDP	
	% of total		% of total
Agriculture	9.5	Private consumption	42.9
Industry, of which:	45.4	Public consumption	13.3
manufacturing	31.2	Investment	22.4
Services	45.1	Exports	121.8
		Imports	-100.4

Structure of employment

	% of total		% of labour force
Agriculture	15	Unemployed 2003	3.6
Industry	30	Av. ann. rate 1995–2003	3.2
Services	55		

Energy

	m TOE		
Total output	83.8	Net energy imports as %	
Total consumption	56.7	of energy use	-48
Consumption per head,			
kg oil equivalent	2,318		

Inflation and finance

Consumer price		*av. ann. increase 1999–2004*	
inflation 2005	3.1%	Narrow money (M1)	8.6%
Av. ann. inflation 2000–05	1.8%	Broad money	9.2%
Money market rate, 2005	2.72%		

Exchange rates

	end 2005		December 2005
M$ per $	3.78	Effective rates	2000 = 100
M$ per SDR	5.40	– nominal	97.9
M$ per €	4.45	– real	97.9

Trade

Principal exports

	$bn fob
Electronics & electrical mach.	67.6
Chemicals & products	7.3
Petroleum & gas	7.3
Palm oil	5.3
Textiles, clothing & footwear	2.7
Total incl. others	**126.5**

Principal imports

	$bn cif
Intermediate goods	75.6
Capital goods & transport equipment	14.6
Consumption goods	6.1
Re-exports	4.5
Total incl. others	**105.3**

Main export destinations

	% of total
United States	18.8
Singapore	15.0
Japan	10.1
China	6.7
Hong Kong	6.0

Main origins of imports

	% of total
Japan	15.9
United States	14.5
Singapore	11.1
China	9.8
Thailand	5.5

Balance of payments, reserves and debt, $bn

Visible exports fob	126.6	Change in reserves	21.9
Visible imports fob	-99.1	Level of reserves	
Trade balance	27.5	end Dec.	66.9
Invisibles inflows	21.0	No. months of import cover	6.2
Invisibles outflows	-29.9	Official gold holdings, m oz	1.2
Net transfers	-3.9	Foreign debt	52.1
Current account balance	14.8	– as % of GDP	52
– as % of GDP	12.5	– as % of total exports	42
Capital balance[a]	-3.2	Debt service ratio	7
Overall balance[a]	10.2		

Health and education

Health spending, % of GDP	3.8	Education spending, % of GDP	8.1
Doctors per 1,000 pop.	0.6	Enrolment, %: primary	93
Hospital beds per 1,000 pop.	1.9	secondary	70
Improved-water source access,		tertiary	29
% of pop.	95		

Society

No. of households	5.5m	Colour TVs per 100 households	90.3
Av. no. per household	4.7	Telephone lines per 100 pop.	17.4
Marriages per 1,000 pop.	...	Mobile telephone subscribers	
Divorces per 1,000 pop.	...	per 100 pop.	57.1
Cost of living, Dec. 2005		Computers per 100 pop.	19.2
New York = 100	65	Internet hosts per 1,000 pop.	6.2

MEXICO

Area	1,972,545 sq km	Capital	Mexico city
Arable as % of total land	13	Currency	Mexican peso (PS)

People

Population	104.9m	Life expectancy:	men	73.7 yrs
Pop. per sq km	53.2		women	78.6 yrs
Av. ann. growth		Adult literacy		91.0%
in pop. 2000–05	1.34%	Fertility rate (per woman)		2.4
Pop. under 15	31.0%	Urban population		76.0%
Pop. over 60	7.8%			per 1,000 pop.
No. of men per 100 women	96	Crude birth rate		22.4
Human Development Index	81.4	Crude death rate		4.5

The economy

GDP	7,635bn pesos	GDP per head	$6,450
GDP	$677bn	GDP per head in purchasing	
Av. ann. growth in real		power parity (USA=100)	24.7
GDP 1994–2004	2.7%	Economic freedom index	2.83

Origins of GDP

	% of total
Agriculture	4.1
Industry, of which:	26.4
manufacturing & mining	19.5
Services	69.5

Components of GDP

	% of total
Private consumption	68.5
Public consumption	11.7
Investment	21.8
Exports	30.1
Imports	-31.9

Structure of employment

	% of total		% of labour force
Agriculture	17	Unemployed 2004	2.5
Industry	25	Av. ann. rate 1995–2004	2.5
Services	58		

Energy

	m TOE		
Total output	242.5	Net energy imports as %	
Total consumption	159.9	of energy use	-52
Consumption per head,			
kg oil equivalent	1,564		

Inflation and finance

Consumer price		*av. ann. increase 1999–2004*	
inflation 2005	4.0%	Narrow money (M1)	12.6%
Av. ann. inflation 2000–05	4.9%	Broad money	6.6%
Money market rate, 2005	9.59%		

Exchange rates

	end 2005		December 2005
PS per $	10.78	Effective rates	2000 = 100
PS per SDR	15.40	– nominal	...
PS per €	12.68	– real	...

Trade

Principal exports		Principal imports	
	$bn fob		*$bn fob*
Manufactured products	172.5	Intermediate goods	149.3
(Maquiladora[a]	*87.0)*	*(Maquiladora[a]*	*68.6)*
Crude oil & products	29.9	Consumer goods	25.4
Agricultural products	5.6	Capital goods	22.6
Total incl. others	**188.0**	Total	**196.8**

Main export destinations		Main origins of imports	
	% of total		*% of total*
United States	87.5	United States	56.3
Canada	1.8	China	3.8
Japan	1.1	Germany	3.6
Spain	1.0	South Korea	3.0

Balance of payments, reserves and debt, $bn

Visible exports fob	188.0	Change in reserves	5.2
Visible imports fob	-196.8	Level of reserves	
Trade balance	-8.8	end Dec.	64.2
Invisibles inflows	19.1	No. months of import cover	3.3
Invisibles outflows	-34.7	Official gold holdings, m oz	0.1
Net transfers	17.0	Foreign debt	138.7
Current account balance	-7.4	– as % of GDP	22
– as % of GDP	-1.1	– as % of total exports	69
Capital balance	12.3	Debt service ratio	25
Overall balance	4.1		

Health and education

Health spending, % of GDP	6.2	Education spending, % of GDP	5.3
Doctors per 1,000 pop.	1.9	Enrolment, %: primary	110
Hospital beds per 1,000 pop.	1.0	secondary	79
Improved-water source access,		tertiary	22
% of pop.	91		

Society

No. of households	24.1m	Colour TVs per 100 households	90.5
Av. no. per household	4.3	Telephone lines per 100 pop.	17.2
Marriages per 1,000 pop.	6.5	Mobile telephone subscribers	
Divorces per 1,000 pop.	0.5	per 100 pop.	36.6
Cost of living, Dec. 2005		Computers per 100 pop.	10.7
New York = 100	84	Internet hosts per 1,000 pop.	24.4

a Manufacturing assembly plants near the Mexican-US border where goods for
processing may be imported duty-free and all output is exported.

MOROCCO

Area	446,550 sq km	Capital	Rabat
Arable as % of total land	19	Currency	Dirham (Dh)

People

Population	31.1m	Life expectancy: men		68.8 yrs
Pop. per sq km	69.7		women	73.3 yrs
Av. ann. growth		Adult literacy		52.3%
in pop. 2000–05	1.48%	Fertility rate (per woman)		2.8
Pop. under 15	31.1%	Urban population		58.8%
Pop. over 60	6.8%			per 1,000 pop.
No. of men per 100 women	99	Crude birth rate		23.2
Human Development Index	63.1	Crude death rate		5.6

The economy

GDP	Dh444bn	GDP per head	$1,610
GDP	$50.0bn	GDP per head in purchasing	
Av. ann. growth in real		power parity (USA=100)	10.9
GDP 1994–2004	3.0%	Economic freedom index	3.21

Origins of GDP		**Components of GDP**	
	% of total		% of total
Agriculture	15.3	Private consumption	61.4
Industry, of which:	29.8	Public consumption	19.8
manufacturing	17.5	Investment	22.7
Services	54.9	Exports	26.3
		Imports	-30.2

Structure of employment

	% of total		% of labour force
Agriculture	44	Unemployed 2003	11.9
Industry	20	Av. ann. rate 1995–2003	15.6
Services	36		

Energy

	m TOE		
Total output	0.6	Net energy imports as %	
Total consumption	10.9	of energy use	94
Consumption per head,			
kg oil equivalent	378		

Inflation and finance

		av. ann. increase 1999–2004	
Consumer price			
inflation 2005	1.0%	Narrow money (M1)	10.4%
Av. ann. inflation 2000–05	1.4%	Broad money	9.1%
Money market rate, 2005	2.78%		

Exchange rates

	end 2005		December 2005
Dh per $	9.25	Effective rates	2000 = 100
Dh per SDR	13.22	– nominal	95.7
Dh per €	10.88	– real	92.2

Trade

Principal exports		Principal imports	
	$bn fob		$bn cif
Textiles	2.0	Semi-finished goods	4.1
Phosphoric acid	0.7	Consumer goods	4.0
Electrical components	0.6	Capital goods	3.9
Phosphate rock	0.5	Energy & lubricants	2.9
Citrus fruits	0.2	Food, drink & tobacco	1.5
Total incl. others	**9.9**	Total incl. others	**17.8**

Main export destinations		Main origins of imports	
	% of total		% of total
France	25.4	France	20.3
Spain	19.1	Spain	14.9
United Kingdom	8.0	Germany	7.0
Italy	4.9	Italy	6.7

Balance of payments, reserves and debt, $bn

Visible exports fob	9.9	Change in reserves	2.5
Visible imports fob	-16.4	Level of reserves	
Trade balance	-6.5	end Dec.	16.6
Invisibles inflows	7.2	No. months of import cover	9.5
Invisibles outflows	-4.6	Official gold holdings, m oz	0.7
Net transfers	4.8	Foreign debt	17.7
Current account balance	0.9	– as % of GDP	41
– as % of GDP	1.8	– as % of total exports	96
Capital balance	0.1	Debt service ratio	16
Overall balance	0.7		

Health and education

Health spending, % of GDP	5.1	Education spending, % of GDP	6.5
Doctors per 1,000 pop.	0.5	Enrolment, %: primary	110
Hospital beds per 1,000 pop.	0.8	secondary	45
Improved-water source access,		tertiary	11
% of pop.	80		

Society

No. of households	5.9m	Colour TVs per 100 households	48.1
Av. no. per household	5.2	Telephone lines per 100 pop.	4.4
Marriages per 1,000 pop.	...	Mobile telephone subscribers	
Divorces per 1,000 pop.	...	per 100 pop.	31.2
Cost of living, Dec. 2005		Computers per 100 pop.	2.1
New York = 100	73	Internet hosts per 1,000 pop.	8.0

NETHERLANDS

Area[a]	41,526 sq km	Capital	Amsterdam
Arable as % of total land	27	Currency	Euro (€)

People

Population	16.2m	Life expectancy: men	76.3 yrs
Pop. per sq km	390.1	women	81.6 yrs
Av. ann. growth		Adult literacy	99.0%
in pop. 2000–05	0.50%	Fertility rate (per woman)	1.7
Pop. under 15	18.2%	Urban population	66.8%
Pop. over 60	19.2%		per 1,000 pop.
No. of men per 100 women	99	Crude birth rate	12.1
Human Development Index	94.3	Crude death rate	9.1

The economy

GDP	€466bn	GDP per head	$35,740
GDP	$579bn	GDP per head in purchasing	
Av. ann. growth in real		power parity (USA=100)	80.1
GDP 1994–2004	2.4%	Economic freedom index	1.90

Origins of GDP		Components of GDP	
	% of total		% of total
Agriculture	2.7	Private consumption	49.4
Industry, of which:	24.1	Public consumption	23.5
manufacturing	...	Investment	19.7
Services	73.2	Exports	73.9
		Imports	-66.7

Structure of employment

	% of total		% of labour force
Agriculture	4	Unemployed 2003	4.3
Industry	22	Av. ann. rate 1995–2003	4.7
Services	74		

Energy

	m TOE		
Total output	58.5	Net energy imports as %	
Total consumption	80.8	of energy use	28
Consumption per head,			
kg oil equivalent	4,982		

Inflation and finance

Consumer price		av. ann. increase 1999–2004	
inflation 2005	1.7%	Euro area:	
Av. ann. inflation 2000–05	2.5%	Narrow money (M1)	8.4%
Lending rate, 2004	2.75%	Broad money	6.9%
Deposit rate, households, 2005	3.18%	Household saving rate, 2004	7.3%

Exchange rates

	end 2005		December 2005
€ per $	0.85	Effective rates	2000 = 100
€ per SDR	1.21	– nominal	107.0
		– real	111.3

Trade

Principal exports		Principal imports	
	$bn fob		*$bn cif*
Machinery & transport equipment	103	Machinery & transport equipment	108
Chemicals	54	Chemicals	36
Food, drink & tobacco	46	Food, drink & tobacco	33
Fuels	29	Fuels	26
Total incl. others	**318**	Total incl. others	**284**

Main export destinations		Main origins of imports	
	% of total		*% of total*
Germany	23.8	Germany	19.6
Belgium	11.9	Belgium	11.1
United Kingdom	10.0	United States	8.0
France	9.7	United Kingdom	6.5
EU25	79.5	EU25	52.8

Balance of payments, reserves and aid, $bn

Visible exports fob	304.3	Overall balance	-1.0
Visible imports fob	-273.3	Change in reserves	-0.4
Trade balance	31.0	Level of reserves	
Invisibles inflows	139.1	end Dec.	21.1
Invisibles outflows	-137.9	No. months of import cover	0.6
Net transfers	-9.0	Official gold holdings, m oz	25.0
Current account balance	23.2	Aid given	4.20
– as % of GDP	4.0	– as % of GDP	0.73
Capital balance	-13.3		

Health and education

Health spending, % of GDP	9.8	Education spending, % of GDP	5.1
Doctors per 1,000 pop.	3.1	Enrolment, %: primary	108
Hospital beds per 1,000 pop.	4.7	secondary	122
Improved-water source access, % of pop.	100	tertiary	58

Society

No. of households	7.1m	Colour TVs per 100 households	98.7
Av. no. per household	2.3	Telephone lines per 100 pop.	48.4
Marriages per 1,000 pop.	5.2	Mobile telephone subscribers	
Divorces per 1,000 pop.	1.9	per 100 pop.	91.2
Cost of living, Dec. 2005		Computers per 100 pop.	68.5
New York = 100	104	Internet hosts per 1,000 pop.	448.0

a   Includes water.

NEW ZEALAND

Area	270,534 sq km	Capital	Wellington
Arable as % of total land	6	Currency	New Zealand dollar (NZ$)

People

Population	3.9m	Life expectancy:	men	77.7 yrs
Pop. per sq km	14.4		women	82.0 yrs
Av. ann. growth		Adult literacy		99.0%
in pop. 2000–05	1.07%	Fertility rate (per woman)		2.0
Pop. under 15	21.3%	Urban population		86.0%
Pop. over 60	16.7%			per 1,000 pop.
No. of men per 100 women	97	Crude birth rate		14.0
Human Development Index	93.3	Crude death rate		7.4

The economy

GDP	NZ$149bn	GDP per head	$25,370
GDP	$98.9bn	GDP per head in purchasing	
Av. ann. growth in real		power parity (USA=100)	59.0
GDP 1994–2004	3.3%	Economic freedom index	1.84

Origins of GDP		Components of GDP	
	% of total		% of total
Agriculture & mining	7.3	Private consumption	58.7
Manufacturing	15.2	Public consumption	17.8
Other	77.5	Investment	24.0
		Exports	29.2
		Imports	-29.6

Structure of employment

	% of total		% of labour force
Agriculture	9	Unemployed 2004	3.9
Industry	22	Av. ann. rate 1995–2004	5.8
Services	69		

Energy

	m TOE		
Total output	13.2	Net energy imports as %	
Total consumption	17.4	of energy use	24
Consumption per head,			
kg oil equivalent	4,333		

Inflation and finance

Consumer price		av. ann. increase 1999–2004	
inflation 2005	3.0%	Narrow money (M1)	8.3%
Av. ann. inflation 2000–05	2.5%	Broad money	6.5%
Money market rate, 2005	6.76%	Household saving rate, 2003	-6.5%

Exchange rates

	end 2005		December 2005
NZ$ per $	1.47	Effective rates	2000 = 100
NZ$ per SDR	2.10	– nominal	135.7
NZ$ per €	1.73	– real	139.7

Trade

Principal exports		Principal imports	
	$bn fob		*$bn cif*
Dairy produce	3.5	Machinery & electrical	
Meat	3.1	equipment	4.6
Forestry products	1.4	Transport equipment	3.6
Fish	1.0	Mineral fuels	2.4
Total incl. others	**20.3**	Total incl. others	**23.2**

Main export destinations		Main origins of imports	
	% of total		*% of total*
Australia	20.8	Australia	22.4
United States	14.4	Japan	11.2
Japan	11.2	United States	11.2
China	5.7	China	9.7

Balance of payments, reserves and aid, $bn

Visible exports fob	20.5	Overall balance	0.6
Visible imports fob	-21.9	Change in reserves	0.4
Trade balance	-1.4	Level of reserves	
Invisibles inflows	9.4	end Dec.	5.3
Invisibles outflows	-14.2	No. months of import cover	1.8
Net transfers	0.1	Official gold holdings, m oz	0.0
Current account balance	-6.2	Aid given	0.21
– as % of GDP	-6.3	– as % of GDP	0.23
Capital balance	9.2		

Health and education

Health spending, % of GDP	8.1	Education spending, % of GDP	6.7
Doctors per 1,000 pop.	2.3	Enrolment, %: primary	102
Hospital beds per 1,000 pop.	6.1	secondary	120
Improved-water source access,		tertiary	77
% of pop.	95		

Society

No. of households	1.5m	Colour TVs per 100 households	98.0
Av. no. per household	2.7	Telephone lines per 100 pop.	46.1
Marriages per 1,000 pop.	4.6	Mobile telephone subscribers	
Divorces per 1,000 pop.	3.3	per 100 pop.	77.5
Cost of living, Dec. 2005		Computers per 100 pop.	49.3
New York = 100	96	Internet hosts per 1,000 pop.	249.2

NIGERIA

Area	923,768 sq km	Capital	Abuja
Arable as % of total land	33	Currency	Naira (N)

People

Population	127.1m	Life expectancy: men	44.1 yrs
Pop. per sq km	137.6	women	44.3 yrs
Av. ann. growth		Adult literacy	68.0%
in pop. 2000–05	2.24%	Fertility rate (per woman)	5.6
Pop. under 15	44.3%	Urban population	48.3%
Pop. over 60	4.8%		per 1,000 pop.
No. of men per 100 women	102	Crude birth rate	39.1
Human Development Index	45.3	Crude death rate	18.4

The economy

GDP	N9,575bn	GDP per head	$570
GDP	$72.1bn	GDP per head in purchasing	
Av. ann. growth in real		power parity (USA=100)	2.9
GDP 1994–2004	3.8%	Economic freedom index	4.00

Origins of GDP		**Components of GDP**	
	% of total		% of total
Agriculture	34.8	Private consumption	84.7
Manufacturing	4.6	Public consumption	2.5
Other	60.6	Investment	19.5
		Exports	42.0
		Imports	-48.7

Structure of employment

	% of total		% of labour force
Agriculture	...	Unemployed 2001	3.9
Industry	...	Av. ann. rate 1995–2001	3.7
Services	...		

Energy

	m TOE		
Total output	214.6	Net energy imports as %	
Total consumption	97.8	of energy use	-119
Consumption per head,			
kg oil equivalent	777		

Inflation and finance

		av. ann. increase 1999–2004	
Consumer price			
inflation 2005	13.5%	Narrow money (M1)	27.1%
Av. ann. inflation 2000–05	15.7%	Broad money	26.5%
Treasury bill rate 2005	7.63%		

Exchange rates

	end 2005		December 2005
N per $	129.0	Effective rates	2000 = 100
N per SDR	184.4	– nominal	71.5
N per €	151.8	– real	129.6

Trade

Principal exports		Principal imports	
	$bn fob		$bn cif
Oil	20.7	Manufactured goods	4.4
Gas	2.0	Chemicals	2.8
		Machinery & transport equipment	2.8
		Agric products & foodstuffs	1.1
Total incl. others	**31.1**	Total incl. others	**14.2**

Main export destinations[a]		Main origins of imports[a]	
	% of total		% of total
United States	49.9	United States	8.9
India	10.2	China	8.5
Spain	7.5	United Kingdom	8.3
Brazil	6.9	Netherlands	6.2

Balance of payments, reserves and debt, $bn

Visible exports fob	23.7	Change in reserves	9.8
Visible imports fob	-11.1	Level of reserves	
Trade balance	12.6	end Dec.	17.3
Invisibles inflows	3.5	No. months of import cover	12.1
Invisibles outflows	-6.0	Official gold holdings, m oz	0.7
Net transfers	2.3	Foreign debt	35.9
Current account balance	12.3	– as % of GDP	72
– as % of GDP	17.0	– as % of total exports	141
Capital balance	-4.5	Debt service ratio	9
Overall balance	-8.5		

Health and education

Health spending, % of GDP	5.0	Education spending, % of GDP	...
Doctors per 1,000 pop.	0.3	Enrolment, %: primary	119
Hospital beds per 1,000 pop.	...	secondary	36
Improved-water source access,		tertiary	8
% of pop.	60		

Society

No. of households	26.1m	Colour TVs per 100 households	53.1
Av. no. per household	4.8	Telephone lines per 100 pop.	0.8
Marriages per 1,000 pop.	...	Mobile telephone subscribers	
Divorces per 1,000 pop.	...	per 100 pop.	7.2
Cost of living, Dec. 2005		Computers per 100 pop.	0.7
New York = 100	82	Internet hosts per 1,000 pop.	...

a Estimate.

NORWAY

Area	323,878 sq km	Capital	Oslo
Arable as % of total land	3	Currency	Norwegian krone (Nkr)

People

Population	4.6m	Life expectancy: men	77.8 yrs
Pop. per sq km	14.2	women	82.5 yrs
Av. ann. growth		Adult literacy	99.0%
in pop. 2000–05	0.52%	Fertility rate (per woman)	1.8
Pop. under 15	19.6%	Urban population	80.5%
Pop. over 60	20.0%		per 1,000 pop.
No. of men per 100 women	99	Crude birth rate	12.0
Human Development Index	96.3	Crude death rate	9.3

The economy

GDP	Nkr1,686bn	GDP per head	$54,360
GDP	$250bn	GDP per head in purchasing	
Av. ann. growth in real		power parity (USA=100)	96.9
GDP 1994–2004	2.9%	Economic freedom index	2.29

Origins of GDP		**Components of GDP**	
	% of total		% of total
Agriculture	1.9	Private consumption	44.8
Industry, of which:	39.9	Public consumption	22.0
manufacturing	...	Investment	19.0
Services	58.2	Exports	43.7
		Imports	-29.5

Structure of employment

	% of total		% of labour force
Agriculture	4	Unemployed 2004	4.5
Industry	22	Av. ann. rate 1995–2004	4.0
Services	74		

Energy

	m TOE		
Total output	233.2	Net energy imports as %	
Total consumption	23.3	of energy use	-899
Consumption per head,			
kg oil equivalent	5,100		

Inflation and finance

Consumer price		av. ann. increase 1999–2004	
inflation 2005	1.5%	Narrow money (M1)	6.6%
Av. ann. inflation 2000–05	1.7%	Broad money	6.9%
Interbank rate, 2005	2.21%	Household saving rate, 2004	10.2%

Exchange rates

	end 2005		December 2005
Nkr per $	6.78	Effective rates	2000 = 100
Nkr per SDR	9.68	– nominal	110.3
Nkr per €	7.98	– real	127.5

Trade

Principal exports	$bn fob
Oil, gas & products	64.2
Machinery & transport equip.	9.8
Manufactured materials	6.8
Food, drink & tobacco	4.5
Total incl. others	**82**

Principal imports	$bn cif
Machinery & transport equip.	18.7
Manufactured materials	8.3
Misc. manufactures	7.6
Chemicals	4.7
Total incl. others	**49**

Main export destinations	% of total
United Kingdom	22.3
Germany	12.9
Netherlands	9.9
France	9.6
United States	8.4
Sweden	6.7
EU25	78.2

Main origins of imports	% of total
Sweden	15.7
Germany	13.6
Denmark	7.3
United Kingdom	6.5
United States	4.9
Netherlands	4.4
EU25	70.8

Balance of payments, reserves and aid, $bn

Visible exports fob	83.0	Overall balance	5.2
Visible imports fob	-49.4	Change in reserves	6.6
Trade balance	33.6	Level of reserves	
Invisibles inflows	38.5	end Dec.	44.3
Invisibles outflows	-34.9	No. months of import cover	6.3
Net transfers	-2.6	Official gold holdings, m oz	1.2
Current account balance	34.4	Aid given	2.20
– as % of GDP	13.8	– as % of GDP	0.87
Capital balance	-20.9		

Health and education

Health spending, % of GDP	10.3	Education spending, % of GDP	7.6
Doctors per 1,000 pop.	3.1	Enrolment, %: primary	101
Hospital beds per 1,000 pop.	3.8	secondary	115
Improved-water source access,		tertiary	81
% of pop.	100		

Society

No. of households	2.0m	Colour TVs per 100 households	93.5
Av. no. per household	2.3	Telephone lines per 100 pop.	47.2
Marriages per 1,000 pop.	5.2	Mobile telephone subscribers	
Divorces per 1,000 pop.	2.4	per 100 pop.	103.6
Cost of living, Dec. 2005		Computers per 100 pop.	57.8
New York = 100	140	Internet hosts per 1,000 pop.	458.5

PAKISTAN

Area	803,940 sq km	Capital	Islamabad
Arable as % of total land	25	Currency	Pakistan rupee (PRs)

People

Population	157.3m	Life expectancy:	men	64.6 yrs
Pop. per sq km	195.7		women	64.9 yrs
Av. ann. growth		Adult literacy		49.9%
in pop. 2000–05	2.04%	Fertility rate (per woman)		4.3
Pop. under 15	38.3%	Urban population		34.8%
Pop. over 60	5.8%			per 1,000 pop.
No. of men per 100 women	106	Crude birth rate		35.9
Human Development Index	52.7	Crude death rate		7.5

The economy

GDP	PRs5,533bn	GDP per head	$610
GDP	$96.1bn	GDP per head in purchasing	
Av. ann. growth in real		power parity (USA=100)	5.6
GDP 1994–2004	3.8%	Economic freedom index	3.33

Origins of GDP		Components of GDP[a]	
	% of total		% of total
Agriculture	21.6	Private consumption	80.0
Industry, of which:	25.0	Public consumption	7.8
manufacturing & mining	20.2	Investment	16.9
Other	53.4	Exports	15.3
		Imports	-19.9

Structure of employment

	% of total		% of labour force
Agriculture	42	Unemployed 2002	8.3
Industry	21	Av. ann. rate 1995–2002	6.4
Services	37		

Energy

	m TOE		
Total output	55.5	Net energy imports as %	
Total consumption	69.3	of energy use	20
Consumption per head,			
kg oil equivalent	467		

Inflation and finance

Consumer price		av. ann. increase 1999–2004	
inflation 2005	9.1%	Narrow money (M1)	16.2%
Av. ann. inflation 2000–05	5.1%	Broad money	15.7%
Money market rate, 2005	6.83%		

Exchange rates

	end 2005		December 2005
PRs per $	59.83	Effective rates	2000 = 100
PRs per SDR	85.51	– nominal	82.52
PRs per €	70.39	– real	97.63

Trade

Principal exports[a]	$bn fob	Principal imports[a]	$bn fob
Cotton fabrics	1.9	Machinery & transport equip.	6.0
Knitwear	1.6	Fuels etc	4.3
Bedwear	1.5	Chemicals	3.6
Cotton yarn & thread	1.1	Manufactures	2.3
Rice	0.9		
Total incl. others	**13.4**	Total incl. others	**17.9**

Main export destinations[a]	% of total	Main origins of imports[a]	% of total
United States	24.0	Saudi Arabia	12.3
United Arab Emirates	7.6	China	8.9
United Kingdom	6.2	United Arab Emirates	8.3
Afghanistan	5.2	United States	7.6

Balance of payments, reserves and debt, $bn

Visible exports fob	13.4	Change in reserves	-1.1
Visible imports fob	-16.7	Level of reserves	
Trade balance	-3.4	end Dec.	10.7
Invisibles inflows	2.9	No. months of import cover	5.2
Invisibles outflows	-7.9	Official gold holdings, m oz	2.1
Net transfers	7.5	Foreign debt	35.7
Current account balance	-0.8	– as % of GDP	44
– as % of GDP	-0.8	– as % of total exports	194
Capital balance	-1.1	Debt service ratio	23
Overall balance	-1.4		

Health and education

Health spending, % of GDP	2.4	Education spending, % of GDP	1.8
Doctors per 1,000 pop.	0.7	Enrolment, %: primary	68
Hospital beds per 1,000 pop.	0.7	secondary	23
Improved-water source access,		tertiary	3
% of pop.	90		

Society

No. of households	21.5m	Colour TVs per 100 households	38.3
Av. no. per household	7.2	Telephone lines per 100 pop.	3.0
Marriages per 1,000 pop.	...	Mobile telephone subscribers	
Divorces per 1,000 pop.	...	per 100 pop.	3.3
Cost of living, Dec. 2005		Computers per 100 pop.	...
New York = 100	43	Internet hosts per 1,000 pop.	0.4

a Fiscal year ending June 30, 2005.

PERU

Area	1,285,216 sq km	Capital	Lima
Arable as % of total land	3	Currency	Nuevo Sol (New Sol)

People

Population	27.6m	Life expectancy: men	68.7 yrs
Pop. per sq km	21.5	women	73.9 yrs
Av. ann. growth		Adult literacy	89.7%
in pop. 2000–05	1.50%	Fertility rate (per woman)	2.9
Pop. under 15	32.2%	Urban population	74.6%
Pop. over 60	7.8%		per 1,000 pop.
No. of men per 100 women	101	Crude birth rate	23.3
Human Development Index	76.2	Crude death rate	5.9

The economy

GDP	New Soles 234bn	GDP per head	$2,490
GDP	$68.6bn	GDP per head in purchasing	
Av. ann. growth in real		power parity (USA=100)	14.3
GDP 1994–2004	3.5%	Economic freedom index	2.86

Origins of GDP		Components of GDP	
	% of total		% of total
Agriculture	8.8	Private consumption	68.7
Industry, of which:	26.3	Public consumption	10.1
manufacturing	14.9	Investment	18.5
Services	64.9	Exports	20.9
		Imports	-18.3

Structure of employment

	% of total		% of labour force
Agriculture	1	Unemployed 2004	10.5
Industry	20	Av. ann. rate 1996–2004	8.3
Services	79		

Energy

	m TOE		
Total output	9.4	Net energy imports as %	
Total consumption	12.0	of energy use	21
Consumption per head,			
kg oil equivalent	442		

Inflation and finance

Consumer price		av. ann. increase 1999–2004	
inflation 2005	1.6%	Narrow money (M1)	1.3%
Av. ann. inflation 2000–05	1.9%	Broad money	1.5%
Deposit rate, 2005	3.43%		

Exchange rates

	end 2005		December 2005
New Soles per $	3.28	Effective rates	2000 = 100
New Soles per SDR	2.10	– nominal	...
New Soles per €	3.86	– real	...

Trade

Principal exports		Principal imports	
	$bn fob		*$bn fob*
Copper	2.4	Intermediate goods	5.4
Gold	2.4	Capital goods	2.4
Fishmeal	1.1	Consumer goods	2.0
Zinc	0.6	Other goods	0.1
Total incl. others	**12.6**	Total incl. others	**9.8**

Main export destinations		Main origins of imports	
	% of total		*% of total*
United States	29.0	United States	28.7
China	9.3	Spain	7.4
United Kingdom	7.5	Chile	6.6
Chile	5.0	Brazil	6.0

Balance of payments, reserves and debt, $bn

Visible exports fob	12.6	Change in reserves	2.4
Visible imports fob	-9.8	Level of reserves	
Trade balance	2.8	end Dec.	12.7
Invisibles inflows	2.2	No. months of import cover	9.3
Invisibles outflows	-6.5	Official gold holdings, m oz	1.1
Net transfers	1.5	Foreign debt	31.3
Current account balance	-0.0	– as % of GDP	52
– as % of GDP	-0.0	– as % of total exports	245
Capital balance	2.3	Debt service ratio	21
Overall balance	2.5		

Health and education

Health spending, % of GDP	4.4	Education spending, % of GDP	3.0
Doctors per 1,000 pop.	1.1	Enrolment, %: primary	118
Hospital beds per 1,000 pop.	1.4	secondary	90
Improved-water source access,		tertiary	32
% of pop.	81		

Society

No. of households	5.7m	Colour TVs per 100 households	49.6
Av. no. per household	4.8	Telephone lines per 100 pop.	7.4
Marriages per 1,000 pop.	4.0	Mobile telephone subscribers	
Divorces per 1,000 pop.	...	per 100 pop.	14.8
Cost of living, Dec. 2005		Computers per 100 pop.	10.0
New York = 100	61	Internet hosts per 1,000 pop.	9.6

PHILIPPINES

Area	300,000 sq km	Capital	Manila
Arable as % of total land	19	Currency	Philippine peso (P)

People

Population	81.4m	Life expectancy: men	69.5 yrs
Pop. per sq km	271.3	women	73.8 yrs
Av. ann. growth		Adult literacy	92.6%
in pop. 2000–05	1.84%	Fertility rate (per woman)	3.2
Pop. under 15	35.1%	Urban population	62.6%
Pop. over 60	6.1%		per 1,000 pop.
No. of men per 100 women	101	Crude birth rate	25.3
Human Development Index	75.8	Crude death rate	4.8

The economy

GDP	P4,739bn	GDP per head	$1,040
GDP	$84.6bn	GDP per head in purchasing	
Av. ann. growth in real		power parity (USA=100)	11.6
GDP 1994–2004	4.0%	Economic freedom index	3.23

Origins of GDP		Components of GDP	
	% of total		% of total
Agriculture	15.2	Private consumption	69.3
Industry, of which:	31.9	Public consumption	10.2
manufacturing	23.1	Investment	17.1
Services	52.9	Exports	50.6
		Imports	-50.0

Structure of employment

	% of total		% of labour force
Agriculture	37	Unemployed 2004	10.9
Industry	16	Av. ann. rate 1995–2004	9.2
Services	47		

Energy

	m TOE		
Total output	22.5	Net energy imports as %	
Total consumption	42.1	of energy use	47
Consumption per head,			
kg oil equivalent	525		

Inflation and finance

Consumer price		av. ann. increase 1999–2004	
inflation 2005	7.6%	Narrow money (M1)	7.5%
Av. ann. inflation 2000–05	5.4%	Broad money	7.1%
Money market rate, 2005	7.31%		

Exchange rates

	end 2005		December 2005
P per $	53.07	Effective rates	2000 = 100
P per SDR	75.85	– nominal	80.5
P per €	62.44	– real	98.6

Trade

Principal exports		Principal imports	
	$bn fob		$bn fob
Electrical & electronic		Semi-processed raw	
equipment	26.6	materials	13.7
Semiconductors	18.6	Telecom & electrical machinery	8.7
Clothing	2.2	Electrical equipment parts	6.2
Coconut products	0.6	Chemicals	3.2
Petroleum products	0.4	Crude petroleum	2.5
Total incl. others	**39.6**	Total incl. others	**42.3**

Main export destinations		Main origins of imports	
	% of total		% of total
Japan	20.1	Japan	19.8
United States	17.9	United States	13.7
Netherlands	9.1	China	7.7
Hong Kong	7.9	Singapore	7.4
China	6.7	Taiwan	7.0
Singapore	6.6	South Korea	5.6

Balance of payments, reserves and debt, $bn

Visible exports fob	38.7	Change in reserves	-0.8
Visible imports fob	-45.1	Level of reserves	
Trade balance	-6.4	end Dec.	16.2
Invisibles inflows	7.7	No. months of import cover	3.6
Invisibles outflows	-8.8	Official gold holdings, m oz	7.1
Net transfers	9.6	Foreign debt	60.6
Current account balance	2.1	– as % of GDP	71
– as % of GDP	2.5	– as % of total exports	120
Capital balance	-3.0	Debt service ratio	23
Overall balance	-1.6		

Health and education

Health spending, % of GDP	3.2	Education spending, % of GDP	3.1
Doctors per 1,000 pop.	0.5	Enrolment, %: primary	112
Hospital beds per 1,000 pop.	1.0	secondary	84
Improved-water source access,		tertiary	30
% of pop.	85		

Society

No. of households	16.8m	Colour TVs per 100 households	67.4
Av. no. per household	4.9	Telephone lines per 100 pop.	4.2
Marriages per 1,000 pop.	6.6	Mobile telephone subscribers	
Divorces per 1,000 pop.	...	per 100 pop.	39.9
Cost of living, Dec. 2005		Computers per 100 pop.	4.5
New York = 100	39	Internet hosts per 1,000 pop.	1.3

POLAND

Area	312,683 sq km	Capital	Warsaw
Arable as % of total land	41	Currency	Zloty (Zl)

People

Population	38.6m	Life expectancy: men	71.2 yrs
Pop. per sq km	123.4	women	79.0 yrs
Av. ann. growth		Adult literacy	99.7%
in pop. 2000–05	-0.06%	Fertility rate (per woman)	1.3
Pop. under 15	16.3%	Urban population	62.0%
Pop. over 60	16.8%		*per 1,000 pop.*
No. of men per 100 women	94	Crude birth rate	9.6
Human Development Index	85.8	Crude death rate	10.1

The economy

GDP	Zl885bn	GDP per head	$6,280
GDP	$242bn	GDP per head in purchasing	
Av. ann. growth in real		power parity (USA=100)	32.7
GDP 1994–2004	4.4%	Economic freedom index	2.49

Origins of GDP[a]		Components of GDP	
	% of total		*% of total*
Agriculture	3	Private consumption	63.2
Industry, of which:	33	Public consumption	18.8
manufacturing	20	Investment	20.0
Services	64	Exports	37.6
		Imports	-39.6

Structure of employment

	% of total		*% of labour force*
Agriculture	18	Unemployed 2004	19.0
Industry	29	Av. ann. rate 1995–2004	15.4
Services	53		

Energy

	m TOE		
Total output	80.0	Net energy imports as %	
Total consumption	93.7	of energy use	15
Consumption per head,			
kg oil equivalent	2,452		

Inflation and finance

Consumer price		*av. ann. increase 1999–2004*	
inflation 2005	2.1%	Narrow money (M1)	10.6%
Av. ann. inflation 2000–05	2.8%	Broad money	7.2%
Money market rate, 2005	5.3%		

Exchange rates

	end 2005		*December 2005*
Zl per $	3.26	Effective rates	*2000 = 100*
Zl per SDR	4.66	– nominal	108.7
Zl per €	3.84	– real	110.3

Trade

Principal exports		Principal imports	
	$bn fob		*$bn cif*
Machinery &		Machinery &	
transport equipment	28.6	transport equipment	34.0
Manufactured goods	17.6	Manufactured goods	18.6
Other manufactured goods	11.3	Chemicals	12.6
Agric. products & foodstuffs	5.8	Mineral fuels	8.1
Total incl. others	**73.8**	Total incl. others	**88.2**

Main export destinations		Main origins of imports	
	% of total		*% of total*
Germany	29.5	Germany	23.8
Italy	6.0	Italy	7.7
France	5.9	Russia	7.2
United Kingdom	5.4	France	6.6

Balance of payments, reserves and debt, $bn

Visible exports fob	81.9	Change in reserves	2.8
Visible imports fob	-87.5	Level of reserves	
Trade balance	-5.6	end Dec.	36.8
Invisibles inflows	15.6	No. months of import cover	3.9
Invisibles outflows	-26.0	Official gold holdings, m oz	3.3
Net transfers	5.6	Foreign debt	99.2
Current account balance	-10.4	– as % of GDP	47
– as % of GDP	-4.3	– as % of total exports	126
Capital balance	9.2	Debt service ratio	44
Overall balance	0.8		

Health and education

Health spending, % of GDP	6.5	Education spending, % of GDP	5.6
Doctors per 1,000 pop.	2.5	Enrolment, %: primary	99
Hospital beds per 1,000 pop.	5.6	secondary	105
Improved-water source access,		tertiary	60
% of pop.	...		

Society

No. of households	13.5m	Colour TVs per 100 households	85.6
Av. no. per household	2.9	Telephone lines per 100 pop.	31.9
Marriages per 1,000 pop.	3.2	Mobile telephone subscribers	
Divorces per 1,000 pop.	1.1	per 100 pop.	59.9
Cost of living, Dec. 2005		Computers per 100 pop.	19.1
New York = 100	82	Internet hosts per 1,000 pop.	102.1

a 2002

PORTUGAL

Area	88,940 sq km	Capital	Lisbon
Arable as % of total land	17	Currency	Euro (€)

People

Population	10.1m	Life expectancy: men	74.6 yrs
Pop. per sq km	113.6	women	81.2 yrs
Av. ann. growth		Adult literacy	93.3%
in pop. 2000–05	0.52%	Fertility rate (per woman)	1.5
Pop. under 15	15.9%	Urban population	55.6%
Pop. over 60	22.3%		per 1,000 pop.
No. of men per 100 women	94	Crude birth rate	11.0
Human Development Index	90.4	Crude death rate	10.9

The economy

GDP	€135bn	GDP per head	$16,610
GDP	$168bn	GDP per head in purchasing	
Av. ann. growth in real		power parity (USA=100)	49.5
GDP 1994–2004	2.5%	Economic freedom index	2.29

Origins of GDP		Components of GDP	
	% of total		% of total
Agriculture	3.7	Private consumption	64.1
Industry, of which:	26.7	Public consumption	20.7
manufacturing	...	Investment	23.0
Services	69.6	Exports	28.9
		Imports	-36.7

Structure of employment

	% of total		% of labour force
Agriculture	13	Unemployed 2003	6.3
Industry	33	Av. ann. rate 1995–2003	5.5
Services	55		

Energy

	m TOE		
Total output	3.4	Net energy imports as %	
Total consumption	25.8	of energy use	83
Consumption per head,			
kg oil equivalent	2,469		

Inflation and finance

Consumer price		av. ann. increase 1999–2004	
inflation 2005	2.3%	Euro area:	
Av. ann. inflation 2000–05	3.2%	Narrow money (M1)	8.4%
Deposit rate, h'holds, 2005	1.94%	Broad money	6.9%
		Household saving rate, 2004	11.8%

Exchange rates

	end 2005		December 2005
€ per $	0.85	Effective rates	2000 = 100
€ per SDR	1.21	– nominal	105.1
		– real	110.5

Trade

Principal exports		**Principal imports**	
	$bn fob		*$bn cif*
Transport goods	6.3	Machinery	13.1
Machinery	6.2	Transport goods	8.9
Clothing	4.1	Chemicals	6.1
Shoes	2.0	Agricultural goods	4.6
Total incl. others	**37**	Total incl. others	**58**

Main export destinations		**Main origins of imports**	
	% of total		*% of total*
Spain	24.9	Spain	29.3
France	14.0	Germany	14.3
Germany	13.5	France	9.3
United Kingdom	9.6	Italy	6.1
United States	6.1	United Kingdom	4.6
EU25	79.4	EU25	76.6

Balance of payments, reserves and debt, $bn

Visible exports fob	37.3	Overall balance	-1.9
Visible imports fob	-55.4	Change in reserves	-1.1
Trade balance	-18.1	Level of reserves	
Invisibles inflows	21.3	end Dec.	11.7
Invisibles outflows	-19.3	No. months of import cover	1.9
Net transfers	3.5	Official gold holdings, m oz	14.9
Current account balance	-12.7	Aid given	1.03
– as % of GDP	-7.6	– as % of GDP	0.63
Capital balance	12.6		

Health and education

Health spending, % of GDP	9.6	Education spending, % of GDP	5.8
Doctors per 1,000 pop.	3.4	Enrolment, %: primary	115
Hospital beds per 1,000 pop.	3.6	secondary[a]	113
Improved-water source access,		tertiary	56
% of pop.	...		

Society

No. of households	3.8m	Colour TVs per 100 households	98.1
Av. no. per household	2.7	Telephone lines per 100 pop.	40.3
Marriages per 1,000 pop.	6.4	Mobile telephone subscribers	
Divorces per 1,000 pop.	1.7	per 100 pop.	98.4
Cost of living, Dec. 2005		Computers per 100 pop.	13.3
New York = 100	83	Internet hosts per 1,000 pop.	136.5

a   Includes training for unemployed.

ROMANIA

Area	237,500 sq km	Capital	Bucharest
Arable as % of total land	41	Currency	Leu (RON)

People

Population	22.3m	Life expectancy: men	68.7 yrs
Pop. per sq km	93.9	women	75.7 yrs
Av. ann. growth		Adult literacy	97.3%
in pop. 2000–05	-0.37%	Fertility rate (per woman)	1.3
Pop. under 15	15.4%	Urban population	54.7%
Pop. over 60	19.3%		per 1,000 pop.
No. of men per 100 women	95	Crude birth rate	10.4
Human Development Index	79.2	Crude death rate	12.6

The economy

GDP	L2,388trn	GDP per head	$3,280
GDP	$73.2bn	GDP per head in purchasing	
Av. ann. growth in real		power parity (USA=100)	21.4
GDP 1994–2004	2.4%	Economic freedom index	3.19

Origins of GDP		Components of GDP	
	% of total		% of total
Agriculture	14.7	Private consumption	70.4
Industry, of which:	31.8	Public consumption	15.9
manufacturing	...	Investment	23.1
Services	48.8	Exports	37.1
		Imports	-46.4

Structure of employment

	% of total		% of labour force
Agriculture	35	Unemployed 2004	8.0
Industry	30	Av. ann. rate 1995–2004	7.1
Services	35		

Energy

	m TOE		
Total output	28.9	Net energy imports as %	
Total consumption	39.0	of energy use	26
Consumption per head,			
kg oil equivalent	1,794		

Inflation and finance

		av. ann. increase 1999–2004	
Consumer price			
inflation 2005	9.0%	Narrow money (M1)	38.4%
Av. ann. inflation 2000–05	18.3%	Broad money	36.9%
Bank rate, 2005	9.6%		

Exchange rates

	end 2005		December 2005
RON per $	3.11	Effective rates	2000 = 100
RON per SDR	4.44	– nominal	58.09
RON per €	3.66	– real	121.31

Trade

Principal exports

	$bn fob
Textiles	5.2
Machinery & equipment	4.1
Basic metals & products	3.6
Minerals & fuels	1.7
Total incl. others	**23.5**

Principal imports

	$bn cif
Machinery & equipment	7.8
Fuels & minerals	4.4
Textiles & footwear	4.1
Chemicals	2.6
Total incl. others	**32.7**

Main export destinations

	% of total
Italy	21.2
Germany	15.0
France	8.5
EU25	73.1

Main origins of imports

	% of total
Italy	17.2
Germany	14.9
Russia	6.8
EU25	65.1

Balance of payments, reserves and debt, $bn

Visible exports fob	23.5	Change in reserves	6.6
Visible imports fob	-30.2	Level of reserves	
Trade balance	-6.7	end Dec.	16.1
Invisibles inflows	4.0	No. months of import cover	5.3
Invisibles outflows	-6.0	Official gold holdings, m oz	3.4
Net transfers	3.1	Foreign debt	30.0
Current account balance	-5.6	– as % of GDP	52
– as % of GDP	-7.6	– as % of total exports	138
Capital balance	10.3	Debt service ratio	22
Overall balance	6.0		

Health and education

Health spending, % of GDP	6.1	Education spending, % of GDP	3.5
Doctors per 1,000 pop.	1.9	Enrolment, %: primary	99
Hospital beds per 1,000 pop.	6.6	secondary	85
Improved-water source access,		tertiary	35
% of pop.	57		

Society

No. of households	7.6m	Colour TVs per 100 households	52.7
Av. no. per household	3.0	Telephone lines per 100 pop.	20.3
Marriages per 1,000 pop.	5.3	Mobile telephone subscribers	
Divorces per 1,000 pop.	2.1	per 100 pop.	47.1
Cost of living, Dec. 2005		Computers per 100 pop.	11.3
New York = 100	65	Internet hosts per 1,000 pop.	20.0

RUSSIA

Area	17,075,400 sq km	Capital	Moscow
Arable as % of total land	7	Currency	Rouble (Rb)

People

Population	142.4m	Life expectancy: men		58.7 yrs
Pop. per sq km	8.3		women	71.8 yrs
Av. ann. growth		Adult literacy		99.4%
in pop. 2000–05	-0.46%	Fertility rate (per woman)		1.3
Pop. under 15	15.3%	Urban population		73.3%
Pop. over 60	17.1%			per 1,000 pop.
No. of men per 100 women	87	Crude birth rate		8.6
Human Development Index	79.5	Crude death rate		16.0

The economy

GDP	Rb16,752bn	GDP per head	$4,080
GDP	$581bn	GDP per head in purchasing	
Av. ann. growth in real		power parity (USA=100)	25.0
GDP 1994–2004	2.8%	Economic freedom index	3.50

Origins of GDP		Components of GDP[a]	
	% of total		% of total
Agriculture	5.0	Private consumption	48.8
Industry, of which:	36.0	Public consumption	16.5
manufacturing	...	Investment	21.1
Services	58.9	Exports	35.0
		Imports	-22.3

Structure of employment

	% of total		% of labour force
Agriculture	10	Unemployed 2004	7.8
Industry	31	Av. ann. rate 1995–2004	10.6
Services	59		

Energy

	m TOE		
Total output	1,106.9	Net energy imports as %	
Total consumption	639.7	of energy use	-73
Consumption per head,			
kg oil equivalent	4,424		

Inflation and finance

Consumer price		av. ann. increase 1999–2004	
inflation 2005	12.7%	Narrow money (M1)	40.1%
Av. ann. inflation 2000–05	14.8%	Broad money	39.8%
Money market rate, 2005	2.68%		

Exchange rates

	end 2005		December 2005
Rb per $	28.78	Effective rates	2000 = 100
Rb per SDR	41.14	– nominal	96.55
Rb per 7	33.86	– real	151.94

Trade

Principal exports		Principal imports	
	$bn fob		*$bn fob*
Fuels	100.0	Machinery & equipment	20.9
Metals	28.9	Food & drink	9.3
Machinery & equipment	12.5	Chemicals	8.3
Chemicals	11.0	Metals	3.7
Total incl. others	**183.2**	Total incl. others	**75.6**

Main export destinations		Main origins of imports	
	% of total		*% of total*
Germany	7.9	Germany	13.0
China	6.1	China	5.8
Netherlands	6.1	Ukraine	5.8
United States	5.7	Italy	5.1

Balance of payments, reserves and debt, $bn

Visible exports fob	183.5	Change in reserves	47.8
Visible imports fob	-96.3	Level of reserves	
Trade balance	87.1	end Dec.	126.3
Invisibles inflows	30.7	No. months of import cover	9.9
Invisibles outflows	-57.1	Official gold holdings, m oz	12.4
Net transfers	0.8	Foreign debt	197.3
Current account balance	59.9	– as % of GDP	45
– as % of GDP	10.3	– as % of total exports	117
Capital balance	-4.9	Debt service ratio	13
Overall balance	46.6		

Health and education

Health spending, % of GDP	5.6	Education spending, % of GDP	3.8
Doctors per 1,000 pop.	4.3	Enrolment, %: primary	118
Hospital beds per 1,000 pop.	10.5	secondary	95
Improved-water source access,		tertiary	69
% of pop.	96		

Society

No. of households	52.9m	Colour TVs per 100 households	75.2
Av. no. per household	2.7	Telephone lines per 100 pop.	27.5
Marriages per 1,000 pop.	4.6	Mobile telephone subscribers	
Divorces per 1,000 pop.	3.0	per 100 pop.	51.6
Cost of living, Dec. 2005		Computers per 100 pop.	13.2
New York = 100	98	Internet hosts per 1,000 pop.	11.4

a   Production based.

SAUDI ARABIA

Area	2,200,000 sq km	Capital	Riyadh
Arable as % of total land	2	Currency	Riyal (SR)

People

Population	24.9m	Life expectancy: men	71.1 yrs
Pop. per sq km	11.3	women	75.1 yrs
Av. ann. growth		Adult literacy	79.4%
in pop. 2000–05	2.69%	Fertility rate (per woman)	4.1
Pop. under 15	37.3%	Urban population	88.5%
Pop. over 60	4.6%		per 1,000 pop.
No. of men per 100 women	117	Crude birth rate	31.5
Human Development Index	77.2	Crude death rate	3.7

The economy

GDP	SR940bn	GDP per head	$10,060
GDP	$251bn	GDP per head in purchasing	
Av. ann. growth in real		power parity (USA=100)	34.8
GDP 1994–2004	2.6%	Economic freedom index	2.84

Origins of GDP		Components of GDP	
	% of total		% of total
Agriculture	4.0	Private consumption	30.1
Industry, of which:	49.2	Public consumption	23.2
manufacturing	5.5	Investment	19.0
Services	46.8	Exports	52.7
		Imports	-24.9

Structure of employment

	% of total		% of labour force
Agriculture	5	Unemployed 2002	5.2
Industry	21	Av. ann. rate 1995–2002	4.4
Services	74		

Energy

	m TOE		
Total output	533.7	Net energy imports as %	
Total consumption	130.8	of energy use	-308
Consumption per head,			
kg oil equivalent	5,607		

Inflation and finance

Consumer price		av. ann. increase 1999–2004	
inflation 2005	0.7%	Narrow money (M1)	11.0%
Av. ann. inflation 2000–05	0.1%	Broad money	10.0%
Deposit rate, 2005	3.75%		

Exchange rates

	end 2005		December 2005
SR per $	3.75	Effective rates	2000 = 100
SR per SDR	5.35	– nominal	93.3
SRE per €	4.41	– real	84.4

Trade

Principal exports	$bn fob	Principal imports	$bn cif
Crude oil & refined petroleum	77.8	Machinery & transport equipment	15.9
Oil products	15.6	Foodstuffs	6.0
Total incl. others	**126.0**	Total incl. others	**38.8**

Main export destinations	% of total	Main origins of imports	% of total
United States	18.5	United States	9.3
Japan	15.2	Germany	7.6
South Korea	10.1	Japan	7.2
China	5.7	United Kingdom	6.1

Balance of payments, reserves and aid, $bn

Visible exports fob	126.1	Overall balance	4.5
Visible imports fob	-40.8	Change in reserves	4.8
Trade balance	85.2	Level of reserves	
Invisibles inflows	9.7	end Dec.	29.3
Invisibles outflows	-29.8	No. months of import cover	5.0
Net transfers	-13.7	Official gold holdings, m oz	4.6
Current account balance	51.5	Aid given	1.73
– as % of GDP	20.5	– as % of GDP	0.69
Capital balance	-47.0		

Health and education

Health spending, % of GDP	4.0	Education spending, % of GDP	...
Doctors per 1,000 pop.	1.4	Enrolment, %: primary	67
Hospital beds per 1,000 pop.	2.2	secondary	67
Improved-water source access, % of pop.	...	tertiary	25

Society

No. of households	4.0m	Colour TVs per 100 households	98.9
Av. no. per household	5.9	Telephone lines per 100 pop.	14.8
Marriages per 1,000 pop.	2.9	Mobile telephone subscribers	
Divorces per 1,000 pop.	...	per 100 pop.	36.8
Cost of living, Dec. 2005		Computers per 100 pop.	34.0
New York = 100	68	Internet hosts per 1,000 pop.	2.5

SINGAPORE

Area	639 sq km	Capital	Singapore
Arable as % of total land	1	Currency	Singapore dollar (S$)

People

Population	4.3m	Life expectancy: men	77.6 yrs
Pop. per sq km	6,729.3	women	81.3 yrs
Av. ann. growth		Adult literacy	92.5%
in pop. 2000–05	1.48%	Fertility rate (per woman)	1.4
Pop. under 15	19.5%	Urban population	100.0%
Pop. over 60	12.2%		per 1,000 pop.
No. of men per 100 women	101	Crude birth rate	10.2
Human Development Index	90.7	Crude death rate	5.5

The economy

GDP	S$181bn	GDP per head	$24,840
GDP	$107bn	GDP per head in purchasing	
Av. ann. growth in real		power parity (USA=100)	70.8
GDP 1994–2004	5.1%	Economic freedom index	1.56

Origins of GDP		Components of GDP	
	% of total		% of total
Agriculture	0	Private consumption	42.2
Industry, of which:	32.9	Public consumption	10.6
manufacturing	27.1	Investment	18.3
Services	67.1	Exports	223.2
		Imports	-193.5

Structure of employment

	% of total		% of labour force
Agriculture	0	Unemployed 2003	5.4
Industry	24	Av. ann. rate 1995–2003	3.8
Services	76		

Energy

	m TOE		
Total output	0.1	Net energy imports as %	
Total consumption	22.4	of energy use	99
Consumption per head,			
kg oil equivalent	5,359		

Inflation and finance

Consumer price		av. ann. increase 1999–2004	
inflation 2005	0.5%	Narrow money (M1)	7.4%
Av. ann. inflation 2000–05	0.6%	Broad money	3.5%
Money market rate, 2005	2.28%		

Exchange rates

	end 2005		December 2005
S$ per $	1.66	Effective rates	2000 = 100
S$ per SDR	2.38	– nominal	100.4
S$ per 7	1.95	– real	93.2

Trade

Principal exports	$bn fob	Principal imports	$bn cif
Machinery & equipment	109.7	Machinery & equipment	96.2
Chemicals	21.0	Petroleum	12.2
Mineral fuels	17.0	Manufactured products	11.0
Manufactured products	6.7	Chemicals	10.6
Food	1.9	Food	3.4
Total incl. others	**180**	Total incl. others	**164**

Main export destinations	% of total	Main origins of imports	% of total
Malaysia	15.2	Malaysia	15.2
United States	12.4	United States	12.5
Hong Kong	9.8	Japan	11.7
China	8.6	China	9.9
Japan	6.4	Taiwan	5.7
Taiwan	4.6	Thailand	4.1
Thailand	4.3	Saudi Arabia	3.4

Balance of payments, reserves and debt, $bn

Visible exports fob	197.3	Change in reserves	16.5
Visible imports fob	166.1	Level of reserves	
Trade balance	31.2	end Dec.	112.2
Invisibles inflows	56.6	No. months of import cover	6.0
Invisibles outflows	-58.8	Official gold holdings, m oz	...
Net transfers	-1.1	Foreign debt	23.6
Current account balance	27.9	– as % of GDP	22
– as % of GDP	26.1	– as % of total exports	9
Capital balance	-13.0	Debt service ratio	2
Overall balance	12.1		

Health and education

Health spending, % of GDP	4.5	Education spending, % of GDP	3.7
Doctors per 1,000 pop.	1.3	Enrolment, %: primary	...
Hospital beds per 1,000 pop.	2.9	secondary	...
Improved-water source access,		tertiary	...
% of pop.	...		

Society

No. of households	1.0m	Colour TVs per 100 households	98.7
Av. no. per household	3.5	Telephone lines per 100 pop.	43.2
Marriages per 1,000 pop.	6.3	Mobile telephone subscribers	
Divorces per 1,000 pop.	1.8	per 100 pop.	89.5
Cost of living, Dec. 2005		Computers per 100 pop.	62.2
New York = 100	103	Internet hosts per 1,000 pop.	187.0

SLOVAKIA

Area	49,035 sq km	Capital	Bratislava
Arable as % of total land	30	Currency	Koruna (Kc)

People

Population	5.4m	Life expectancy: men	71.1 yrs
Pop. per sq km	110.1	women	78.7 yrs
Av. ann. growth		Adult literacy	99.6%
in pop. 2000–05	0.00%	Fertility rate (per woman)	1.2
Pop. under 15	16.7%	Urban population	58.0%
Pop. over 60	16.2%		per 1,000 pop.
No. of men per 100 women	94	Crude birth rate	10.2
Human Development Index	84.9	Crude death rate	9.8

The economy

GDP	Kc1,326bn	GDP per head	$7,610
GDP	$41.1bn	GDP per head in purchasing	
Av. ann. growth in real		power parity (USA=100)	36.9
GDP 1994–2004	4.3%	Economic freedom index	2.35

Origins of GDP

	% of total
Agriculture	3.6
Industry, of which:	29.7
manufacturing	19.0
Services	66.7

Components of GDP

	% of total
Private consumption	56.6
Public consumption	19.4
Investment	24.7
Exports	76.8
Imports	-79.5

Structure of employment

	% of total		% of labour force
Agriculture	6	Unemployed 2004	18.1
Industry	38	Av. ann. rate 1995–2004	15.7
Services	56		

Energy

	m TOE		
Total output	6.4	Net energy imports as %	
Total consumption	18.5	of energy use	65
Consumption per head,			
kg oil equivalent	3,443		

Inflation and finance

Consumer price		av. ann. increase 1999–2004	
inflation 2005	2.7%	Narrow money	21.5
Av. ann. inflation 2000–05	5.9%	Broad money	9.5%
Money market rate, 2005	3.02%	Household saving rate, 2003	6.6%

Exchange rates

	end 2005		December 2005
Kc per $	31.95	Effective rates	2000 = 100
Kc per SDR	45.66	– nominal	113.94
Kc per €	37.59	– real	134.86

Trade

Principal exports		Principal imports	
	$bn fob		*$bn fob*
Machinery & transport equipment	12.7	Machinery & transport equipment	11.6
Semi-manufactures	6.5	Semi-manufactures	5.5
Other manufactured goods	3.1	Fuels	3.7
Chemicals	1.5	Chemicals	2.9
Fuels	1.4		
Total incl. others	**27.6**	Total incl. others	**29.2**

Main export destinations		Main origins of imports	
	% of total		*% of total*
Germany	28.7	United States	23.6
Czech Republic	13.3	United Kingdom	13.1
Austria	7.8	Austria	9.3
Italy	6.4	Denmark	5.6
EU25	85.2	EU25	73.6

Balance of payments, reserves and debt, $bn

Visible exports fob	27.6	Change in reserves	2.8
Visible imports fob	-29.2	Level of reserves	
Trade balance	-1.5	end Dec.	14.9
Invisibles inflows	4.7	No. months of import cover	5.3
Invisibles outflows	-4.8	Official gold holdings, m oz	1.1
Net transfers	0.2	Foreign debt	22.1
Current account balance	-1.5	– as % of GDP	68
– as % of GDP	-3.5	– as % of total exports	87
Capital balance	3.3	Debt service ratio	20
Overall balance	1.7		

Health and education

Health spending, % of GDP	5.9	Education spending, % of GDP	4.4
Doctors per 1,000 pop.	3.2	Enrolment, %: primary	101
Hospital beds per 1,000 pop.	7.2	secondary	92
Improved-water source access, % of pop.	100	tertiary	34

Society

No. of households	2.1m	Colour TVs per 100 households	84.0
Av. no. per household	2.5	Telephone lines per 100 pop.	23.2
Marriages per 1,000 pop.	4.8	Mobile telephone subscribers	
Divorces per 1,000 pop.	1.7	per 100 pop.	79.4
Cost of living, Dec. 2005		Computers per 100 pop.	29.6
New York = 100	...	Internet hosts per 1,000 pop.	59.8

SLOVENIA

Area	20,253 sq km	Capital	Ljubljana
Arable as % of total land	9	Currency	Tolars (SIT)

People

Population	2.0m	Life expectancy: men		73.5 yrs
Pop. per sq km	98.8	women		80.7 yrs
Av. ann. growth		Adult literacy		99.7%
in pop. 2000–05	0.00%	Fertility rate (per woman)		1.2
Pop. under 15	13.9%	Urban population		50.8%
Pop. over 60	20.5%			per 1,000 pop.
No. of men per 100 women	95	Crude birth rate		8.3
Human Development Index	90.4	Crude death rate		10.4

The economy

GDP	SIT6,191bn	GDP per head	$16,090
GDP	$32.2bn	GDP per head in purchasing	
Av. ann. growth in real		power parity (USA=100)	52.8
GDP 1994–2004	3.8%	Economic freedom index	2.41

Origins of GDP		**Components of GDP**	
	% of total		% of total
Agriculture	2.7	Private consumption	54.0
Industry, of which:	38.2	Public consumption	19.8
manufacturing	29.0	Investment	26.8
Services	59.1	Exports	59.9
		Imports	-60.5

Structure of employment

	% of total		% of labour force
Agriculture	8	Unemployed 2004	6.1
Industry	38	Av. ann. rate 1995–2004	6.9
Services	54		

Energy

	m TOE		
Total output	3.3	Net energy imports as %	
Total consumption	7.0	of energy use	53
Consumption per head,			
kg oil equivalent	3,518		

Inflation and finance

Consumer price		av. ann. increase 1999–2004	
inflation 2005	2.5%	Narrow money (M1)	22.0%
Av. ann. inflation 2000–05	5.5%	Broad money	14.6%
Money market rate, 2005	3.73%		

Exchange rates

	end 2005		December 2005
SIT per $	202.4	Effective rates	2000 = 100
SIT per SDR	289.3	– nominal	...
SIT per €	238.2	– real	...

Trade

Principal exports		Principal imports	
	$bn fob		*$bn fob*
Manufactures	6.6	Machinery & transport	
Machinery & transport		equipment	5.8
equipment	5.9	Manufactures	5.7
Chemicals	2.1	Chemicals	2.2
Food & live animals	0.3	Mineral fuels	1.4
Total incl. others	**15.6**	Total incl. others	**17.2**

Main export destinations		Main origins of imports	
	% of total		*% of total*
Germany	21.2	Germany	19.9
Italy	12.9	Italy	18.6
Croatia	9.2	Austria	12.9
Austria	7.4	France	8.1
France	6.4	Croatia	3.7
EU25	67.3	EU25	82.6

Balance of payments, reserves and debt, $bn

Visible exports fob	16.1	Change in reserves	0.3
Visible imports fob	-17.3	Level of reserves	
Trade balance	-1.3	end Dec.	8.9
Invisibles inflows	4.2	No. months of import cover	5.1
Invisibles outflows	-3.6	Official gold holdings, m oz	0.2
Net transfers	0.0	Foreign debt	14.8
Current account balance	-0.7	– as % of GDP	46
– as % of GDP	-2.1	– as % of total exports	73
Capital balance	0.5	Debt service ratio	15
Overall balance	-0.3		

Health and education

Health spending, % of GDP	8.8	Education spending, % of GDP	6.1
Doctors per 1,000 pop.	2.2	Enrolment, %: primary	108
Hospital beds per 1,000 pop.	5.0	secondary	109
Improved-water source access,		tertiary	68
% of pop.	...		

Society

No. of households	0.7m	Colour TVs per 100 households	92.6
Av. no. per household	2.9	Telephone lines per 100 pop.	40.7
Marriages per 1,000 pop.	3.5	Mobile telephone subscribers	
Divorces per 1,000 pop.	1.0	per 100 pop.	100.5
Cost of living, Dec. 2005		Computers per 100 pop.	35.5
New York = 100	...	Internet hosts per 1,000 pop.	30.7

SOUTH AFRICA

Area	1,225,815 sq km	Capital	Pretoria
Arable as % of total land	12	Currency	Rand (R)

People

Population	45.2m	Life expectancy:	men	44.2 yrs
Pop. per sq km	36.9		women	43.8 yrs
Av. ann. growth		Adult literacy		82.4%
in pop. 2000–05	0.78%	Fertility rate (per woman)		2.8
Pop. under 15	32.6%	Urban population		57.9%
Pop. over 60	6.8%		*per 1,000 pop.*	
No. of men per 100 women	96	Crude birth rate		22.6
Human Development Index	65.8	Crude death rate		20.6

The economy

GDP	R1,375bn	GDP per head	$4,710
GDP	$213bn	GDP per head in purchasing	
Av. ann. growth in real		power parity (USA=100)	28.2
GDP 1994–2004	3.0%	Economic freedom index	2.74

Origins of GDP		**Components of GDP**	
	% of total		*% of total*
Agriculture	3.6	Private consumption	63.3
Industry, of which:	31.9	Public consumption	19.6
manufacturing	20.0	Investment	18.9
Services	64.5	Exports	26.6
		Imports	-28.4

Structure of employment

	% of total		*% of labour force*
Agriculture	10	Unemployed 2004	27.1
Industry	25	Av. ann. rate 1995–2004	24.1
Services	65		

Energy

	m TOE		
Total output	154.5	Net energy imports as %	
Total consumption	118.6	of energy use	-30
Consumption per head,			
kg oil equivalent	2,587		

Inflation and finance

		av. ann. increase 1999–2004	
Consumer price			
inflation 2005	4.0%	Narrow money (M1)	10.3%
Av. ann. inflation 2000–05	5.1%	Broad money	14.5%
Money market rate, 2005	6.62%		

Exchange rates

	end 2005		*December 2005*
R per $	6.33	Effective rates	*2000 = 100*
R per SDR	9.04	– nominal	111.9
R per €	7.45	– real	113.8

Trade

Principal exports		**Principal imports**	
	$bn fob		*$bn cif*
Manufactures	26.7	Manufactures	39.4
Ores & metals	10.1	Fuels	8.0
Food	4.1	Food	2.9
Fuels	4.1		
Total incl. others	**46.0**	Total incl. others	**57.1**

Main export destinations		**Main origins of imports**	
	% of total		*% of total*
United States	10.1	Germany	13.5
United Kingdom	9.1	United States	8.0
Japan	8.8	United Kingdom	7.2
Germany	7.0	Japan	6.5

Balance of payments, reserves and debt, $bn

Visible exports fob	48.4	Change in reserves	6.7
Visible imports fob	-48.5	Level of reserves	
Trade balance	-0.1	end Dec.	14.9
Invisibles inflows	11.5	No. months of import cover	2.7
Invisibles outflows	-16.9	Official gold holdings, m oz	4.0
Net transfers	-1.5	Foreign debt	28.5
Current account balance	-7.0	– as % of GDP	18
– as % of GDP	-3.2	– as % of total exports	58
Capital balance	10.4	Debt service ratio	8
Overall balance	8.5		

Health and education

Health spending, % of GDP	8.4	Education spending, % of GDP	5.3
Doctors per 1,000 pop.	0.8	Enrolment, %: primary	106
Hospital beds per 1,000 pop.	...	secondary	89
Improved-water source access,		tertiary	15
% of pop.	87		

Society

No. of households	12.2m	Colour TVs per 100 households	65.6
Av. no. per household	3.9	Telephone lines per 100 pop.	10.4
Marriages per 1,000 pop.	4.4	Mobile telephone subscribers	
Divorces per 1,000 pop.	1.0	per 100 pop.	43.1
Cost of living, Dec. 2005		Computers per 100 pop.	8.3
New York = 100	74	Internet hosts per 1,000 pop.	11.0

SOUTH KOREA

Area	99,274 sq km	Capital	Seoul
Arable as % of total land	17	Currency	Won (W)

People

Population	48.0m	Life expectancy:	men	74.5 yrs
Pop. per sq km	483.5		women	81.9 yrs
Av. ann. growth		Adult literacy		97.9%
in pop. 2000–05	0.4%	Fertility rate (per woman)		1.2
Pop. under 15	18.6%	Urban population		80.8%
Pop. over 60	13.7%			per 1,000 pop.
No. of men per 100 women	101	Crude birth rate		11.9
Human Development Index	90.1	Crude death rate		6.0

The economy

GDP	W778trn	GDP per head	$14,160
GDP	$680bn	GDP per head in purchasing	
Av. ann. growth in real		power parity (USA=100)	51.7
GDP 1994–2004	4.9%	Economic freedom index	2.63

Origins of GDP		Components of GDP	
	% of total		% of total
Agriculture	4	Private consumption	53.2
Industry, of which:	41	Public consumption	12.5
manufacturing	29	Investment	30.7
Services	56	Exports	51.6
		Imports	-48.1

Structure of employment

	% of total		% of labour force
Agriculture	8	Unemployed 2004	3.7
Industry	28	Av. ann. rate 1995–2004	3.8
Services	64		

Energy

	m TOE		
Total output	36.9	Net energy imports as %	
Total consumption	205.3	of energy use	82
Consumption per head,			
kg oil equivalent	4,291		

Inflation and finance

Consumer price		av. ann. increase 1999–2004	
inflation 2005	2.7%	Narrow money (M1)	9.0%
Av. ann. inflation 2000–05	3.3%	Broad money	10.8%
Money market rate, 2005	3.33%	Household saving rate, 2004	5.1%

Exchange rates

	end 2005		December 2005
W per $	1,012	Effective rates	2000 = 100
W per SDR	1,446	– nominal	...
W per €	1,190	– real	...

Trade

Principal exports		Principal imports	
	$bn fob		*$bn cif*
Electronic products	87.8	Electrical machinery	50.0
Motor vehicles	24.6	Crude petroleum	29.9
Machinery	22.6	Machinery & equipment	28.2
Chemicals	20.5	Semiconductors	23.6
Metal goods	18.6	Consumer durables	11.6
Total incl. others	**253.8**	Total incl. others	**224.5**

Main export destinations		Main origins of imports	
	% of total		*% of total*
China	19.6	Japan	20.6
United States	16.9	China	13.2
Japan	8.5	United States	12.8
Hong Kong	7.1	Saudi Arabia	5.3
Taiwan	3.9	Germany	3.8

Balance of payments, reserves and debt, $bn

Visible exports fob	257.7	Change in reserves	43.7
Visible imports fob	-219.6	Level of reserves	
Trade balance	38.2	end Dec.	199.2
Invisibles inflows	51.1	No. months of import cover	8.6
Invisibles outflows	-58.2	Official gold holdings, m oz	0.5
Net transfers	-2.5	Foreign debt	144.8
Current account balance	27.6	– as % of GDP	21
– as % of GDP	4.1	– as % of total exports	47
Capital balance	8.3	Debt service ratio	6
Overall balance	38.7		

Health and education

Health spending, % of GDP	5.6	Education spending, % of GDP	4.9
Doctors per 1,000 pop.	1.6	Enrolment, %: primary	106
Hospital beds per 1,000 pop.	7.1	secondary	91
Improved-water source access,		tertiary	85
% of pop.	92		

Society

No. of households	17.0m	Colour TVs per 100 households	93.6
Av. no. per household	2.8	Telephone lines per 100 pop.	55.3
Marriages per 1,000 pop.	6.3	Mobile telephone subscribers	
Divorces per 1,000 pop.	3.5	per 100 pop.	76.1
Cost of living, Dec. 2005		Computers per 100 pop.	54.5
New York = 100	110	Internet hosts per 1,000 pop.	5.2

SPAIN

Area	504,782 sq km	Capital	Madrid
Arable as % of total land	28	Currency	Euro (€)

People

Population	41.1m	Life expectancy: men	76.5 yrs
Pop. per sq km	81.4	women	83.8 yrs
Av. ann. growth		Adult literacy	97.9%
in pop. 2000–05	1.12%	Fertility rate (per woman)	1.3
Pop. under 15	14.3%	Urban population	76.7%
Pop. over 60	21.4%		per 1,000 pop.
No. of men per 100 women	96	Crude birth rate	9.3
Human Development Index	92.8	Crude death rate	9.1

The economy

GDP	€838bn	GDP per head	$25,300
GDP	$1,040bn	GDP per head in purchasing	
Av. ann. growth in real		power parity (USA=100)	63.1
GDP 1994–2004	3.4%	Economic freedom index	2.33

Origins of GDP		Components of GDP	
	% of total		% of total
Agriculture	3.5	Private consumption	57.7
Industry, of which:	30.1	Public consumption	17.8
manufacturing	...	Investment	28.3
Services	66.4	Exports	25.9
		Imports	-29.7

Structure of employment

	% of total		% of labour force
Agriculture	5	Unemployed 2004	11.0
Industry	31	Av. ann. rate 1995–2004	16.2
Services	64		

Energy

	m TOE		
Total output	33.0	Net energy imports as %	
Total consumption	136.1	of energy use	76
Consumption per head,			
kg oil equivalent	3,240		

Inflation and finance

Consumer price		av. ann. increase 1999–2004	
inflation 2005	3.4%	Euro area:	
Av. ann. inflation 2000–05	3.2%	Narrow money (M1)	8.4%
Money market rate, 2005	2.09%	Broad money	6.9%
		Household saving rate, 2004	7.2%

Exchange rates

	end 2005		December 2005
€ per $	0.85	Effective rates	2000 = 100
€ per SDR	1.21	– nominal	104.9
		– real	115.1

Trade

Principal exports		Principal imports	
	$bn fob		*$bn cif*
Raw materials &		Raw materials & intermediate	
intermediate products	80.5	products (excl. fuels)	113.4
Consumer goods	71.6	Consumer goods	73.7
Capital goods	23.4	Capital goods	42.0
Total incl. others	**182.2**	Total incl. others	**257.8**

Main export destinations		Main origins of imports	
	% of total		*% of total*
France	19.4	Germany	16.1
Germany	11.7	France	15.2
Italy	9.0	Italy	9.1
United Kingdom	9.0	United Kingdom	6.1
United States	4.0	United States	3.6
EU25	73.4	EU25	67.7

Balance of payments, reserves and aid, $bn

Visible exports fob	184.3	Overall balance	-6.4
Visible imports fob	-248.8	Change in reserves	-7.1
Trade balance	-64.5	Level of reserves	
Invisibles inflows	114.2	end Dec.	19.8
Invisibles outflows	-98.9	No. months of import cover	0.7
Net transfers	0.0	Official gold holdings, m oz	16.8
Current account balance	-49.2	Aid given	2.44
– as % of GDP	-4.7	– as % of GDP	0.24
Capital balance	50.0		

Health and education

Health spending, % of GDP	7.7	Education spending, % of GDP	4.5
Doctors per 1,000 pop.	3.3	Enrolment, %: primary	108
Hospital beds per 1,000 pop.	3.8	secondary	117
Improved-water source access,		tertiary	62
% of pop.	...		

Society

No. of households	15.0m	Colour TVs per 100 households	98.5
Av. no. per household	2.7	Telephone lines per 100 pop.	41.5
Marriages per 1,000 pop.	5.0	Mobile telephone subscribers	
Divorces per 1,000 pop.	0.8	per 100 pop.	86.5
Cost of living, Dec. 2005		Computers per 100 pop.	25.4
New York = 100	95	Internet hosts per 1,000 pop.	59.8

SWEDEN

Area	449,964 sq km	Capital	Stockholm
Arable as % of total land	7	Currency	Swedish krona (Skr)

People

Population	8.9m	Life expectancy: men	78.6 yrs
Pop. per sq km	19.8	women	83.0 yrs
Av. ann. growth		Adult literacy	99.0%
in pop. 2000–05	0.37%	Fertility rate (per woman)	1.6
Pop. under 15	17.5%	Urban population	83.4%
Pop. over 60	23.4%		per 1,000 pop.
No. of men per 100 women	98	Crude birth rate	10.3
Human Development Index	94.9	Crude death rate	10.1

The economy

GDP	Skr2,546bn	GDP per head	$38,920
GDP	$346bn	GDP per head in purchasing	
Av. ann. growth in real		power parity (USA=100)	74.5
GDP 1994–2004	2.8%	Economic freedom index	1.96

Origins of GDP

	% of total
Agriculture	1.9
Industry, of which:	27.9
manufacturing	21.0
Services	70.2

Components of GDP

	% of total
Private consumption	47.8
Public consumption	26.9
Investment	17.7
Exports	48.5
Imports	-40.9

Structure of employment

	% of total		% of labour force
Agriculture	2	Unemployed 2004	5.5
Industry	23	Av. ann. rate 1995–2004	5.9
Services	75		

Energy

	m TOE		
Total output	31.7	Net energy imports as %	
Total consumption	51.5	of energy use	39
Consumption per head,			
kg oil equivalent	5,754		

Inflation and finance

Consumer price		av. ann. increase 2001–04	
inflation 2005	0.5%	Narrow money	9.3%
Av. ann. inflation 2000–05	1.5%	Broad money	3.4%
Repurchase rate, end-2005	1.50%	Household saving rate, 2004	8.6%

Exchange rates

	end 2005		December 2005
Skr per $	7.96	Effective rates	2000 = 100
Skr per SDR	11.37	– nominal	95.6
Skr per €	9.36	– real	91.4

Trade

Principal exports		**Principal imports**	
	$bn fob		*$bn cif*
Machinery & transport		Machinery & transport	
equipment	63.0	equipment	45.5
Wood & paper products	15.0	Miscellaneous manufactures	19.6
Chemicals	14.8	Chemicals	12.1
Manufactured goods	13.5	Mineral fuels	9.6
Total incl. others	**123**	Total incl. others	**101**

Main export destinations		**Main origins of imports**	
	% of total		*% of total*
United States	10.7	Germany	18.9
Germany	10.2	Denmark	9.2
Norway	8.5	United Kingdom	7.7
United Kingdom	7.9	Norway	7.6
Denmark	6.6	Netherlands	6.8
EU25	58.8	EU25	73.1

Balance of payments, reserves and aid, $bn

Visible exports fob	125.2	Overall balance	-1.1
Visible imports fob	-101.8	Change in reserves	2.6
Trade balance	23.4	Level of reserves	
Invisibles inflows	67.5	end Dec.	24.7
Invisibles outflows	-58.6	No. months of import cover	1.9
Net transfers	-4.8	Official gold holdings, m oz	6.0
Current account balance	27.5	Aid given	2.72
– as % of GDP	7.9	– as % of GDP	0.78
Capital balance	-34.7		

Health and education

Health spending, % of GDP	9.4	Education spending, % of GDP	7.7
Doctors per 1,000 pop.	3.3	Enrolment, %: primary	111
Hospital beds per 1,000 pop.	3.6	secondary	139
Improved-water source access,		tertiary	83
% of pop.	100		

Society

No. of households	4.2m	Colour TVs per 100 households	97.1
Av. no. per household	2.1	Telephone lines per 100 pop.	71.5
Marriages per 1,000 pop.	4.1	Mobile telephone subscribers	
Divorces per 1,000 pop.	2.1	per 100 pop.	108.5
Cost of living, Dec. 2005		Computers per 100 pop.	76.1
New York = 100	105	Internet hosts per 1,000 pop.	316.5

SWITZERLAND

Area	41,293 sq km	Capital	Berne
Arable as % of total land	10	Currency	Swiss franc (SFr)

People

Population	7.2m	Life expectancy: men	78.2 yrs
Pop. per sq km	174.4	women	83.8 yrs
Av. ann. growth		Adult literacy	86.0%
in pop. 2000–05	0.24%	Fertility rate (per woman)	1.4
Pop. under 15	16.5%	Urban population	67.5%
Pop. over 60	21.8%		per 1,000 pop.
No. of men per 100 women	94	Crude birth rate	8.7
Human Development Index	94.7	Crude death rate	8.8

The economy

GDP	SFr445bn	GDP per head	$49,660
GDP	$358bn	GDP per head in purchasing	
Av. ann. growth in real		power parity (USA=100)	83.3
GDP 1994–2004	1.4%	Economic freedom index	1.89

Origins of GDP[a]		Components of GDP	
	% of total		% of total
Agriculture	1	Private consumption	60.5
Industry, of which:	29	Public consumption	11.9
manufacturing	20	Investment	20.1
Services	70	Exports	46.2
		Imports	-38.8

Structure of employment

	% of total		% of labour force
Agriculture	4	Unemployed 2004	4.3
Industry	24	Av. ann. rate 1995–2004	3.4
Services	72		

Energy

	m TOE		
Total output	12.0	Net energy imports as %	
Total consumption	27.1	of energy use	56
Consumption per head,			
kg oil equivalent	3,689		

Inflation and finance

Consumer price		av. ann. increase 1999–2004	
inflation 2005	1.2%	Narrow money (M1)	6.5%
Av. ann. inflation 2000–05	0.8%	Broad money	0.3%
Money market rate, 2005	0.63%	Household saving rate, 2004	8.9%

Exchange rates

	end 2005		December 2005
SFr per $	1.31	Effective rates	2000 = 100
SFr per SDR	1.88	– nominal	107.5
SFr per €	1.54	– real	115.1

Trade

Principal exports	$bn	Principal imports	$bn
Chemicals	39.9	Chemicals	23.8
Machinery	27.0	Machinery	22.0
Watches & jewellery	9.0	Motor vehicles	10.9
Metals & metal manufactures	8.9	Textiles	7.0
Precision instruments	8.1	Precision instruments	6.6
Total incl. others	**114**	Total incl. others	**107**

Main export destinations	% of total	Main origins of imports	% of total
Germany	20.6	Germany	33.9
United States	10.1	Italy	11.7
France	8.6	France	10.1
Italy	8.5	Netherlands	5.2
United Kingdom	4.8	Austria	4.4
Spain	4.1	United States	4.3
EU25	59.5	EU25	81.1

Balance of payments, reserves and aid, $bn

Visible exports fob	138.2	Overall balance	1.6
Visible imports fob	-122.5	Change in reserves	5.0
Trade balance	15.7	Level of reserves	
Invisibles inflows	114.9	end Dec.	74.6
Invisibles outflows	-64.4	No. months of import cover	4.8
Net transfers	-6.0	Official gold holdings, m oz	43.5
Current account balance	60.2	Aid given	1.55
– as % of GDP	16.9	– as % of GDP	0.41
Capital balance	-67.8		

Health and education

Health spending, % of GDP	11.5	Education spending, % of GDP	5.8
Doctors per 1,000 pop.	3.6	Enrolment, %: primary	108
Hospital beds per 1,000 pop.	6.0	secondary	98
Improved-water source access,		tertiary	49
% of pop.	100		

Society

No. of households	3.3m	Colour TVs per 100 households	96.9
Av. no. per household	2.2	Telephone lines per 100 pop.	71.0
Marriages per 1,000 pop.	4.5	Mobile telephone subscribers	
Divorces per 1,000 pop.	2.8	per 100 pop.	84.6
Cost of living, Dec. 2005		Computers per 100 pop.	82.3
New York = 100	116	Internet hosts per 1,000 pop.	295.2

a Latest available.

TAIWAN

Area	36,179 sq km	Capital	Taipei
Arable as % of total land	25	Currency	Taiwan dollar (T$)

People

Population	22.7m	Life expectancy:[a] men	74.5 yrs
Pop. per sq km	627.4	women	80.3 yrs
Av. ann. growth		Adult literacy	96.1
in pop. 2000–05	0.60%	Fertility rate (per woman)	1.6
Pop. under 15	21.0%	Urban population	...
Pop. over 60	12.1%		per 1,000 pop.
No. of men per 100 women	104	Crude birth rate	13
Human Development Index	...	Crude death rate[a]	6.4

The economy

GDP	T$10,206bn	GDP per head	$13,450
GDP	$305bn	GDP per head in purchasing	
Av. ann. growth in real		power parity (USA=100)	68.3
GDP 1994–2004	4.5%	Economic freedom index	2.38

Origins of GDP		Components of GDP	
	% of total		% of total
Agriculture	1.7	Private consumption	63.0
Industry, of which:	29.5	Public consumption	12.5
manufacturing	25.5	Investment	20.7
Services	68.7	Exports	65.8
		Imports	-62.0

Structure of employment

	% of total		% of labour force
Agriculture	8	Unemployed 2004	4.4
Industry	36	Av. ann. rate 1995–2004	3.3
Services	56		

Energy

	m TOE		
Total output	...	Net energy imports as %	
Total consumption	...	of energy use	...
Consumption per head,			
kg oil equivalent	...		

Inflation and finance

Consumer price		av. ann. increase 1999–2004	
inflation 2005	2.3%	Narrow money (M1)	10.3%
Av. ann. inflation 2000–05	0.7%	Broad money	5.3%
Money market rate, 2005	1.45%		

Exchange rates

	end 2005		December 2005
T$ per $	32.95	Effective rates	2000 = 100
T$ per SDR	47.78	– nominal	...
T$ per €	38.76	– real	...

Trade

Principal exports		Principal imports	
	$bn fob		*$bn cif*
Machinery & electrical equipment	87.9	Machinery & electrical equipment	66.2
Base metals & manufactures	18.3	Minerals	23.0
Plastics and rubber products	12.5	Metals	18.4
Textiles & clothing	12.5	Chemicals	17.6
Vehicles, aircraft & ships	6.5	Precision instruments, clocks & watches	12.5
Total incl. others	**174.0**	Total incl. others	**167.9**

Main export destinations		Main origins of imports	
	% of total		*% of total*
China	19.6	Japan	26.0
Hong Kong	17.1	United States	12.9
United States	16.2	China	9.9
Japan	7.6	South Korea	6.9

Balance of payments, reserves and debt, $bn

Visible exports fob	173.2	Change in reserves	35.1
Visible imports fob	-157.0	Level of reserves	
Trade balance	16.1	end Dec.	242.5
Invisibles inflows	41.1	No. months of import cover	15.2
Invisibles outflows	-34.7	Official gold holdings, m oz	0.0
Net transfers	-3.8	Foreign debt	81.9
Current account balance	18.7	– as % of GDP	25
– as % of GDP	6.1	– as % of total exports	38
Capital balance	6.8	Debt service ratio	3
Overall balance	26.6		

Health and education

Health spending, % of GDP	...	Education spending, % of GDP	...
Doctors per 1,000 pop.	...	Enrolment, %: primary	...
Hospital beds per 1,000 pop.	...	secondary	...
Improved-water source access, % of pop.	...	tertiary	...

Society

No. of households	7.0m	Colour TVs per 100 households	99.4
Av. no. per household	3.2	Telephone lines per 100 pop.	59.6
Marriages per 1,000 pop.	7.2	Mobile telephone subscribers	
Divorces per 1,000 pop.	1.9	per 100 pop.	100.3
Cost of living, Dec. 2005		Computers per 100 pop.	52.8
New York = 100	88	Internet hosts per 1,000 pop.	173.7

a   2002 estimate.

THAILAND

Area	513,115 sq km	Capital	Bangkok
Arable as % of total land	28	Currency	Baht (Bt)

People

Population	63.5m	Life expectancy:	men	68.5 yrs
Pop. per sq km	123.8		women	75.0 yrs
Av. ann. growth		Adult literacy		92.6%
in pop. 2000–05	0.89%	Fertility rate (per woman)		1.9
Pop. under 15	23.8%	Urban population		32.5%
Pop. over 60	10.5%			per 1,000 pop.
No. of men per 100 women	96	Crude birth rate		17.3
Human Development Index	77.8	Crude death rate		7.2

The economy

GDP	Bt6,504bn	GDP per head	$2,550
GDP	$162bn	GDP per head in purchasing	
Av. ann. growth in real		power parity (USA=100)	20.4
GDP 1994–2004	3.2%	Economic freedom index	2.99

Origins of GDP		**Components of GDP**	
	% of total		% of total
Agriculture	9.9	Private consumption	55.7
Industry, of which:	44.1	Public consumption	10.9
manufacturing	35.2	Investment	27.1
Services	46.0	Exports	70.0
		Imports	-65.0

Structure of employment

	% of total		% of labour force
Agriculture	45	Unemployed 2004	1.5
Industry	20	Av. ann. rate 1995–2004	1.9
Services	35		

Energy

	m TOE		
Total output	48.3	Net energy imports as %	
Total consumption	88.8	of energy use	46
Consumption per head,			
kg oil equivalent	1,406		

Inflation and finance

Consumer price		av. ann. increase 1999–2004	
inflation 2005	4.5%	Narrow money (M1)	5.1%
Av. ann. inflation 2000–05	2.3%	Broad money	3.8%
Money market rate, 2005	2.62%		

Exchange rates

	end 2005		December 2005
Bt per $	41.03	Effective rates	2000 = 100
Bt per SDR	58.64	– nominal	...
Bt per €	48.27	– real	...

Trade

Principal exports		Principal imports	
	$bn fob		*$bn cif*
Machinery & mech. appliances	13.0	Capital goods	40.8
Integrated circuits	12.7	Raw materials & intermediates	26.5
Computer parts	9.0	Petroleum & products	10.2
Electrical appliances	8.5	Consumer goods	8.9
Total incl. others	**96.2**	Total incl. others	**94.4**

Main export destinations		Main origins of imports	
	% of total		*% of total*
United States	15.9	Japan	23.6
Japan	13.9	China	8.6
Singapore	7.2	United States	7.6
China	7.1	Malaysia	5.8
Hong Kong	5.1	Singapore	4.4

Balance of payments, reserves and debt, $bn

Visible exports fob	96.1	Change in reserves	7.7
Visible imports fob	-85.0	Level of reserves	
Trade balance	11.1	end Dec.	49.8
Invisibles inflows	22.2	No. months of import cover	5.3
Invisibles outflows	-28.4	Official gold holdings, m oz	2.7
Net transfers	2.1	Foreign debt	51.3
Current account balance	7.1	– as % of GDP	36
– as % of GDP	4.4	– as % of total exports	52
Capital balance	0.7	Debt service ratio	12
Overall balance	5.7		

Health and education

Health spending, % of GDP	3.3	Education spending, % of GDP	4.6
Doctors per 1,000 pop.	0.4	Enrolment, %: primary	97
Hospital beds per 1,000 pop.	...	secondary	77
Improved-water source access,		tertiary	39
% of pop.	85		

Society

No. of households	16.9m	Colour TVs per 100 households	83.9
Av. no. per household	3.6	Telephone lines per 100 pop.	11.0
Marriages per 1,000 pop.	6.5	Mobile telephone subscribers	
Divorces per 1,000 pop.	1.0	per 100 pop.	44.2
Cost of living, Dec. 2005		Computers per 100 pop.	6.0
New York = 100	61	Internet hosts per 1,000 pop.	12.4

TURKEY

Area	779,452 sq km	Capital	Ankara
Arable as % of total land	30	Currency	Turkish Lira (YTL)[a]

People

Population	72.3m	Life expectancy: men	67.5 yrs
Pop. per sq km	92.8	women	72.1 yrs
Av. ann. growth		Adult literacy	97.7%
in pop. 2000–05	1.40%	Fertility rate (per woman)	2.5
Pop. under 15	29.2%	Urban population	67.3%
Pop. over 60	8.0%		per 1,000 pop.
No. of men per 100 women	102	Crude birth rate	20.9
Human Development Index	75.0	Crude death rate	6.6

The economy

GDP	YTL431bn	GDP per head	$4,190
GDP	$303bn	GDP per head in purchasing	
Av. ann. growth in real		power parity (USA=100)	19.5
GDP 1994–2004	4.1%	Economic freedom index	3.11

Origins of GDP		Components of GDP	
	% of total		% of total
Agriculture	11.3	Private consumption	66.6
Industry, of which:	28.6	Public consumption	13.3
manufacturing	...	Investment	26.0
Services	60.1	Exports	29.1
		Imports	-35.0

Structure of employment

	% of total		% of labour force
Agriculture	34	Unemployed 2004	10.3
Industry	23	Av. ann. rate 1995–2004	8.2
Services	43		

Energy

	m TOE		
Total output	23.6	Net energy imports as %	
Total consumption	79.0	of energy use	70
Consumption per head,			
kg oil equivalent	1,117		

Inflation and finance

Consumer price		av. ann. increase 1999–2004	
inflation 2005	8.2%	Narrow money (M1)	41.6%
Av. ann. inflation 2000–05	26.9%	Broad money	36.4%
Money market rate, 2005	14.73%		

Exchange rates[a]

	end 2005		December 2005
YTL per $	1.35	Effective rates	2000 = 100
YTL per SDR	1.92	– nominal	...
YTL per €	1.59	– real	...

Trade

Principal exports		**Principal imports**	
	$bn fob		*$bn cif*
Textiles	17.8	Chemicals & products	15.1
Motor vehicles & parts	8.8	Motor vehicles & parts	11.7
Metals	6.8	Metals	11.1
Machinery & equipment	3.9	Machinery & equipment	10.4
Total incl. others	**63.2**	Total incl. others	**97.5**

Main export destinations		**Main origins of imports**	
	% of total		*% of total*
Germany	13.9	Germany	12.9
United Kingdom	8.8	Russia	9.3
United States	7.7	Italy	7.1
Italy	7.3	France	6.4
France	5.8	United States	4.8
EU25	54.6	EU25	46.7

Balance of payments, reserves and debt, $bn

Visible exports fob	67.0	Change in reserves	1.8
Visible imports fob	-90.9	Level of reserves	
Trade balance	-23.9	end Dec.	37.3
Invisibles inflows	26.7	No. months of import cover	4.1
Invisibles outflows	-19.4	Official gold holdings, m oz	3.7
Net transfers	1.1	Foreign debt	161.6
Current account balance	-15.5	– as % of GDP	67
– as % of GDP	-5.1	– as % of total exports	213
Capital balance	17.0	Debt service ratio	45
Overall balance	4.3		

Health and education

Health spending, % of GDP	7.6	Education spending, % of GDP	3.6
Doctors per 1,000 pop.	1.3	Enrolment, %: primary	91
Hospital beds per 1,000 pop.	2.6	secondary	79
Improved-water source access,		tertiary	28
% of pop.	93		

Society

No. of households	15.1m	Colour TVs per 100 households	68.0
Av. no. per household	4.7	Telephone lines per 100 pop.	26.5
Marriages per 1,000 pop.	8.5	Mobile telephone subscribers	
Divorces per 1,000 pop.	0.6	per 100 pop.	48.0
Cost of living, Dec. 2005		Computers per 100 pop.	5.1
New York = 100	88	Internet hosts per 1,000 pop.	11.0

a   On January 1 2005 the currency dropped six noughts; L1,000,000 = YTL 1.

UKRAINE

Area	603,700 sq km	Capital	Kiev
Arable as % of total land	56	Currency	Hryvnya (UAH)

People

Population	48.2m	Life expectancy:	men	60.7 yrs
Pop. per sq km	79.8		women	72.5 yrs
Av. ann. growth		Adult literacy		99.4%
in pop. 2000–05	-1.10%	Fertility rate (per woman)		1.1
Pop. under 15	14.9%	Urban population		67.3%
Pop. over 60	20.9%			per 1,000 pop.
No. of men per 100 women	85	Crude birth rate		8.4
Human Development Index	76.6	Crude death rate		16.9

The economy

GDP	UAH345bn	GDP per head	$1,340
GDP	$64.8bn	GDP per head in purchasing	
Av. ann. growth in real		power parity (USA=100)	16.1
GDP 1994–2004	1.1%	Economic freedom index	3.24

Origins of GDP		**Components of GDP**	
	% of total		% of total
Agriculture	12	Private consumption	66.5
Industry, of which:	37	Public consumption	6.9
manufacturing	23	Investment	18.8
Services	51	Exports	60.9
		Imports	-53.8

Structure of employment

	% of total		% of labour force
Agriculture	19	Unemployed 2004	8.6
Industry	30	Av. ann. rate 1995–2004	9.6
Services	51		

Energy

	m TOE		
Total output	75.5	Net energy imports as %	
Total consumption	132.6	of energy use	43
Consumption per head,			
kg oil equivalent	2,772		

Inflation and finance

		av. ann. increase 1999–2004	
Consumer price			
inflation 2005	13.5%	Narrow money (M1)	36.9%
Av. ann. inflation 2000–05	8.0%	Broad money	41.8%
Money market rate, 2005	4.16%		

Exchange rates

	end 2005		December 2005
UAH per $	5.05	Effective rates	2000 = 100
UAII per SDR	7.22	– nominal	103.17
UAH per €	5.94	– real	112.35

Trade

Principal exports		**Principal imports**	
	$bn fob		*$bn cif*
Metals	13.0	Fuels, mineral products	10.7
Machinery & equipment	5.5	Machinery & equipment	7.8
Fuels & mineral products	4.1	Chemicals	2.3
Food & agricultural produce	3.5	Food & agricultural produce	1.9
Chemicals	2.8		
Total incl. others	**32.7**	Total incl. others	**29.0**

Main export destinations		**Main origins of imports**	
	% of total		*% of total*
Russia	18.0	Russia	39.8
Germany	5.8	Germany	9.2
Turkey	5.7	Turkmenistan	6.6
Italy	5.0	Italy	2.7

Balance of payments, reserves and debt, $bn

Visible exports fob	33.4	Change in reserves	2.6
Visible imports fob	-29.7	Level of reserves	
Trade balance	3.7	end Dec.	9.5
Invisibles inflows	6.7	No. months of import cover	3.2
Invisibles outflows	-6.2	Official gold holdings, m oz	0.5
Net transfers	2.6	Foreign debt	21.7
Current account balance	6.8	– as % of GDP	42
– as % of GDP	10.5	– as % of total exports	70
Capital balance	-4.2	Debt service ratio	14
Overall balance	2.5		

Health and education

Health spending, % of GDP	5.7	Education spending, % of GDP	5.4
Doctors per 1,000 pop.	3.0	Enrolment, %: primary	93
Hospital beds per 1,000 pop.	8.8	secondary	97
Improved-water source access,		tertiary	62
% of pop.	98		

Society

No. of households	19.8m	Colour TVs per 100 households	76.9
Av. no. per household	2.4	Telephone lines per 100 pop.	25.2
Marriages per 1,000 pop.	5.7	Mobile telephone subscribers	
Divorces per 1,000 pop.	3.4	per 100 pop.	28.5
Cost of living, Dec. 2005		Computers per 100 pop.	2.8
New York = 100	...	Internet hosts per 1,000 pop.	4.0

UNITED ARAB EMIRATES

Area	83,600 sq km	Capital	Abu Dhabi
Arable as % of total land	1	Currency	Dirham (AED)

People

Population	3.1m	Life expectancy: men	77.4 yrs
Pop. per sq km	37.1	women	82.2 yrs
Av. ann. growth		Adult literacy	77.3%
in pop. 2000–05	6.51%	Fertility rate (per woman)	2.5
Pop. under 15	22.0%	Urban population	85.5%
Pop. over 60	1.6%		per 1,000 pop.
No. of men per 100 women	214	Crude birth rate	16.7
Human Development Index	84.9	Crude death rate	1.3

The economy

GDP	AED383bn	GDP per head	$33,610
GDP	$104bn	GDP per head in purchasing	
Av. ann. growth in real		power parity (USA=100)	60.6
GDP 1994–2004	6.6%	Economic freedom index	2.93

Origins of GDP

Components of GDP[a]

	% of total		% of total
Agriculture	3	Private consumption	49.5
Industry, of which:	55	Public consumption	21.5
manufacturing	13	Investment	15.0
Services	42	Exports	86.0
		Imports	-72.1

Structure of employment

	% of total		% of labour force
Agriculture	8	Unemployed 2001	2.3
Industry	33	Av. ann. rate 1995–2001	2.1
Services	59		

Energy

			m TOE
Total output	159.2	Net energy imports as %	
Total consumption	39.2	of energy use	-306
Consumption per head,			
kg oil equivalent	9,707		

Inflation and finance

		av. ann. increase 1999–2004	
Consumer price			
inflation 2005	6.0%	Narrow money (M1)	21.7%
Av. ann. inflation 2000–05	3.8%	Broad money	17.7%

Exchange rates

	end 2005		December 2005
AED per $	...	Effective rates	2000 = 100
AED per SDR	...	– nominal	93.6
AED per €	...	– real	...

Trade

Principal exports

	$bn fob
Re-exports	33.9
Crude oil	29.6
Gas	4.7
Total incl. others	**90.6**

Principal imports[a]

	$bn cif
Machinery & electrical equip.	9.2
Precious stones & metals	5.8
Transport equipment	5.8
Total incl. others	**52.1**

Main export destinations

	% of total
Japan	25.7
South Korea	10.7
Thailand	5.4
Iran	3.9

Main origins of imports

	% of total
China	10.3
India	8.9
Japan	6.8
Germany	6.3

Balance of payments, reserves and debt, $bn

Visible exports fob	82.7	Change in reserves	3.4
Visible imports fob	-54.2	Level of reserves	
Trade balance	28.5	end Dec.	18.5
Invisibles inflows	6.7	No. months of import cover	2.7
Invisibles outflows	-17.4	Official gold holdings, m oz	0.0
Net transfers	-5.1	Foreign debt	30.1
Current account balance	12.7	– as % of GDP	30
– as % of GDP	9.7	– as % of total exports	33
Capital balance[b]	-9.5	Debt service ratio	2
Overall balance[b]	0.5		

Health and education

Health spending, % of GDP	3.3	Education spending, % of GDP	1.6
Doctors per 1,000 pop.	1.9	Enrolment, %: primary	97
Hospital beds per 1,000 pop.	2.2	secondary	79
Improved-water source access,		tertiary	35
% of pop.	...		

Society

No. of households	0.7m	Colour TVs per 100 households	97.0
Av. no. per household	6.4	Telephone lines per 100 pop.	27.3
Marriages per 1,000 pop.	3.1	Mobile telephone subscribers	
Divorces per 1,000 pop.	1.1	per 100 pop.	84.7
Cost of living, Dec. 2005		Computers per 100 pop.	12.0
New York = 100	71	Internet hosts per 1,000 pop.	42.1

a 2003
b 1999

UNITED KINGDOM

Area	242,534 sq km	Capital	London
Arable as % of total land	23	Currency	Pound (£)

People

Population	59.4m	Life expectancy: men	76.7 yrs
Pop. per sq km	244.9	women	81.2 yrs
Av. ann. growth		Adult literacy	99.0%
in pop. 2000–05	0.34%	Fertility rate (per woman)	1.7
Pop. under 15	17.9%	Urban population	89.2%
Pop. over 60	21.2%		per 1,000 pop.
No. of men per 100 women	96	Crude birth rate	11.0
Human Development Index	93.9	Crude death rate	10.2

The economy

GDP	£1,160bn	GDP per head	$35,760
GDP	$2,124bn	GDP per head in purchasing	
Av. ann. growth in real		power parity (USA=100)	77.7
GDP 1994–2004	2.8%	Economic freedom index	1.74

Origins of GDP		Components of GDP	
	% of total		% of total
Agriculture	0.9	Private consumption	65.1
Industry, of which:	26.0	Public consumption	21.3
manufacturing	15.0	Investment	17.0
Services	73.1	Exports	24.7
		Imports	-28.0

Structure of employment

	% of total		% of labour force
Agriculture	1	Unemployed 2004	4.6
Industry	24	Av. ann. rate 1995–2004	6.1
Services	75		

Energy

	m TOE		
Total output	246.1	Net energy imports as %	
Total consumption	232.0	of energy use	-6
Consumption per head,			
kg oil equivalent	3,893		

Inflation and finance

Consumer price		av. ann. increase 1999–2004	
inflation 2005	2.8%	Narrow money (M0)	6.3%
Av. ann. inflation 2000–05	2.4%	Broad money (M4)	9.0%
Money market rate, 2005	4.70%	Household saving rate, 2004	4.4%

Exchange rates

	end 2005		December 2005
£ per $	0.58	Effective rates	2000 = 100
£ per SDR	0.83	– nominal	96.5
£ per €	0.68	– real	97.0

Trade

Principal exports

	$bn fob
Finished manufactured products	184.8
Semi-manufactured products	103.4
Fuels	33.2
Food, drink & tobacco	19.4
Basic materials	6.9
Total incl. others	**350**

Principal imports

	$bn fob
Finished manufactured products	259.2
Semi-manufactured products	109.9
Food, drink & tobacco	40.2
Fuels	30.5
Basic materials	11.7
Total incl. others	**460**

Main export destinations

	% of total
United States	15.0
Germany	11.6
France	9.8
Ireland	7.0
Netherlands	6.3
EU25	58.1

Main origins of imports

	% of total
Germany	14.0
United States	8.8
France	8.0
Netherlands	7.2
Belgium-Luxembourg	5.6
EU25	55.0

Balance of payments, reserves and aid, $bn

Visible exports fob	349.6	Overall balance	0.4
Visible imports fob	-456.9	Change in reserves	3.7
Trade balance	-107.3	Level of reserves	
Invisibles inflows	437.3	end Dec.	49.7
Invisibles outflows	-352.3	No. months of import cover	0.7
Net transfers	-19.6	Official gold holdings, m oz	10.0
Current account balance	-41.9	Aid given	7.88
– as % of GDP	-2.0	– as % of GDP	0.36
Capital balance	25.9		

Health and education

Health spending, % of GDP	8.0	Education spending, % of GDP	5.3
Doctors per 1,000 pop.	2.2	Enrolment, %: primary	100
Hospital beds per 1,000 pop.	4.2	secondary	170
Improved-water source access,		tertiary	64
% of pop.	...		

Society

No. of households	25.3m	Colour TVs per 100 households	98.2
Av. no. per household	2.4	Telephone lines per 100 pop.	56.4
Marriages per 1,000 pop.	5.2	Mobile telephone subscribers	
Divorces per 1,000 pop.	3.0	per 100 pop.	102.2
Cost of living, Dec. 2005		Computers per 100 pop.	60.0
New York = 100	125	Internet hosts per 1,000 pop.	97.3

UNITED STATES

Area	9,372,610 sq km	Capital	Washington DC
Arable as % of total land	19	Currency	US dollar ($)

People

Population	297.0m	Life expectancy: men		75.2 yrs
Pop. per sq km	31.7	women		80.6 yrs
Av. ann. growth		Adult literacy		99.0%
in pop. 2000–05	0.97%	Fertility rate (per woman)		2.0
Pop. under 15	20.8%	Urban population		80.8%
Pop. over 60	16.7%		per 1,000 pop.	
No. of men per 100 women	97	Crude birth rate		14.5
Human Development Index	94.4	Crude death rate		8.4

The economy

GDP	$11,712bn	GDP per head	$39,430
Av. ann. growth in real		GDP per head in purchasing	
GDP 1994–2004	3.3%	power parity (USA=100)	100
		Economic freedom index	1.84

Origins of GDP		Components of GDP	
	% of total		% of total
Agriculture	1.2	Private consumption	70.1
Industry, of which:	18.2	Public consumption	18.6
manufacturing	12.1	Non-government investment	16.4
Services[a]	80.6	Exports	10.0
		Imports	-15.2

Structure of employment

	% of total		% of labour force
Agriculture	2	Unemployed 2004	5.5
Industry	22	Av. ann. rate 1995–2004	5.1
Services	76		

Energy

	m TOE		
Total output	1,631.4	Net energy imports as %	
Total consumption	2,280.8	of energy use	28
Consumption per head,			
kg oil equivalent	7,843		

Inflation and finance

		av. ann. increase 1999–2004	
Consumer price inflation 2005	3.4%	Narrow money	5.6%
Av. ann. inflation 2000–05	2.5%	Broad money	6.1%
Treasury bill rate, 2005	3.17%	Household saving rate, 2004	1.8%

Exchange rates

	end 2005		December 2005
$ per SDR	1.45	Effective rates	2000 = 100
$ per €	1.18	– nominal	85.1
		– real	93.0

Trade

Principal exports		Principal imports	
	$bn fob		*$bn fob*
Capital goods, excl. vehicles	331.1	Industrial supplies	412.4
Industrial supplies	203.6	Consumer goods, excl. vehicles	373.2
Consumer goods, excl. vehicles	102.8	Capital goods, excl. vehicles	343.8
Vehicles & products	88.2	Vehicles & products	228.4
Food & beverages	56.3	Food & beverages	62.2
Total incl. others	**819**	Total incl. others	**1,470**

Main export destinations		Main origins of imports	
	% of total		*% of total*
Canada	23.5	Canada	17.4
Mexico	13.7	China	13.3
Japan	6.7	Mexico	10.6
United Kingdom	4.6	Japan	8.8
China	4.3	Germany	5.2
EU25	21.4	EU25	19.1

Balance of payments, reserves and aid, $bn

Visible exports fob	811.0	Overall balance	-2.8
Visible imports fob	-1,473.0	Change in reserves	6.4
Trade balance	-661.9	Level of reserves	
Invisibles inflows	720.0	end Dec.	190.5
Invisibles outflows	-645.2	No. months of import cover	1.0
Net transfers	-80.9	Official gold holdings, m oz	261.6
Current account balance	-668.1	Aid given	19.71
– as % of GDP	-5.7	– as % of GDP	0.17
Capital balance	580.1		

Health and education

Health spending, % of GDP	15.2	Education spending, % of GDP	5.7
Doctors per 1,000 pop.	2.5	Enrolment, %: primary	98
Hospital beds per 1,000 pop.	3.3	secondary	106
Improved-water source access,		tertiary	83
% of pop.	100		

Society

No. of households	110.2m	Colour TVs per 100 households	99.6
Av. no. per household	2.6	Telephone lines per 100 pop.	60.6
Marriages per 1,000 pop.	8.2	Mobile telephone subscribers	
Divorces per 1,000 pop.	4.8	per 100 pop.	62.1
Cost of living, Dec. 2005		Computers per 100 pop.	76.2
New York = 100	100	Internet hosts per 1,000 pop.[b]	830.8

a   Including utilities.
b   Includes all hosts ending ".com", ".net" and ".org" which exaggerates the numbers.

VENEZUELA

Area	912,050 sq km	Capital	Caracas
Arable as % of total land	3	Currency	Bolivar (Bs)

People

Population	26.2m	Life expectancy:	men	70.9 yrs
Pop. per sq km	28.7		women	76.8 yrs
Av. ann. growth		Adult literacy		93.0%
in pop. 2000–05	1.82%	Fertility rate (per woman)		2.7
Pop. under 15	31.2%	Urban population		88.1%
Pop. over 60	7.6%			per 1,000 pop.
No. of men per 100 women	101	Crude birth rate		22.8
Human Development Index	77.2	Crude death rate		5.0

The economy

GDP	Bs208trn	GDP per head	$4,200
GDP	$110bn	GDP per head in purchasing	
Av. ann. growth in real		power parity (USA=100)	15.2
GDP 1994–2004	1.0%	Economic freedom index	4.16

Origins of GDP

Components of GDP

	% of total		% of total
Agriculture	5.7	Private consumption	67.8
Industry, of which:	47.1	Public consumption	7.5
manufacturing	16.2	Investment	9.2
Services	47.2	Exports	30.6
		Imports	-15.0

Structure of employment

	% of total		% of labour force
Agriculture	11	Unemployed 2002	15.8
Industry	20	Av. ann. rate 1995–2002	12.8
Services	69		

Energy

	m TOE		
Total output	179.6	Net energy imports as %	
Total consumption	54.2	of energy use	-231
Consumption per head,			
kg oil equivalent	2,112		

Inflation and finance

		av. ann. increase 1999–2004	
Consumer price			
inflation 2005	16.0%	Narrow money	34.2%
Av. ann. inflation 2000–05	20.6%	Broad money	30.6%
Money market rate, 2005	2.62%		

Exchange rates

	end 2005		December 2005
Bs per $	2,147	Effective rates	2000 = 100
Bs per SDR	3,069	– nominal	31.2
Bs per €	2,526	– real	70.5

Trade

Principal exports		Principal imports	
	$bn fob		*$bn fob*
Oil	27.9	Non-oil	15.9
Non-oil	7.5	Oil	1.4
Total incl. others	**35.4**	Total incl. others	**16.7**

Main export destinations		Main origins of imports	
	% of total		*% of total*
United States	67.6	United States	31.5
Netherlands Antilles	5.8	Colombia	6.0
Dominican Rep	3.4	Brazil	5.2
Canada	2.9	Germany	3.7

Balance of payments, reserves and debt, $bn

Visible exports fob	38.7	Change in reserves	2.6
Visible imports fob	-17.3	Level of reserves	
Trade balance	21.4	end Dec.	23.4
Invisibles inflows	2.7	No. months of import cover	10.2
Invisibles outflows	-10.2	Official gold holdings, m oz	11.5
Net transfers	-0.0	Foreign debt	35.6
Current account balance	13.8	– as % of GDP	38
– as % of GDP	12.6	– as % of total exports	106
Capital balance	-8.7	Debt service ratio	20
Overall balance	2.2		

Health and education

Health spending, % of GDP	4.5	Education spending, % of GDP	...
Doctors per 1,000 pop.	1.8	Enrolment, %: primary	104
Hospital beds per 1,000 pop.	0.8	secondary	70
Improved-water source access,		tertiary	40
% of pop.	83		

Society

No. of households	5.7m	Colour TVs per 100 households	95.1
Av. no. per household	4.6	Telephone lines per 100 pop.	12.8
Marriages per 1,000 pop.	4.2	Mobile telephone subscribers	
Divorces per 1,000 pop.	0.9	per 100 pop.	32.2
Cost of living, Dec. 2005		Computers per 100 pop.	8.2
New York = 100	58	Internet hosts per 1,000 pop.	1.8

VIETNAM

Area	331,114 sq km	Capital	Hanoi
Arable as % of total land	21	Currency	Dong (D)

People

Population	82.5m	Life expectancy:	men	69.9 yrs
Pop. per sq km	249.2		women	73.9 yrs
Av. ann. growth		Adult literacy		90.3%
in pop. 2000–05	1.37%	Fertility rate (per woman)		2.3
Pop. under 15	29.5%	Urban population		26.7%
Pop. over 60	7.5%			per 1,000 pop.
No. of men per 100 women	100	Crude birth rate		20.2
Human Development Index	70.4	Crude death rate		5.8

The economy

GDP	D713trn	GDP per head	$550
GDP	$45.2bn	GDP per head in purchasing	
Av. ann. growth in real		power parity (USA=100)	6.9
GDP 1994–2004	7.3%	Economic freedom index	3.89

Origins of GDP		Components of GDP	
	% of total		% of total
Agriculture	22	Private consumption	62.7
Industry, of which:	40	Public consumption	6.5
manufacturing	20	Investment	37.7
Services	38	Exports	69.6
		Imports	-76.5

Structure of employment

	% of total		% of labour force
Agriculture	60	Unemployed 2003	2.3
Industry	16	Av. ann. rate 1995–2003	...
Services	24		

Energy

	m TOE		
Total output	54.5	Net energy imports as %	
Total consumption	44.3	of energy use	-23
Consumption per head,			
kg oil equivalent	544		

Inflation and finance

Consumer price		av. ann. increase 1999–2004	
inflation 2005	8.3%	Narrow money (M1)	23.7
Av. ann. inflation 2000–05	4.5%	Broad money	27.8
Treasury bill rate, Oct 2005	6.13%		

Exchange rates

	end 2005		December 2005
D per $	...	Effective rates	2000 = 100
D per SDR	...	– nominal	...
D per €	...	– real	...

Trade

Principal exports		Principal imports	
	$bn fob		*$bn cif*
Crude oil	5.9	Machinery & equipment	5.5
Textiles & garments	4.5	Textiles	4.2
Footwear	2.8	Petroleum products	3.6
Fisheries products	2.5	Steel	2.6
Total incl. others	**26.5**	Total incl. others	**31.5**

Main export destinations		Main origins of imports	
	% of total		*% of total*
United States	18.8	China	13.9
Japan	13.2	Taiwan	11.6
China	10.3	Singapore	11.3
Australia	6.9	Japan	11.1
Singapore	5.2	South Korea	10.4
Germany	4.0	Thailand	5.8
United Kingdom	3.8	Malaysia	3.8

Balance of payments[a], reserves and debt, $bn

Visible exports fob	16.7	Change in reserves	0.8
Visible imports fob	-17.8	Level of reserves	
Trade balance	-1.1	end Dec.	7.2
Invisibles inflows	3.1	No. months of import cover[a]	2.6
Invisibles outflows	-4.6	Official gold holdings, m oz	0.0
Net transfers	1.9	Foreign debt	17.8
Current account balance	-0.6	– as % of GDP	45
– as % of GDP	-1.3	– as % of total exports	75
Capital balance	2.1	Debt service ratio	3
Overall balance	0.4		

Health and education

Health spending, % of GDP	5.4	Education spending, % of GDP	...
Doctors per 1,000 pop.	0.5	Enrolment, %: primary	101
Hospital beds per 1,000 pop.	2.4	secondary	72
Improved-water source access,		tertiary	10
% of pop.	80		

Society

No. of households	24.7m	Colour TVs per 100 households	41.0
Av. no. per household	3.3	Telephone lines per 100 pop.	12.3
Marriages per 1,000 pop.	12.1	Mobile telephone subscribers	
Divorces per 1,000 pop.	0.5	per 100 pop.	6.0
Cost of living, Dec. 2005		Computers per 100 pop.	1.3
New York = 100	67	Internet hosts per 1,000 pop.	0.1

ZIMBABWE

Area	390,759 sq km	Capital	Harare
Arable as % of total land	8	Currency	Zimbabwe dollar (Z$)

People

Population	12.9m	Life expectancy: men	38.2 yrs
Pop. per sq km	33.0	women	36.3 yrs
Av. ann. growth		Adult literacy	90%
in pop. 2000–05	0.65%	Fertility rate (per woman)	3.6
Pop. under 15	40.0%	Urban population	35.9%
Pop. over 60	5.4%		per 1,000 pop.
No. of men per 100 women	98	Crude birth rate	32.1
Human Development Index	50.4	Crude death rate	23.0

The economy

GDP	Z$23,802bn	GDP per head	$360
GDP	$4.7bn	GDP per head in purchasing	
Av. ann. growth in real		power parity (USA=100)	5.2
GDP 1994–2004	-1.9%	Economic freedom index	4.23

Origins of GDP		Components of GDP[a]	
	% of total		% of total
Agriculture	18	Private consumption	112.6
Industry, of which:	23	Public consumption	2.2
manufacturing	14	Investment	-13.0
Services	60	Net exports	-1.8

Structure of employment

	% of total		% of labour force
Agriculture	...	Unemployed 1999	6
Industry	...	Av. ann. rate 1995–99	6.5
Services	...		

Energy

	m TOE		
Total output	8.5	Net energy imports as %	
Total consumption	9.7	of energy use	12
Consumption per head,			
kg oil equivalent	752		

Inflation and finance

Consumer price		av. ann. increase 1999–2004	
inflation 2002	140.1%	Narrow money (M1)	186.6%
Av. ann. inflation 2000–02	106.0%	Broad money	187.5%
Interbank rate, Sep 2005	132.5%		

Exchange rates

	end 2005		December 2005
Z$ per $	77,965	Effective rates	2000 = 100
Z$ per SDR	111,432	– nominal	...
Z$ per €	91,724	– real	...

Trade[b]

Principal exports		Principal imports	
	$m fob		$m cif
Gold	366	Fuels	413
Tobacco	227	Chemicals	401
Ferro-alloys	185	Machinery & transport equip.	271
Platinum	121	Manufactured products	269
Total incl. others	**1,770**	Total incl. others	**2,422**

Main export destinations		Main origins of imports	
	% of total		% of total
South Africa	33.2	South Africa	46.9
Switzerland	7.8	Botswana	3.6
United Kingdom	7.6	United Kingdom	3.4
China	6.4	Zambia	3.1
Germany	4.5	China	2.4

Balance of payments[b], reserves and debt, $bn

Visible exports fob	1.7	Change in reserves[d]	0.0
Visible imports fob	-2.0	Level of reserves[d]	
Trade balance	-0.3	end Dec.	0.1
Net invisibles outflows	-0.3	No. months of import cover[d]	0.6
Net transfers	0.2	Official gold holdings, m oz[d]	0.1
Current account balance	-0.4	Foreign debt	4.8
– as % of GDP	-8.3	– as % of GDP	33
Capital balance[c]	-0.4	– as % of total exports	264
Overall balance[c]	-0.4	Debt service ratio	5

Health and education

Health spending, % of GDP	7.9	Education spending, % of GDP	4.7
Doctors per 1,000 pop.	0.2	Enrolment, %: primary	93
Hospital beds per 1,000 pop.	...	secondary	36
Improved-water source access,		tertiary	4
% of pop.	83		

Society

No. of households	3.2m	Colour TVs per 100 households	2.1
Av. no. per household	4.1	Telephone lines per 100 pop.	2.7
Marriages per 1,000 pop.	...	Mobile telephone subscribers	
Divorces per 1,000 pop.	...	per 100 pop.	3.6
Cost of living, Dec. 2005		Computers per 100 pop.	8.4
New York = 100	...	Internet hosts per 1,000 pop.	0.5

a   2003
b   Estimates.
c   2001 estimates.
d   2002

EURO AREA[a]

Area	2,497,000 sq km	Capital	–
Arable as % of total land	26	Currency	Euro (€)

People

Population	306.7m	Life expectancy:	men	76.6 yrs
Pop. per sq km	122.7		women	82.8 yrs
Av. ann. growth		Adult literacy		98.3%
in pop. 2000–05	0.4%	Fertility rate (per woman)		1.5
Pop. under 15	16.2%	Urban population		76.5%
Pop. over 60	21.9%			per 1,000 pop.
No. of men per 100 women	96	Crude birth rate		9.9
Human Development Index	93.2	Crude death rate[b]		10.1

The economy

GDP	€7,652bn	GDP per head	$30,980
GDP	$9,500bn	GDP per head in purchasing	
Av. ann. growth in real		power parity (USA=100)	70.9
GDP 1994–2004	2.2%	Economic freedom index	2.26

Origins of GDP		Components of GDP	
	% of total		% of total
Agriculture	2	Private consumption	56.9
Industry, of which:	27	Public consumption	20.5
manufacturing	19	Investment	20.5
Services	71	Exports	36.7
		Imports	-34.6

Structure of employment

	% of total		% of labour force
Agriculture	4.4	Unemployed 2004	8.9
Industry	31.2	Av. ann. rate 1995–2004	9.3
Services	64.3		

Energy

	m TOE		
Total output	445.2	Net energy imports as %	
Total consumption	1,221.3	of energy use	64
Consumption per head,			
kg oil equivalent	3,964		

Inflation and finance

Consumer price		av. ann. increase 1999–2004	
inflation 2005	2.2%	Narrow money (M1)	8.4%
Av. ann. inflation 2000–05	2.2%	Broad money	6.9%
Repo rate, 2005	2.10%	Household saving rate, 2004	10.2%

Exchange rates

	end 2005		December 2005
€ per $	0.85	Effective rates	2000 = 100
€ per SDR	1.21	– nominal	116.7
		– real	117.8

Trade[b]

Principal exports

	$bn fob
Machinery & transport equip.	544
Manufactures	295
Chemicals	189
Energy and raw materials	62
Food & drink	60
Total incl. others	**1,205**

Principal imports

	$bn cif
Machinery & transport equip.	437
Manufactures	325
Food, drink & tobacco	282
Energy & raw materials	107
Chemicals	72
Total incl. others	**1,284**

Main export destinations

	% of total
United States	24.2
Switzerland	7.7
China	5.0
Russia	4.7
Japan	4.5

Main origins of imports

	% of total
United States	15.3
China	12.4
Russia	7.8
Japan	7.2
Switzerland	6.0

Balance of payments, reserves and aid, $bn

Visible exports fob	1,404.4	Overall balance	-15.4
Visible imports fob	-1,277.2	Change in reserves	-4.8
Trade balance	127.2	Level of reserves	
Invisibles inflows	757.5	end Dec.	382.1
Invisibles outflows	-757.0	No. months of import cover	2.3
Net transfers	-67.0	Official gold holdings, m oz	390.0
Current account balance	58.7	Aid given	30.2
– as % of GDP	0.6	– as % of GDP	0.32
Capital balance	-69.0		

Health and education

Health spending, % of GDP	9.6	Education spending, % of GDP	4.81
Doctors per 1,000 pop.	3.9	Enrolment, %: primary	104
Hospital beds per 1,000 pop.	6.6	secondary	106
Improved-water source access,		tertiary	54
% of pop.	...		

Society

No. of households	127.4m	Colour TVs per 100 households	97.0
Av. no. per household	2.41	Telephone lines per 100 pop.	53.0
Marriages per 1,000 pop.	5.0	Mobile telephone subscribers	
Divorces per 1,000 pop.	1.6	per 100 pop.	89.7
Cost of living, Dec. 2005		Computers per 100 pop.	40.5
New York = 100	...	Internet hosts per 1,000 pop.	152.9

a   Data refer to the 12 EU members that have adopted the euro.
b   EU25 data.

WORLD

Area	148,698,382 sq km	Capital	...
Arable as % of total land	10.8	Currency	...

People

Population	6,377.6m	Life expectancy:	men	64.3 yrs
Pop. per sq km	42.9		women	68.7 yrs
Av. ann. growth		Adult literacy		79.0%
in pop. 2000–05	1.21%	Fertility rate (per woman)		2.7
Pop. under 15	28.2%	Urban population		49.2%
Pop. over 60	10.4%			per 1,000 pop.
No. of men per 100 women	101	Crude birth rate		21.3
Human Development Index	74.1	Crude death rate		8.9

The economy

GDP	$41.3trn	GDP per head	$6,460
Av. ann. growth in real		GDP per head in purchasing	
GDP 1994–2004	3.0%	power parity (USA=100)	22.5
		Economic freedom index	3.21

Origins of GDP		**Components of GDP**	
	% of total		% of total
Agriculture	4	Private consumption	62
Industry, of which:	28	Public consumption	17
manufacturing	18	Investment	21
Services	68	Exports	24
		Imports	-24

Structure of employment[a]

	% of total		% of labour force
Agriculture	4	Unemployed 2004	7.1
Industry	26	Av. ann. rate 1995–2004	6.9
Services	70		

Energy

	m TOE		
Total output	10,672.0	Net energy imports as %	
Total consumption	10,543.7	of energy use	-1
Consumption per head,			
kg oil equivalent	1,734		

Inflation and finance[a]

		av. ann. increase 1999–2004	
Consumer price			
inflation 2005	3.6%	Narrow money (M1)	8.9%
Av. ann. inflation 2000–05	3.7%	Broad money	5.8%
LIBOR $ rate, 3-month, 2005	3.56%	Household saving rate, 2004	5.4%

Trade

World exports

	$bn fob		$bn fob
Manufactures	7,042	Ores & metals	274
Fuels	732	Agricultural raw materials	183
Food	640	Total incl. others	**9,145**

Main export destinations

	% of total	Main origins of imports	% of total
United States	15.7	Germany	9.4
Germany	7.7	United States	9.3
China	5.4	China	8.5
France	5.1	Japan	6.5
United Kingdom	5.1	France	4.5
Japan	4.5	United Kingdom	3.5

Balance of payments, reserves and aid, $bn

Visible exports fob	9,043	Overall balance	0
Visible imports fob	-8,990	Change in reserves	723
Trade balance	53	Level of reserves	
Invisibles inflows	3,981	end Dec.	4,260
Invisibles outflows	-4,038	No. months of import cover	4
Net transfers	-25	Official gold holdings, m oz	900.8
Current account balance	-27	Aid given[b]	82.7
– as % of GDP	-0.1	– as % of GDP[b]	0.25
Capital balance	-94		

Health and education

Health spending, % of GDP	10.2	Education spending, % of GDP	4.5
Doctors per 1,000 pop.	1.5	Enrolment, %: primary	103
Hospital beds per 1,000 pop.	...	secondary	70
Improved-water source access,		tertiary	24
% of pop.	82		

Society

No. of households	...	TVs per 100 households	...
Av. no. per household	...	Telephone lines per 100 pop.	19.0
Marriages per 1,000 pop.	...	Mobile telephone subscribers	
Divorces per 1,000 pop.	...	per 100 pop.	27.6
Cost of living, Dec. 2005		Computers per 100 pop.	12.9
New York = 100	...	Internet hosts per 1,000 pop.	61.8

a OECD countries.
b OECD and Middle East countries.

Glossary

Balance of payments The record of a country's transactions with the rest of the world. The **current account** of the balance of payments consists of: visible trade (goods); "invisible" trade (services and income); private transfer payments (eg, remittances from those working abroad); official transfers (eg, payments to international organisations, famine relief). Visible imports and exports are normally compiled on rather different definitions to those used in the trade statistics (shown in principal imports and exports) and therefore the statistics do not match. The **capital account** consists of long- and short-term transactions relating to a country's assets and liabilities (eg, loans and borrowings). The current account and the capital account, plus an errors and omissions item, make up the **overall balance**. In the country pages of this book this item is included in the overall balance. **Changes in reserves** include gold at market prices and are shown without the practice often followed in balance of payments presentations of reversing the sign.

Big Mac index A light-hearted way of looking at exchange rates. If the dollar price of a burger at McDonald's in any country is higher than the price in the United States, converting at market exchange rates, then that country's currency could be thought to be over-valued against the dollar and vice versa.

Body-mass index A measure for assessing obesity – weight in kilograms divided by height in metres squared. An index of 30 or more is regarded as an indicator of obesity; 25 to 29.9 as over-weight. Guidelines vary for men and for women and may be adjusted for age.

CFA Communauté Financière Africaine. Its members, most of the francophone African nations, share a common currency, the CFA franc, which used to be pegged to the French franc but is now pegged to the euro.

Cif/fob Measures of the value of merchandise trade. Imports include the cost of "carriage, insurance and freight" (cif) from the exporting country to the importing. The value of exports does not include these elements and is recorded "free on board" (fob). Balance of payments statistics are generally adjusted so that both exports and imports are shown fob; the cif elements are included in invisibles.

Crude birth rate The number of live births in a year per 1,000 population. The crude rate will automatically be relatively high if a large proportion of the population is of childbearing age.

Crude death rate The number of deaths in a year per 1,000 population. Also affected by the population's age structure.

Debt, foreign Financial obligations owed by a country to the rest of the world and repayable in foreign currency. **The debt service ratio** is debt service (principal repayments plus interest payments) expressed as a percentage of the country's earnings from exports of goods and services.

EU European Union. Members are: Austria, Belgium, Denmark, Finland, France, Germany, Greece, Ireland, Italy, Luxembourg, Netherlands, Portugal, Spain, Sweden and the United Kingdom and, as of May 1 2004, Cyprus, Czech Republic, Estonia, Hungary, Latvia, Lithuania, Malta, Poland, Slovakia and Slovenia.

Effective exchange rate The nominal index measures a currency's depreciation (figures below 100) or appreciation (figures over 100) from a base date against a trade-weighted basket of the currencies of the country's main trading partners. The real effective exchange rate reflects adjustments for relative movements in prices or costs.

Euro area The 12 euro area members of the EU are Austria, Belgium, Finland, France, Germany, Greece, Ireland, Italy,

Luxembourg, Netherlands, Portugal and Spain. Their common currency is the euro, which came into circulation on January 1 2002.

Fertility rate The average number of children born to a woman who completes her childbearing years.

GDP Gross domestic product. The sum of all output produced by economic activity within a country. GNP (gross national product) and GNI (gross national income) include net income from abroad eg, rent, profits.

Household saving rate Household savings as % of disposable household income.

Import cover The number of months of imports covered by reserves, ie reserves ÷ $1/12$ annual imports (visibles and invisibles).

Inflation The annual rate at which prices are increasing. The most common measure and the one shown here is the increase in the consumer price index.

Internet hosts Websites and other computers that sit permanently on the internet.

Life expectancy The average length of time a baby born today can expect to live.

Literacy is defined by UNESCO as the ability to read and write a simple sentence, but definitions can vary from country to country.

Median age Divides the age distribution into two halves. Half of the population is above and half below the median age.

Money supply A measure of the "money" available to buy goods and services. Various definitions exist. The measures shown here are based on definitions used by the IMF and may differ from measures used nationally. Narrow money (M1) consists of cash in circulation and

demand deposits (bank deposits that can be withdrawn on demand). "Quasi-money" (time, savings and foreign currency deposits) is added to this to create broad money.

OECD Organisation for Economic Co-operation and Development. The "rich countries" club was established in 1961 to promote economic growth and the expansion of world trade. It is based in Paris and now has 30 members.

Opec Organisation of Petroleum Exporting Countries. Set up in 1960 and based in Vienna, Opec is mainly concerned with oil pricing and production issues. Members are; Algeria, Indonesia, Iran, Iraq, Kuwait, Libya, Nigeria, Qatar, Saudi Arabia, United Arab Emirates and Venezuela.

PPP Purchasing power parity. PPP statistics adjust for cost of living differences by replacing normal exchange rates with rates designed to equalise the prices of a standard "basket"of goods and services. These are used to obtain PPP estimates of GDP per head. PPP estimates are shown on an index, taking the United States as 100.

Real terms Figures adjusted to exclude the effect of inflation.

Reserves The stock of gold and foreign currency held by a country to finance any calls that may be made for the settlement of foreign debt.

SDR Special drawing right. The reserve currency, introduced by the IMF in 1970, was intended to replace gold and national currencies in settling international transactions. The IMF uses SDRs for book-keeping purposes and issues them to member countries. Their value is based on a basket of the US dollar (with a weight of 45%), the euro (29%), the Japanese yen (15%) and the pound sterling (11%).

List of countries

Whenever data is available, the world rankings consider 183 countries: all those which had (in 2004) or have recently had a population of at least 1m or a GDP of at least $1bn. Here is a list of them.

	Population	GDP	GDP per head	Area	Median age
	m	$bn	$PPP	'000 sq km	years
Afghanistan	24.9	5.8	800[a]	652	16.7
Albania	3.2	7.6	4,980	29	28.3
Algeria	32.3	84.6	6,600	2,382	24.0
Andorra	0.1	1.8[a]	26,290[a]	0.4	37.0
Angola	14.1	19.5	2,180	1,247	16.6
Argentina	38.9	153.0	13,300	2,767	28.9
Armenia	3.1	3.1	4,100	30	31.7
Aruba	0.1	1.9[b]	21,800[ab]	0.2	34.0
Australia	19.9	637.3	30,330	7,682	36.6
Austria	8.1	292.3	32,280	84	40.6
Azerbaijan	8.4	8.5	4,150	87	27.5
Bahamas	0.3	5.3[b]	17,520[b]	14	27.6
Bahrain	0.7	11.0	20,760	1	29.8
Bangladesh	149.7	56.6	1,870	144	22.1
Barbados	0.3	2.8	16,230[a]	0.4	34.7
Belarus	9.9	22.9	6,970	208	37.8
Belgium	10.3	352.3	31,100	31	40.6
Belize	0.3	1.1	6,750	23	21.2
Benin	6.9	4.1	1,090	113	17.6
Bermuda	0.1	4.5[a]	69,230[a]	1	36.0
Bhutan	2.3	0.7	1,400[ab]	47	20.1
Bolivia	9.0	8.8	2,720	1,099	20.8
Bosnia	4.2	8.5	7,030	51	38.0
Botswana	1.8	9.0	9,950	581	19.9
Brazil	180.7	604.0	8,200	8,512	26.8
Brunei	0.4	6.8[ab]	18,690[ab]	6	26.2
Bulgaria	7.8	24.1	8,080	111	40.6
Burkina Faso	13.4	4.8	1,170	274	16.2
Burundi	7.1	0.7	680	28	17.0
Cambodia	14.5	4.9	2,420	181	20.3
Cameroon	16.3	14.4	2,170	475	18.8
Canada	31.7	978.0	31,260	9,971	38.6
Cayman Islands	0.0	1.4[a]	32,350[a]	0.3	34.0
Central African Rep	3.9	1.3	1,090	622	18.1
Chad	8.9	4.2	2,090	1,284	16.3
Channel Islands	0.1	6.2[ab]	61,900[ab]	0.2	39.7
Chile	16.0	94.1	10,870	757	30.6
China	1,313.3	1,931.7	5,900	9,561	32.6
Colombia	44.9	97.7	7,260	1,142	25.4
Congo-Kinshasa	54.4	6.6	710	2,345	16.3

	Population	GDP	GDP per head	Area	Median age
	m	*$bn*	*$PPP*	*'000 sq km*	*years*
Congo-Brazzaville	3.8	4.3	980	342	16.3
Costa Rica	4.3	18.5	9,480	51	26.1
Côte d'Ivoire	16.9	15.5	1,550	322	18.5
Croatia	4.4	34.3	12,190	57	40.6
Cuba	11.3	32.5[a]	2,870[a]	111	35.6
Cyprus	0.8	15.4	22,810	9	35.3
Czech Republic	10.2	107.0	19,410	79	39.0
Denmark	5.4	241.4	31,910	43	39.5
Dominican Republic	8.9	18.7	7,450	48	23.3
Ecuador	13.2	30.3	3,960	272	24.0
Egypt	73.4	78.8	4,210	1,000	22.8
El Salvador	6.6	15.8	5,040	21	23.3
Equatorial Guinea	0.5	3.2	19,300[b]	28	17.6
Eritrea	4.3	0.9	980	117	17.4
Estonia	1.3	11.2	14,560	45	38.9
Ethiopia	72.4	8.0	760	1,134	17.5
Faroe Islands	0.0	1.0[ab]	21,300[ab]	1	34.0
Fiji	0.8	2.6	6,070	18	24.5
Finland	5.2	185.9	29,950	338	40.9
France	60.4	2,046.6[c]	29,300[c]	544	39.3
French Polynesia	0.2	4.6[ab]	17,500[ab]	3	28.9
Gabon	1.4	7.2	6,620	268	19.4
Gambia, The	1.5	0.4	1,990	11	19.8
Georgia	5.1	5.2	2,840	70	35.5
Germany	82.5	2,740.6	28,300	358	42.1
Ghana	21.4	8.9	2,240	239	19.8
Greece	11.0	205.2	22,210	132	39.7
Greenland	0.1	1.1	19,640[ab]	2,176	31.0
Guadeloupe	0.4	3.5	7,930[ab]	2	34.1
Guam	0.2	2.5	15,150[a]	1	28.1
Guatemala	12.7	27.5	4,310	109	18.1
Guinea	8.6	3.9	2,180	246	18.0
Guinea-Bissau	1.5	0.3	720	36	16.2
Haiti	8.4	3.5	1,840[a]	28	20.0
Honduras	7.1	7.4	2,880	112	19.8
Hong Kong	7.1	163.0	30,820	1	38.9
Hungary	9.8	100.7	16,810	93	38.8
Iceland	0.3	12.2	33,050	103	34.1
India	1,081.2	691.2	3,140	3,287	24.3
Indonesia	222.6	257.6	3,610	1,904	26.5
Iran	69.8	163.4	7,530	1,648	23.4

	Population	GDP	GDP per head	Area	Median age
	m	$bn	$PPP	'000 sq km	years
Iraq	25.9	12.6[ab]	2,400[a]	438	19.1
Ireland	4.0	181.6	38,830	70	34.2
Israel	6.6	116.9	24,380	21	28.9
Italy	57.3	1,677.8	28,180	301	42.3
Jamaica	2.7	8.9	4,160	11	24.9
Japan	127.8	4,622.8	29,250	378	42.9
Jordan	5.6	11.5	4,690	89	21.3
Kazakhstan	15.4	40.7	7,440	2,717	29.4
Kenya	32.4	16.1	1,140	583	17.9
Kuwait	2.6	55.7	19,380	18	29.5
Kyrgyzstan	5.2	2.2	1,940	583	23.8
Laos	5.8	2.5	1,950	237	19.1
Latvia	2.3	13.6	11,650	64	39.5
Lebanon	3.7	21.8	5,840	10	26.8
Lesotho	1.8	1.3	2,620	30	19.2
Liberia	3.5	0.5	900[a]	111	16.3
Libya	5.7	29.1	8,400[a]	1,760	23.9
Lithuania	3.4	22.3	13,110	65	37.8
Luxembourg	0.5	31.9	69,960	3	38.1
Macau	0.4	6.8[b]	22,000[a]	0.02	36.6
Macedonia	2.1	5.4	6,610	26	34.2
Madagascar	17.9	4.4	860	587	17.8
Malawi	12.3	1.9	650	118	16.3
Malaysia	24.9	118.3	10,280	333	24.7
Mali	13.4	4.9	1,000	1,240	15.8
Malta	0.4	5.3	18,880	0.3	38.1
Martinique	0.4	6.1[ab]	15,490[ab]	1	36.4
Mauritania	3.0	1.5	1,940	1,031	18.4
Mauritius	1.2	6.0	12,030	2	30.4
Mexico	104.9	676.5	9,800	1,973	25.0
Moldova	4.3	2.6	1,730	34	33.0
Mongolia	2.6	1.6	2,060	1,565	23.7
Morocco	31.1	50.0	4,310	447	24.2
Mozambique	19.2	6.1	1,240	799	17.7
Myanmar	50.1	8.0[a]	1,600[a]	677	25.5
Namibia	2.0	5.7	7,420	824	18.6
Nepal	25.7	6.7	1,490	147	20.1
Netherlands	16.2	579.0	31,790	42	39.3
Netherlands Antilles	0.2	2.8	15,470[a]	1	36.2
New Caledonia	0.2	3.2	13,550[ab]	19	28.4
New Zealand	3.9	98.9	23,410	271	35.8
Nicaragua	5.6	4.6	3,630	130	19.7

	Population	GDP	GDP per head	Area	Median age
	m	*$bn*	*$PPP*	*'000 sq km*	*years*
Niger	12.4	3.1	780	1,267	15.5
Nigeria	127.1	72.1	1,150	924	17.5
North Korea	22.8	40.0	1,750[a]	121	31.1
Norway	4.6	250.1	38,450	324	38.2
Oman	2.9	24.3	15,260	310	22.3
Pakistan	157.3	96.1	2,230	804	20.0
Panama	3.2	13.7	7,280	77	26.1
Papua New Guinea	5.8	3.9	2,540	463	19.7
Paraguay	6.0	7.3	4,810	407	20.8
Peru	27.6	68.6	5,680	1,285	24.2
Philippines	81.4	84.6	4,610	300	22.2
Poland	38.6	242.3	12,970	313	36.5
Portugal	10.1	167.7	19,630	89	39.5
Puerto Rico	3.9	67.9[b]	24,920[b]	9	33.3
Qatar	0.6	20.4[b]	26,100[a]	11	30.9
Réunion	0.8	4.8[ab]	6,270[a]	3	29.3
Romania	22.3	73.2	8,480	238	36.7
Russia	142.4	581.4	9,900	17,075	37.3
Rwanda	8.5	1.8	1,260	26	17.5
Saudi Arabia	24.9	250.6	13,830	2,200	21.6
Senegal	10.3	7.8	1,710	197	18.2
Serbia	10.5	24.0	2,700[a]	102	36.5
Sierra Leone	5.2	1.1	560	72	18.4
Singapore	4.3	106.8	28,080	1	37.5
Slovakia	5.4	41.1	14,620	49	35.6
Slovenia	2.0	32.2	20,940	20	40.2
Somalia	10.3	4.8[ab]	470[a]	638	17.9
South Africa	45.2	212.8	11,190	1,226	23.5
South Korea	48.0	679.7	20,500	99	35.1
Spain	41.1	1,039.9	25,050	505	38.6
Sri Lanka	19.2	20.1	4,390	66	29.6
Sudan	34.3	21.1	1,950	2,506	20.1
Suriname	0.4	1.1	4,100[a]	164	25.1
Swaziland	1.1	2.4	5,640	17	18.1
Sweden	8.9	346.4	29,540	450	40.1
Switzerland	7.2	357.5	33,040	41	40.8
Syria	18.2	24.0	3,610	185	20.6
Taiwan	22.7	305.3	27,100[a]	36	31.0
Tajikistan	6.3	2.1	1,200	143	19.3
Tanzania	37.7	10.9	670	945	18.2
Thailand	63.5	161.7	8,090	513	30.5

	Population	GDP	GDP per head	Area	Median age
	m	*$bn*	*$PPP*	*'000 sq km*	*years*
Togo	5.0	2.1	1,540	57	17.9
Trinidad & Tobago	1.3	12.5	12,180	5	29.4
Tunisia	9.9	28.2	7,770	164	26.8
Turkey	72.3	302.8	7,750	779	26.3
Turkmenistan	4.9	6.2	4,320	488	23.3
Uganda	26.7	6.8	1,480	241	14.8
Ukraine	48.2	64.8	6,390	604	39.0
United Arab Emirates	3.1	104.2	24,060	84	29.0
United Kingdom	59.4	2,124.4	30,820	243	39.0
United States	297.0	11,711.8	39,680	9,373	36.1
Uruguay	3.4	13.2	9,420	176	32.1
Uzbekistan	26.5	12.0	1,870	447	22.6
Venezuela	26.2	110.1	6,040	912	24.7
Vietnam	82.5	45.2	2,750	331	24.9
Virgin Islands	0.1	2.5[ab]	22,940[ab]	0.4	35.0
West Bank and Gaza	3.7	3.5[b]	950[ab]	6	17.1
Yemen	20.7	12.8	880	528	16.5
Zambia	10.9	5.4	940	753	16.7
Zimbabwe	12.9	4.7	2,070	391	18.7
Euro area (12)	306.7	9,500.9	27,960	2,497	40.6
World	6,377.7	41,290.4	8,920	148,698	28.1

a Estimate.
b Latest available year.
c Including French Guiana, Guadeloupe, Martinique and Réunion.
d Populations less than 50,000.

Sources

Airports Council International, *Worldwide Airport Traffic Report*

BP, *Statistical Review of World Energy*

British Mountaineering Council

CB Richard Ellis, *Global Market Rents*

Central Intelligence Agency, *The World Factbook*

Centre for International Earth Science Information Network, Columbia University

Confederation of Swedish Enterprise

Corporate Resources Group, *Quality of Living Report*

Council of Europe

The Economist
www.economist.com

Economist Intelligence Unit, *Cost of Living Survey*; *Country Forecasts*; *Country Reports*; *F-readiness rankings*; *Global Outlook – Business Environment Rankings*; Quality of Life index

ERC Statistics International, *World Cigarette Report*

Euromonitor, *International Marketing Data and Statistics*; *European Marketing Data and Statistics*

Europa Publications, *The Europa World Yearbook*

Eurostat, *Statistics in Focus*

FAO, *FAOSTAT database*; *State of the World's Forests*

Financial Times Business Information, *The Banker*

The Heritage Foundation, *Index of Economic Freedom*

IMD, *World Competitiveness Yearbook*

IMF, *Direction of Trade*; *International Financial Statistics*; *World Economic Outlook*

International Cocoa Organisation, *Quarterly Bulletin of Cocoa Statistics*

International Coffee Organisation

International Cotton Advisory Committee, *Bulletin*

International Road Federation, *World Road Statistics*

International Rubber Study Group, *Rubber Statistical Bulletin*

International Federation of the Phonographic Industry

International Grains Council, *The Grain Market Report*

International Obesity Task Force

International Sugar Organisation, *Statistical Bulletin*

International Tea Committee, *Annual Bulletin of Statistics*

International Telecommunication Union, *ITU Indicators*

ISTA Mielke, *Oil World*

Johnson Matthey

Lloyd's Register, *World Fleet Statistics*

Mercer Human Resource
  Consulting

National statistics offices
Network Wizards
Nobel Foundation

OECD, *Development Assistance
  Committee Report*;
  Environmental Data; *Main
  Economic Indicators*

Space.com
Standard & Poor's *Emerging
  Stock Markets Factbook*
Swiss Re, *sigma*

Taiwan Statistical Data Book
The Times, *Atlas of the World*
Time Inc Magazines, *Fortune
  International*
Transparency International

UN, *Demographic Yearbook;
  Global Refugee Trends*; *State
  of World Population Report*;
  *Statistical Chart on World
  Families*; *Survey on Crime
  Trends*; *Trends in Total
  Migrant Stock*; *World
  Contraceptive Use*; *World
  Population Prospects*; *World
  Urbanisation Prospects*
UNAIDS, *Report on the Global
  AIDS Epidemic*
UNCTAD, *World Investment
  Report*
UN Development Programme,
  Human Development Report
UNESCO, website: unescostat.
  unesco.org

Union Internationale des
  Chemins de Fer, *Statistiques
  Internationales des Chemins
  de Fer*
US Census Bureau
US Department of Agriculture
University of Michigan,
  Windows to the Universe
  website

WHO, *Atlas of Heart Disease
  and Stroke*; *Health Behaviour
  in School-aged Children*;
  Mortality Database; *Weekly
  Epidemiological Record*;
  *World Health Statistics
  Annual*; *World Report on
  Violence and Health*
The Woolmark Company
World Bank, *Doing Business;
  Global Development Finance*;
  *World Development
  Indicators*; *World
  Development Report*
World Bureau of Metal
  Statistics, *World Metal
  Statistics*
World Economic
  Forum/Harvard University,
  *Global Competitiveness
  Yearbook*
World Resources Institute,
  World Resources
World Tourist Organisation,
  Yearbook of Tourism Statistics
World Trade Organisation,
  Annual Report
World Water Council
World Wide Fund for Nature